POCKET GUIDES TO
SOCIAL WORK RESEARCH METHODS

Series Editor
Tony Tripodi, DSW
Professor Emeritus, Ohio State University

Determining Sample Size
Balancing Power, Precision, and Practicality
Patrick Dattalo

Preparing Research Articles
Bruce A. Thyer

Systematic Reviews and Meta-Analysis
Julia H. Littell, Jacqueline Corcoran, and Vijayan Pillai

Historical Research
Elizabeth Ann Danto

Confirmatory Factor Analysis
Donna Harrington

Randomized Controlled Trials
Design and Implementation for
Community-Based Psychosocial Interventions
Phyllis Solomon, Mary M. Cavanaugh, and Jeffrey Draine

Multiple Regression with Discrete Dependent Variables
John G. Orme and Terri Combs-Orme

Needs Assessment
David Royse, Michele Staton-Tindall, Karen Badger, and
J. Matthew Webster

Developing Cross-Cultural Measurement
Thanh V. Tran

Intervention Research
Developing Social Programs
Mark W. Fraser, Jack M. Richman, Maeda J. Galinsky, and
Steven H. Day

Developing and Validating Rapid Assessment Instruments
Neil Abell, David W. Springer, and Akihito Kamata

NEIL ABELL
DAVID W. SPRINGER
AKIHITO KAMATA

Developing and Validating Rapid Assessment Instruments

OXFORD
UNIVERSITY PRESS

2009

OXFORD

UNIVERSITY PRESS

Oxford University Press, Inc., publishes works that further
Oxford University's objective of excellence
in research, scholarship, and education.

Oxford   New York
Auckland   Cape Town   Dar es Salaam   Hong Kong   Karachi
Kuala Lumpur   Madrid   Melbourne   Mexico City   Nairobi
New Delhi   Shanghai   Taipei   Toronto

With offices in
Argentina   Austria   Brazil   Chile   Czech Republic   France   Greece
Guatemala   Hungary   Italy   Japan   Poland   Portugal   Singapore
South Korea   Switzerland   Thailand   Turkey   Ukraine   Vietnam

Published by Oxford University Press, Inc.
198 Madison Avenue, New York, New York 10016

www.oup.com

Oxford is a registered trademark of Oxford University Press

Library of Congress Cataloging-in-Publication Data

Abell, Neil.
Developing and validating rapid assessment instruments / Neil Abell,
David W. Springer, Akihito Kamata.
p.   cm. — (Pocket guides to social work research methods)
Includes bibliographical references and index.
ISBN 978-0-19-533336-7
1. Psychological tests.   2. Psychometrics.   3. Social service.
I. Springer, David W.   II. Kamata, Akihito.   III. Title.
BF176.A34 2008
150.28′7—dc22
2008044056

1   3   5   7   9   8   6   4   2

Printed in the United States of America
on acid-free paper

To the memory of Walter W. Hudson, a mentor without peer who, through his generosity, became one. His influence continues to instigate, enlighten, and inspire.

Acknowledgments

M ost important, we thank Tony Tripodi for inviting us to contribute this book for inclusion in the *Pocket Guides to Social Work Research Series.*

We are extremely grateful for the support that we received from the team at Oxford University Press, including our editor, Maura Roessner, and particularly Mallory Jensen, Associate Editor.

The systematic support throughout the research, writing, editing, and camera-ready copy preparation process for this book by Nicole Cesnales, Rae Seon Kim, Hollee Ganner, Angie Lippman, and Melissa Torrente is sincerely appreciated.

This book is no doubt better as a result of the helpful feedback that we received from the external reviewers, Kevin Corcoran and Tim Conley.

Neil Abell would especially like to thank Scott Edward Rutledge, James Whyte III, and Scott Ryan for their longstanding collegial support and collaboration, Machelle Madsen Thompson and Julia Buckey for exemplifying the inspiration and ideals of the many enthusiastic students who have helped shape the presentation of this material, and most of all his wife, Terry, for leading him into the garden now and then.

David Springer would like to thank his wife, Sarah, for her steadfast support, lively spirit, and sense of humor.

Aki Kamata would like to thank his wife, Yasuyo, for her continuing support and patience with him while he was so busy working on this project.

Neil Abell, Ph.D.   David W. Springer, Ph.D.   Akihito Kamata, Ph.D.

Tallahassee, FL   Austin, TX   Tallahassee, FL

Contents

Developing and Validating Rapid Assessment Instruments

1

Introduction and Overview

T he use of scales and measures in the behavioral sciences has grown exponentially over the past generation. From the early recognition of their potential value until the present, one resource, *Measures for Clinical Practice: A Sourcebook* (Corcoran & Fischer, 1987) has evolved over four editions into a two-volume set cataloging over 500 entries (Fischer & Corcoran, 2007b). Practitioners and researchers can browse for rapid assessment instruments organized by unit of analysis (couples, families, and children, or adults) and cross-referenced by problem types ranging from abuse and acculturation through treatment satisfaction and substance abuse. In one recent year, entries in a leading journal listed validation studies on new instruments addressing spiritual competence, life domains for at-risk and substance-abusing adolescents, caregivers' compulsions to commit elder abuse, and post-traumatic stress disorder symptoms with persons who have severe mental illness.

Many factors might account for this proliferation: increased sophistication within the behavioral sciences and among social and human service providers, growing demands for accountability, and improved training in the importance of grounding assumptions in valid and reliable evidence. Whatever the inspiration, measurement and scaling has become a certified "growth industry," justifying the call for this book.

In preparing these materials, we draw liberally on the substantial library of existing works tracing the evolution of psychometric methods and are indebted to the foundation so carefully laid by others.

Making no effort to be comprehensive (the task is simply too great for our intended purposes), we nevertheless acknowledge a selection of tools, ranging from the *Standards for Educational and Psychological Testing* (American Educational Research Association, American Psychological Association, & National Council on Measurement in Education, 1999) through *Psychometric Theory* (Nunnally & Bernstein, 1994) and *Scale Development* (R. F. DeVellis, 2003). Collectively, these illustrate an accumulation of efforts to *(a)* establish a basic language for judging the strengths of scales, *(b)* detail the conceptual and analytic strategies needed to design and validate them, and *(c)* distill the essentials into useful guides for practitioners and researchers. These aims we will take as our own and try in the brief space afforded us to strike a balance leaving readers better informed and better equipped to take up the challenges for themselves. Although our text is nominally applied to social workers, whose history with psychometrics we briefly summarize here, the principles addressed will, hopefully, be of equal value across the behavioral sciences.

PSYCHOMETRIC PROGRESS IN SOCIAL WORK PRACTICE AND RESEARCH

Debate over the use of scales and measures in social work has been long and vigorous, capturing the growing pains of an emerging profession in a rapidly changing environment. From Mary Richmond's (1917) early encouragement to base diagnoses on grounded observations through more contemporary pressures from managed care (c.f. Berger & Ai, 2000; J. A. Cohen, 2003), the call for evidence has been constant and contentious. Shifting over time from background to foreground, it has shaped social workers' claims for their conceptualization of client problems and the effectiveness of their efforts to help.

As early as the Milford Conference (American Association of Social Workers, 1929), social workers recognized that the future development of their profession was, in large part, dependent on its developing a scientific character. But what that might mean was not so clear. Leading institutions in that era (i.e., the School of Applied Social Sciences at Case Western Reserve University) defined the scientific method in social casework as the systematic application of psychoanalytic principles, and *The Social Work Yearbook* did not post its first entry under "research" until 1933.

Zimbalist (1977), in his landmark history of social welfare research, cites the calamities leading to and following the U.S. stock market crash of 1929 as motivating the call for social indices documenting dependency, delinquency, and illness. The goal was to collect detailed, standardized statistics on critical social welfare concerns, using the resulting data to call attention to social need and justify plans of action. These culminated in the "social breakdown index" (p. 227), popularized in the late 1930s and early 1940s. The idea, he writes, "was to provide an instrument for the 'measurement and control' of social breakdown, which was defined as 'behavior that does not conform to currently accepted concepts of satisfactory social adjustment'" (p. 227). Zimbalist's summary of the problems encountered and results achieved lays the groundwork for much we will discuss in coming chapters and is worth quoting at length here.

> The measurement, however, was achieved by combining in arbitrary fashion seven different rates based on official records (such as divorce, delinquency, etc.) and assuming that this composite reflected the broad range of social maladjustment in the community. In addition, the authors of this device went on to advocate that this index be used not only as a measure of social needs, thus confounding needs with services, but also as a gauge of the effectiveness of existing services, apparently on the dubious assumption that social agencies could be held substantially accountable for the amount of official breakdown that occurred in a community. It is to the credit of the field's common sense and growing research maturity that this overly ambitious approach was quickly recognized as deficient in many aspects and was subjected to penetrating and effective critique in the literature (p. 227).

Consistently driven by their identification with hands-on responses to social problems, caseworkers often led from the heart and favored education in institutions set apart from related disciplines such as psychology, sociology, and anthropology. The ideological purity afforded by such separation came at the expense of keeping pace with training in the scientific method, much less participation in shaping its development. As a result, social workers came late to the recognition, emerging elsewhere in the social sciences throughout the 1940–1950s, that operationalizing reliable and valid constructs would be key to successfully defending their views in the coming competition for demonstrating practice effectiveness. William Gordon, observing in the 1960s that the concept of a social work scientist was more of a challenging hypothesis than an empirical reality, urged his colleagues to recognize the essential distinction between values and knowledge. "For social work," he wrote, "the minimum first step is the separation of what social work prefers or wants for people from what social work knows about people" (Gordon, 1965, p. 37). With the ascendant appeal of behaviorism in the helping professions, the message for the future seemed clear: "social work would for the first time be in a position to evaluate scientifically rather than simply on the basis of preference the proposed social arrangements and behaviors thought to be good for people" (1965, p. 39).

Spurred by the growing awareness that social workers may not be delivering quite all that they assumed, Joel Fischer undertook a landmark study that effectively pulled the rug out from under the profession's confidence that good works must surely follow good intentions (Fischer, 1976). Following the earlier work of Hans Eysenck in psychology, Fischer critically assessed the arguments for practice effectiveness and found the evidence lacking. Perhaps predictably, the profession turned on itself, kicking off a period of tumult mixing a tendency to "shoot the messenger" with bursts of creativity promoting major changes in both the methods and directions of practice evaluation. Reviving appeals to redefine professional values, Hudson (1982a) urged more critical assessments of the description and diagnosis of client problems, stressing the importance of valid and reliable measurement as a necessary precondition for ethical clinical practice. Challenging his critics to reply with evidence rather than rhetoric, he based his position on the "first axioms of treatment": "if you cannot measure the client's problem, it does not exist", and by extension, if the problem doesn't exist, "you cannot treat it" (1978, p. 65).

Building on his extensive study of psychometrics and a research agenda started in the mid-1970s, Hudson responded to Fischer's critique by publishing a collection of nine scales that he characterized as "partially validated" (Hudson, 1982b). The instruments in *The Clinical Measurement Package* (including measures of depression, self-esteem, marital and family discord, and varying dyadic family and peer relations) were by then available in Chinese, French, German, and Spanish and had been distributed in 15 countries outside the United States. Clearly, the work was underway. Responding to practitioners' concerns that using such measures involved too much time and trouble, Hudson and Nurius (1988) adapted an expanding array of measures for the *Clinical Assessment System (CAS)*. Designed to ease the burdens of administration, scoring, and interpretation of rapid assessment instruments, *CAS* made scales accessible through desktop computers and established Hudson as the leading innovator in the field.

Concurrent with this progress, managed care emerged as a force to be reckoned with in health and mental health service delivery. Nominally a strategy to contain the escalation of costs in service provision (Cornelius, 1994), managed care resulted in the careful monitoring of social workers' efforts and called into question the profession's autonomy in defining client problems and the methods used to treat them. The accompanying expansion of brief treatment models in mental health served the dual purpose of limiting time available with clients (in the interest of efficiency) and defining the terms under which their progress could be assessed (J. A. Cohen, 2003). Increased skill in the use of scales was tied to improved abilities in documenting treatment outcomes, but not without avoiding the "arrogance" of assuming that scales meeting the needs of program managers would simultaneously be of value to clients (Neuman, 2003, p. 9).

For educators, the implications were clear and included the development of more and better measurement tools to demonstrate the relevance and effectiveness of social work interventions (Strom–Gottfried, 1997). Calls to incorporate training in the use of valid and reliable outcome measures emerged in health-care environments (Berger & Ai, 2000), instrument selection was streamlined for family practitioners (Early, 2001), and 94% of field instructors in one study identified evaluation of progress through outcome measures as a critical skill for current and future practitioners (Kane, Hamlin, & Hawkins, 2000).

Still, debate continued over the rush to accommodate what some perceived as environmental pressures risking disregard for the best interests of the client. Witkin, commenting as the editor of *Social Work*, the profession's widest circulation journal, cautioned that the "mystery and power of measurement" (2001, p. 101) encouraged potentially embarrassing misinterpretation of the meaning and limitations associated with reducing complex problems to quantified scale scores. Summarizing a broad critique, he proposed a set of core questions to guide the processes of scale development, administration, and use:

- To what extent are the cultural and life experiences of people of color, gay and lesbian people, people with disabilities, and other disadvantaged groups considered by the test?
- What are the practice implications of having clients complete this test? For example, do they get categorized into psychiatric syndromes?
- Of what theory is this test an expression?
- What can the test tell me beyond what I already know or could know about this individual? (2001, p. 104)

We will return to Witkin's questions as anchors, keeping us honest about both the potentials and limitations of these methods in the text that follows. As we will see, these questions, summarizing many social workers' misgivings about the too-casual use of a technology they find objectionable on both conceptual and methodological grounds, are well-developed in psychometric literature (c.f. American Educational Research Association et al., 1999; Messick, 1989). Today, these questions and others like them are often posed, pondered, and heatedly debated within the context of a broader conversation that is unfolding in social work around evidence-based practice (EBP).

To dispel some of the myths and misconceptions associated with EBP, Rubin (2008, p. 7) provides a comprehensive definition:

EBP is a process for making practice decisions in which practitioners integrate the best research evidence available with their practice expertise and with client attributes, values, preferences, and circumstances. When those decisions involve selecting an intervention to provide, practitioners will attempt to maximize the likelihood that their clients will receive the most effective intervention possible in light of the following:

- The most rigorous scientific evidence available;
- practitioner expertise;
- client attributes, values, preferences, and circumstances;
- assessing for each case whether the chosen intervention is achieving the desired outcome, and;
- if the intervention is not achieving the desired outcome, repeating the process of choosing and evaluating alternative interventions.

In each of these five steps, there is ample room for the consideration and utilization of standardized scales. As we will hopefully show in this book, scales should be developed and validated using the most rigorous psychometric methods available. Practitioners must tap their clinical expertise, and seriously consider the unique needs and circumstances of their clients when choosing a measure. Standardized scales are certainly one way to monitor a client's progress on the targeted goals over the course of treatment. Finally, if the client is not demonstrating treatment progress, certain questions should be asked by the practitioner: "Are the tools that I have selected sensitive enough to detect change?" "Is there an alternative treatment that might produce better results?" "If so, what scales give us the best shot at capturing any change experienced by the client?"

SOME KEY CONCEPTS

The *Standards for Educational and Psychological Testing* (American Educational Research Association et al., 1999), designed to provide criteria for the development and use of measures, defines *scales* or *inventories* as instruments measuring attitudes, interests, or dispositions. These, as distinguished from *tests* measuring performance or abilities, will be our focus. In scales, responses to multiple items are combined into a composite score presumed to be caused by a common latent construct. This feature distinguishes scales from *indexes* whose items may, by contrast, sum to predict a larger outcome without having been found to be its cause (DeVellis, 2003).

At the heart of this process is the identification of target *constructs*, historically defined as characteristics that are not directly observable, but more broadly defined as "any concept or characteristic that a (scale) is designed to measure" (American Educational Research Association et al., 1999, p. 5). As we will see, the identification and definition of target constructs is one of the primary, and often underestimated, challenges in scale development. Careful consideration must be given to the overlapping roles of the many persons involved in development and validation, including those who:

- prepare and develop the scale
- publish and market it
- administer and score it
- use its results in decision-making
- interpret its results for clients
- take the scale by choice, direction, or necessity
- sponsor the scale
- select or review its comparative qualities and suitability for defined purposes (1999, p. 1).

All have a role in shaping the emergent *validity* of the scale, meaning, in the most global sense, the evidence supporting any interpretation of its score. As the *Standards* emphasize, and as we will detail in subsequent chapters, contemporary interpretations of *construct validity* depend on multiple lines of evidence, all of which support a summary conclusion of the extent to which scores can be defended as accurate indications of a meaningful characteristic or trait.

Together, these terms will form the core of our efforts, determining the nature and scope of the construct to be measured and considering it in light of who will use it, with whom, and for what purposes. Collectively, these will be considered our necessary—but not sufficient— foundation for scale development and validation. To these, we will add the range of techniques to be used in reaching conclusions about the validity of scales developed for specific purposes and illustrate design and analytic methods meant to provide the best possible evidence.

In sum, these express the obligations of measurement in applied social sciences: to consider the needs and best interests of those we serve, and to rigorously develop tools enabling them to show or tell us how they really are. In turn, we commit ourselves to understanding what a scale does and does not consistently and accurately reveal and to limit our interpretations (and their implications) accordingly. Although "late to the party" in some respects, social workers over the past three decades have been rapidly making up for lost time. Our hope is that our "lessons learned" will generalize to and provide some inspiration for human and social service providers who take up the challenge of giving voice to our clients through proven and practical tools.

OUR PLAN

Our primary aim is to make the essential components of scale development and validation accessible to both practitioners and researchers, respecting the complexity of the tasks and methods involved in design and analysis while distilling it to essentials meeting contemporary standards. In this relatively brief format, we will set some prior limitations, specifically choosing an emphasis on techniques associated with classical measurement theory (CMT; also known as classical test theory) and factor analysis. We will also, in selected applications (including, for example, tasks associated with bilingual validation), incorporate techniques assessing item invariance.

At the outset, we acknowledge that an understanding of psychometrics, like much of research methodology, is necessarily nonlinear. There are some techniques that can be taught step-by-step, but it is unwise to assume that subsequent elements need only be considered when their time has come up in rotation. Anticipating the complexity of a resulting factor structure, for instance, is best undertaken from the beginning of construct conceptualization. Otherwise, disappointment may lie ahead when validation hypotheses are tested. Successful execution of a validation study requires conceptual understanding of each analytic component and the capacity to anticipate related implications during design of the draft instrument and the various studies required to generate information and data for subsequent analyses. Within this context, our sequence follows.

In Chapter 2, we emphasize instrument design and consider what to measure, with implications for the social relevance of scale interpretation and scoring. Considering how to measure, and for whom, will raise design questions, including composition of a team of relevant actors who, by their roles and/or skills, can contribute meaningfully to the draft form of a scale. The structure and format of the measure will address age, readability, and language considerations, anticipating scale length and the resulting burden on both respondents and administrators. How do we determine the "ideal" length of a scale? Other topics to be addressed include creation of scale items, use of focus groups and expert panels, selection of response options, and consideration of scoring techniques and their resulting interpretations.

In Chapter 3, we move to design of the psychometric study. As the critical vehicle for gathering the raw material from which evidence will be established, numerous sampling issues must be addressed. Who should be recruited? In what numbers? How do analytic strategies drive these decisions? When, if ever, are "nonclinical" samples acceptable? In our discussion, we reflect on "real-world" gaps between methodological ideals (i.e., probability samples) and the accessibility of populations of interest for social service providers. Having considered the nature and goals of sampling, we turn to development of a data collection package, including its components, layout, and sequence. Well-designed scales must be validated in thoughtfully constructed studies where recruitment and training of associates, anticipation of labor and costs, and plans for data management and entry have all been carefully considered.

In Chapter 4, we "buckle down" with reliability, considering the basis in CMT for concepts of consistency or stability in measurement. The origins of common reliability coefficients are identified, along with critiques of their interpretation and use. How good is "good enough?" Do the same standards apply to scores that are composites of subscale scores? What is the meaning of "item-level" reliability, and how is it associated with related interpretations of factor structure? We summarize computation of the standard error of measurement (*SEM*) and illustrate its place in practical interpretations of observed scores for individuals.

Validity is addressed in Chapter 5, where we deconstruct the multiple forms of evidence combined to establish the construct validity of a measure. Some forms (i.e., face and content validity) will be shown as fundamentally intuitive or conceptual, although minimal quantification may apply. Still, they are not to be underestimated. Convergent and discriminant construct validity are traced to their early roots in psychometric theory and presented as opposite sides of a common coin approximating the accuracy of a new scale score. Criterion-related validity is overviewed in both its concurrent and predictive forms, with an overview of receiver operating characteristics (ROC) analysis as a tool for gauging scale sensitivity and specificity.

In Chapter 6, we devote our attention to factor analysis and its broad significance in psychometrics. We examine why it is important in scale construction, introducing concepts of latent traits and latent variables. Issues associated with continuous versus categorical measurement are explored, and we overview the inter-relationships of exploratory and confirmatory factor analytic models (EFAs and CFAs, respectively). We describe and detail in applied illustrations the potentials and limitations of EFA and reconsider the underlying significance of theory in guiding construct conceptualization and identification. Uni- and multidimensional models are examined using CFA, and we deconstruct the language of factorial invariance and differential item functioning (DIF). Finally, we examine CFA with categorical measurement indicators and consider the relationship of these techniques to item–response theory (IRT) applications and interpretations.

In Chapter 7, we tie it all together, integrating the seemingly discrete elements of psychometric analyses into implications for practice and research. How do we make summary sense of the varying forms of evidence accumulated and reach conclusions whether to promote our scale as a new addition to the tool kit or go back to the drawing board? Often, the decision will not be easy. And looking ahead, how do we anticipate the expanding needs for measurement in the social and behavioral sciences? Will we, and can we, respond to increasing calls for diversity and population-specific measures? How and when can we balance the tensions between universally applicable and culturally relevant tools?

We hope, in sum, that these topics will serve readers well as they grapple with the challenges of scaling. To the extent that we succeed, the many actors identified by the *Standards* as players in the measurement game (i.e., developers, respondents, administrators, and interpreters) are all more likely to come out winners.

2

Instrument Design

Each in their own way, Witkin (2001) and *The Standards* (American Educational Research Association et al., 1999) remind us that instrument design begins with respectful consideration of those who will take, score, or interpret a measure. Whether stressing careful consideration of the intended use of a scale, its potential implications for specific or diverse populations, or the broad spectrum of actors involved from its inception through use and interpretation, the message is clear. Although seemingly simple on its surface, instrument design is a subtle and complex process calling for clear understanding of one's starting objectives and appreciation of the care needed at each step to achieve the desired result.

Often, scale developers begin with a sense of urgency, concerned that clients' problems haven't been usefully identified or that existing measures fail to capture some new understanding of a key variable. Whether designers are motivated to improve responses to clinical problems or to stake out new conceptual territory in the literature, they risk making serious errors early on that are difficult, if not impossible, to repair when discovered too late.

Thus, clarity and caution from the beginning are critical to instrument design. In the following sections, we overview and illustrate the processes of clarifying goals—both abstract and substantive—when conceiving and justifying the need for a new measure. Having a good idea regarding the information available and the information missing in the literature is essential. Knowing how to conceptualize an abstraction, identify its underlying components, and translate them into clear statements or items can be much more challenging. Caught up in these processes, it is easy to forget that such intellectual labor is only meaningful when the resulting instrument serves a useful purpose and minimizes risks or harm to others.

Designers must also be familiar with the structural options in scale development. There are choices to be made regarding integrating or distinguishing scale dimensions, phrasing item content, and formatting response options. Each has implications for the resulting psychometric qualities of the scale. Because these tasks almost always benefit from the input of a well-constructed team, we will also consider when and how to invite them into the process.

DECIDING WHAT TO MEASURE

This seems like "the easy part," and sometimes it is. Often, however, what begins as a straightforward sense of focus drifts into a murky mess. Ideas that seemed crystal clear (i.e., stress, resilience, self-efficacy) are revealed as ambiguous or vague and beg for specification as instrument development gets underway. Compiling the work-to-date on stress, for instance, the editors of a comprehensive handbook concluded that its broad interpretations (a cause, a result, a process, depending on who was using it and how) had rendered the term almost useless (Goldberger & Breznitz, 1993). A quick study of the literature on resilience will find it defined as "the ability to bear up in spite of . . .ordeals" (Saleeby, 2002, p. 11), a lack of psychological symptoms following violence (Feinauer & Stuart, 1996), or a static, even biological trait contributing to invulnerability (Anthony & Cohler, 1987). When the same term can define a process, an outcome, or a characteristic, scale developers wishing to capture it have their work cut out for them from the very beginning.

From one point of view, ambiguous definitions provide the scale developer with an opportunity to help settle a debate over whether one use of a term is preferable to others. From another angle, we may find the literature scan frustrating and confusing rather than clarifying. Either way, one of the first issues in deciding what to measure depends on our ability to identify how others are using our term of interest and making a choice based on factors such as history, predominance, or innovation. Each can provide a defensible justification for choosing a starting definition.

Finding a Focus

Identifying a target for scale development is the first critical step. Doing so involves understanding the notion of a *construct* and, once identified, locating it in a context of personal, professional, and social relevance. As indicated earlier, *The Standards* (American Educational Research Association et al., 1999) take a broad view, considering a construct to include any concept or characteristic that becomes the focus of scale development.

Historically, however, constructs referred to characteristics that were not directly observable, including abstract notions that could only be understood by asking others to self-report on an internalized characteristic or trait. Although there may be observable components of anxiety, for instance, or family stress, ultimately these qualities are best understood by providing specific prompts (i.e., questions or statements) linked to clear, consistent response options. In classical measurement theory, the construct or target in scale development is understood as a *latent variable* (not directly observable, and subject to change) that is best expressed through *observable indicators* (quantified responses to individual scale items) (DeVellis, 2003).

In this sense, as we will develop more fully in discussions of the path analyses associated with structural equation modeling, the latent variable is considered to be the "cause" of responses or scores on individual scale items. For instance, how well someone reported being able to "bounce back to normal" after a traumatic event could be seen as driven by their underlying capacity for resilience. Although the resilience itself remains unseen, responses to an intentionally developed set of items reflecting it become the observable indicators. Collectively, they permit the person taking the scale to reveal his or her underlying experience.

Achieving this goal is no easy feat, although scale developers may start out thinking otherwise. Beginning with the search for a clear, easily understandable definition requires striking a balance between oversimplified reductions of complex ideas and overly ambitious attempts to scoop too many concepts into a single, measurable construct.

When shaping a definition, developers must consider how a term has been used in the past. Doing so increases the likelihood that the resulting scale will be useful in grounding previously abstract ideas and in testing hypotheses based on specific theories. However, as illustrated earlier with resilience or stress, the literature can sometimes cloud as much as clarify. Ideas often develop along parallel tracks and become quite advanced before having been adequately tested. In such cases, a good literature review might help scale developers pick their path by demonstrating that one definition has emerged as dominant.

When this cannot be shown (or when the developer's own agenda is to challenge a popular position), another option is to pick a side. Taking this path, the developer's obligation is to justify the reason for selecting one definition over others and to specify that all subsequent aspects of construct refinement and item development reflect that decision. Those who prefer varying definitions are then clearly informed of the focus and limitations of the new measure and are free to adopt or reject it based on how well it fits their needs.

A third option is to innovate. This might evolve from frustration with unresolved debates in the literature or from an insight that two previously independent points of view might be integrated to open up new ways of solving conceptual or applied problems. The resulting composite definition could blend elements from existing streams into some new whole. In best-case scenarios, this advances old arguments by integrating ideas from competing camps. Measures produced in this way may move a field forward by making new propositions testable.

Stigmatizing People Living with HIV/AIDS

Consider a proposal for a scale measuring the stigma experienced or expressed by health-care and social service providers working with people living with HIV/AIDS (PLHA). In this context, the core construct is *stigmatizing*, and a review of the literature finds it defined as assigning to others via labeling, stereotyping, separation, and status loss or discrimination attributes that are deeply discrediting and reduce the recipient "from a whole and usual person to a tainted, discounted one" (Goffman, 1963, in Nyblade, 2006, p. 336). As derived from social cognition theory, this is quite a mouthful, and only provides a foundation for an even more complex construct.

As Link and Phelan (2001) initially proposed, and with others have recently amplified, stigmatizing must also take into consideration the emotional responses of those receiving and expressing the stigma (Link, Yang, Phelan, & Collins, 2004) and their sense of what is morally at stake for them in their relationships with others (Yang et al., 2007). Furthermore, stigmatizing thoughts and actions can be distinguished as felt or enacted, depending on whether the reactions to the PLHA are noticed but held within or expressed overtly in interactions (Van Brakel, 2006).

Finding a focus here means recognizing that a strong organizing theme in the literature centers on social cognition theory and that the construct has matured in such a way that related ideas have taken on increasing significance. Furthermore, because the *latent construct* can at least partly be known only to the person having the particular thoughts or feelings, some of its expression can only be revealed by developing good scale items (*observable indicators*) that invite service providers to show how they feel or think.

As we will demonstrate, developers taking on a construct as complex as this one will need to make some hard choices. How much detail can really be captured? How will the weight given to certain components of the definition guide emphasizing them over others? What, if anything, must be eliminated in setting reasonable goals for scale development, and where will developers find opportunities to integrate or innovate in making final decisions? These and other issues must all be resolved early and, adding even more complexity, will be best considered when developers remember the context in which the scale will eventually be applied.

Putting Things in Context

Ultimately, the meanings and interpretations suggested above are only defensible when the reliability and validity of scale responses have been determined. As Messick (1989) reminds us, the responses we study to establish these qualities are not only functions of the scale items but also of the people taking them and the context in which they do so. Although we will consider the particulars of establishing an evidence base for reliability and validity elsewhere, in the earliest stages of scale development, construct clarification depends on designers being aware of their own motivations and biases.

Scales are ultimately established so they can be scored, and those scores become the basis for reaching conclusions about others' characteristics or qualities that may or may not be in their best interest. In the social and behavioral sciences, these *consequential interpretations* of scale scores mean that, from the start, developers must be aware of their own prejudices regarding the target population and/or the meaning of target construct(s) (Messick, 1989).

Considering our illustration of HIV/AIDS service providers and stigmatization, the new measure might be used to help providers become more aware of their tendencies and be included in interventions designed to reduce stigmatizing in clinics and agencies. Once providers reveal how they really think or feel about PLHAs, do we wish to punish or support them? Parker and Aggleton (2003) emphasize that stigmatizing and discriminating may entrench power and control relationships and legitimize inequities such as those based on gender, sexual orientation, race, or ethnicity. How does our translation of a textbook construct into scale items risk distortion if we, in designing the measure, are unaware of our own biases? What risks do we generate for PLHA or service providers if others, in scoring and interpreting the scale, come to punitive conclusions about them?

Scale developers must consider how the language they use in designing scale items might unintentionally express their own biases or even hide their ignorance about the implications of asking others to reveal controversial thoughts or feelings. Assessment tools are inherently built to help make judgments, but not all of these are innocent or without consequence. In creating an instrument that, when scored, reveals sensitive, personal, or even unacceptable characteristics or views, developers must give careful consideration not only to the risks to those who eventually take the scale but also to any potential harm that might come from others deciding their scores identify them as "good" or "bad."

For Messick (1989), considering the vulnerabilities and strengths of future respondents requires reflection not only on their immediate reactions and circumstances but also on the broader *social consequences* of a scale's administration and interpretation. As we will see in greater depth in Chapter 5, even the selection of a construct label can be critically important, as it communicates to scale users and interpreters a potentially powerful message about the meaning of observed scale scores.

How can we minimize risks associated with subsequent use of the scale? The saying "guns don't kill people; people do" may seem extreme, but it makes the point that our best opportunity to build in safety devices for scales comes in the design phase, not once a measure is released for use. We need to consider the potential uses to which a scale we design might be put and weigh the benefits of designing such a tool against the risk that it will be misinterpreted or used in harmful ways.

Family Stress and Self-Efficacy Among People Living with HIV/AIDS

For families whose members are dealing with HIV/AIDS, managing illness is often complicated by the challenges of ordinary daily life. Health-care and social service providers helping them deal with problems at home may find it hard to separate disruptions caused by everyday struggles from those resulting from the disease itself (Cohen, Nehring, Malm, & Harris, 1995). Given this, the Family Responsibility Scale (FRS) was developed to measure "the feeling of overwhelm a parent may

1. Taking care of my family is overwhelming.
2. The pressure of caring for my family is very great.
3. I feel completely worn out by all I must do at home.
4. The demands placed on me at home are wearing me down.
5. Caring for others is taking over my life.
6. After handling my family needs, I have no energy for anything else.
7. Because of my home responsibilities, I can't keep up with my job.
8. Not getting enough rest makes me upset with my family.
9. Because of all the things I must do, I hurry from one thing to the next.
10. I feel I can't keep up with everything that's expected of me at home.
11. Being responsible for others really wears me out.

Figure 2.1   Original FRS item pool.

experience as a result of fulfilling responsibilities as a head of household" (Abell, Ryan, Kamata, & Citrolo, 2006, p. 197). Selected items are displayed in Figure 2.1.

Several potential bias and interpretation issues might apply when defining this construct and imagining its potential interpretations. What are our attitudes toward HIV-positive women who are heads of household? How are these compounded by our judgments about how they were exposed to the virus (i.e., commercial sex work, injection drug use, or unprotected sex with an unfaithful partner)? How might these associations influence our process of item generation and subsequent scale scoring and interpretation?

If the developer was not clear about his or her own biases, then items designed to measure family responsibility might be written so that unacknowledged judgments about these parents slip through. For instance, "I feel I can't keep up with everything that's expected of me at home" might have been written as "I'm too sick to do a good job as a parent" or "I just can't manage everything needed to keep my child well." Although the language in each variation might legitimately reflect the definition of family responsibility, each could also be interpreted as evidence that the parent was unfit. Taken to the extreme, honest answers to the items might lead to scale score interpretations that jeopardize the parent's custodial rights.

The Parental Self-Care Scale (PSCS; Abell, Ryan, & Kamata, 2006), based on an existing conceptualization of self-efficacy (DeVellis & DeVellis, 2001), was developed as a companion to the FRS. The PSCS was designed to incorporate a dimensional structure adopted in the earlier Willingness to Care (WTC) Scale (Abell, 2001). Whereas the WTC captures one person's capacity to care for another who is ill, the PSCS reverses the perspective, measuring ill HIV-positive parents' capacities to manage their own emotional, instrumental, and nursing needs while maintaining family responsibilities. Parents completing the scale (*see* the initial item pool and instructions in Fig. 2.2) would report on their beliefs that they could care for themselves while also caring for others.

When administered by someone wishing to support an HIV-positive head of household, the PSCS can help target areas where resources or services could make the difference in keeping a family together. The exact same score interpreted in an oppositional or hostile manner (e.g., in criminal or family court contexts) could help make a case against the HIV-positive parent's suitability to retain custody or manage overnight visitation in his or her home. We will return to illustrations based on the FRS and PSCS throughout the text. For now, they serve as examples of the potential for "innocent" scale scores to take on meanings scale developers may not intend and illustrate the importance of considering the future contexts of scale administration, scoring, and interpretation when conceptualizing target constructs.

DECIDING HOW TO MEASURE, AND FOR WHOM

In some cases, reflection on definitional and contextual issues will lead to a clear sense of direction. When scale developers end this process confident that they know what they are after, they can move straight into decisions about the basic mechanics of the scale. In other cases,

Taking good care of yourself while being a parent can be a big job. Please read each item below, showing **how sure you are that you can take care of yourself** in these ways **while still taking care of your family.**

Emotional self-care

1. Find someone to talk to when I'm sad.
2. Get some comfort when I'm upset.
3. Calm my anxiety about the future.
4. Get through the times when I'm afraid.
5. Find a way to deal with feeling hopeless.
6. Get support for my concerns about dying.
7. Keep my spirits up.
8. Connect with others when I feel like crying.
9. Handle the times when I'm angry.
10. Get a grip on things when I can't remember well or am confused.

Instrumental self-care

11. Get to my medical appointments.
12. Get groceries I need.
13. Pay for my medicine.
14. Be sure my meals are made.
15. Get my house clean.
16. Wash the dishes.
17. Do the laundry.
18. Pay for my food and housing.
19. Get someone to stay with me when I need help.
20. Work with my doctor to plan for my medical care.

Nursing self-care

21. Take my medicine the right way.
22. Make sure my bed is changed when it needs it.
23. Take a bath or shower.
24. Clean up if I lose control of my bowels or bladder.
25. Make sure I can eat my meals.
26. Clean up if I throw up.
27. Move around to stay comfortable in bed.
28. Make sure my dressings are changed if I have sores.
29. Get in and out of the bathroom.
30. Get in and out of bed as I need to.

Figure 2.2   Original PSCS item pool.

developers will end the same process realizing that they know less than they thought going in and will recognize the need to ground their ideas before going forward.

On the one hand, it may seem best to seize the momentum from a solid literature review and forge ahead with item development and quantitative validation. After all, from a researcher's point of view, scale development is just another form of hypothesis testing. So long as we are willing to be proven wrong, what harm can come from putting our best ideas forward and seeing whether they stand up to examination? On the other hand, recognizing that not enough is known about the target construct can lead to pulling back and calling for open-ended discussion with people whose life experiences may help the developers avoid serious mistakes or omissions. Although it is potentially time-consuming and even tedious, knowing when to put on the brakes and invite some qualitative analysis can make all the difference in how those quantitative tests turn out. In this spirit of open-ended inquiry, we provide a brief introduction to concept mapping.

CONCEPT MAPPING

In concept mapping, data are generated from participants' own words, and maps are interpreted regarding the meaning of phenomenon in the actual context. Therefore, concept mapping is a useful method to organize and interpret qualitative data with quantitative techniques, resulting in a pictorial representation (Johnsen, Biegel, & Shafran, 2000). In other words, "Concept Mapping . . .displays all of the ideas of the group relative to the topic at hand, shows how these ideas are related to each other, and optionally, shows which ideas are more relevant, important, or appropriate" (Trochim, 1989, p. 2).

Thus, as it relates to scale development, we see concept mapping as a potential tool to tap in response to questions raised earlier in this chapter. What are the social consequences of a scale's use? Do we have a hidden bias or a blind ignorance about the implications of asking others to reveal controversial thoughts or feelings? Are we clear in our conceptualization of a construct and its corresponding scale? What are our attitudes toward HIV-positive women who are heads of household?

There are six general steps in the concept mapping process: preparation, generation of ideas or statements, structuring of statements, concept mapping analysis, interpretation of maps, and utilization (Kane

& Trochim, 2007). A brainstorming session generates statements or phrases from key stakeholders in response to a focus statement. After generating statements, participants group them into similar piles and rate each item's importance (Shern, Trochim, & LaComb, 1995). Trochim (1989) recommends between 10 and 20 people for a suitable sample size in the concept mapping system.

Researchers have also used concept mapping to assist in scale development and validation (cf. Butler et al., 2007; Weert-van Oene et al., 2006). For example, Butler and colleagues (2007) used concept mapping in the development of the Current Opioid Misuse Measure (COMM) for patients already on long-term opioid therapy. "The focus prompt distributed to the participants was: 'Please list specific aberrant drug-related behaviors of chronic pain patients *already taking opioids for pain*. Please list as many indicators as possible that may signal that a patient is having problems with opioid therapy'" (Butler et al., 2007, p. 145). Through the concept mapping process, six primary concepts underlying medication misuse were identified, which were used to develop an initial item pool of the COMM. In the rating phase, the items were rated on importance and relevance by 22 pain and addictions specialists.

The Concept System® software generates the statistical calculation needed to generate maps. The software implements calculations such as data aggregation, multidimensional scaling (MDS), cluster analysis, bridging analysis, and sort pile label analysis (Michalski & Cousins, 2000). Among these methods, MDS and cluster analysis are the major statistical processes (Davison, 1983; Kruskal & Wish, 1978).

This method allows the facilitator to combine the ideas of individuals through statistical analyses and then to formulate visual representations of the data. The result is a pictorial representation of the data in concept maps. The concept maps are visual representations of the topic being explored. The maps show how ideas are related to each other and help to identify which of the ideas are more important to the participants. Although the facilitator manages the concept mapping process, the ideas generated by the group are the impetus for the content of the map (Kane & Trochim, 2007).

For those who may be interested, concept mapping facilitator training and the concept mapping computer program software are available through Concept Systems Incorporated (Ithaca, NY). Concept Systems Incorporated provides the software and a Facilitator Training Seminar Manual for those who complete the facilitator training (Concept Systems Incorporated, 2006).

Using Focus Groups to Refine Understanding

A maxim that pops up where advocacy and human rights are concerned is "nothing about us without us." Applied to scale development, it can remind us that settling on the meaning of terms or selection of language describing others should always include opportunities for them to have their say. Focus groups provide formats for developers to engage in open-ended dialog with others and clarify the meaning of ambiguous terms. They can then learn how those terms are applied or interpreted in various cultural, ethnic, or socioeconomic settings and identify specific words or phrases that best express particular ideas. The payoff for clear conceptualization and item development can be enormous (Gilgun, 2004).

Focus group methodology is a topic in itself, and a rich literature is available to explore it in detail (c.f. Edmunds, 1999; Krueger & Casey, 2000). Here, we concentrate on a few essential components, illustrating where appropriate with examples from two groups conducted in Grenada, West Indies. There, insights offered by PLHA and by workers in the Ministry of Health helped shape an understanding of HIV/AIDS stigma in one Eastern Caribbean country (Rutledge, Abell, Padmore, & McCann, 2007).

Considering Purpose

Focus groups can be invaluable in cross-checking developers' assumptions about the social relevance of a target construct. In Grenada, investigators from the United States sought to confirm whether combating stigma was as high a priority in that developing nation as in other parts of the world. In the United States, medical progress in prevention of HIV transmission and in treatment of HIV-related disease is sometimes stymied by the fears and discrimination associated with seeking care. Was it safe to assume these same dynamics applied in Grenada and, if so, that PLHA would view them as important in comparison to other life challenges? A nurse–midwife participating in a focus group for service providers told us:

> I think . . . we need to have everybody on board. With legislation and so on, but also (with) the aim of letting people know that HIV is here and the stigma, what you are addressing here . . . would be important. Then we could move towards getting rid of . . . the discrimination that exists here and elsewhere. What it does is drive the epidemic underground. That's when they want to be secretive. It's not short term we're talking about. I think that that's where we ought to go. So people have to buy into this . . . even the nurses, the doctors, the lawyers, the teachers, everybody. Get them on board and continue to put the message out there.

When a focus group of PLHA was asked whether stigma should be prioritized, two women had the following exchange:

> Speaker A: I need a job, I have four children and I am unemployed. I need a job.
> Speaker B: I find . . . the stigma first because . . . even though you have a job, you have to eat, so food is something you need everyday, as long as you living with the stigma, there is something about the stigma that gets you unnerved. There's something about the stigma (that) kinda puts you inside a shell, it sort of sends you in. If you are active, you now become inactive; you are afraid to participate in functions and so forth. The stigma is the one that, I think, that needs to be stopped.

Taken together, responses from the two groups seemed to support the relevance of concentrating on stigma, while providing reminders that the challenges of daily life were critical, too.

Focus groups can also be useful in critiquing the applicability and relevance of preferred construct definitions and can provide opportunities for brainstorming potential terms and phrases to be used later in developing meaningful items. In the Grenadian groups, for instance, researchers learned that people usually targeted for stigma and discrimination were labeled with words that were unfamiliar in the United States. Commercial sex workers or prostitutes, for instance, might be called "sketels," and men who have sex with men could be called "battymen." Knowing slang or dialect favored in particular settings can help in writing items that will be more relevant or realistic within specific populations. As a result, questions of "how" to measure are usefully refined.

Recruiting Intentionally and Effectively

The question of "for whom" developers are measuring should be answerable, in part, by who is recruited for focus group membership. If a tool is meant to be used by children who have experienced or witnessed violent trauma, developers will have to seek them out in treatment settings or school environments and adhere to all the precautions necessary to protect their well-being. If it is meant for persons infected with or affected by HIV/AIDS, then elaborate procedures will likely be needed to get permission even to contact them, much less invite their participation in a group.

The "for whom" question is also reflected in the substance and content of the group itself, and will color its primary objectives. For instance, if the new tool is meant for use by professionals serving PLHA, then developers will have to consider in advance how their questions should be refocused to reflect the role of helpers while not assuming prematurely that none of them are also HIV-positive. Questions about stigma, for example, might take on very different meaning depending on whether the respondents are personally or professionally impacted by the illness, or both.

Focus groups are intentionally small to facilitate qualitative analysis of transcribed responses to open-ended questions. The size of the group should also reflect the developer's need for reasonable diversity among a defined set of participants. Members of the Grenadian service providers' group included nurse–midwives, a Ministry of Health medical officer, and a National Infectious Disease Control Unit counselor. Selection criteria balanced a range of roles and skills thought to represent a continuum of care. Researchers also recognized that too few members might mean shy participants would keep quiet, whereas too many could result in important views being drowned out by dominant members.

Scale developers should compose groups by drawing on their own connections where possible. However, gatekeepers can be useful allies when the developer lacks close contacts with others most likely to fill in the gaps in his or her understanding. Sensitivity to unproductive combinations of members is also useful. Where strong views could be reasonably expected based on individual members' characteristics (i.e., sexual orientation, gender, race or ethnicity, or social roles), developers should consider whether diversity or similarity among members is most likely to yield the information they seek. If conflict or tension is possible, developers are better realizing this in advance and making membership decisions accordingly. The goal should be to encourage rather than inhibit candor so members feel free to speak their minds on sensitive topics without going off on unproductive tangents.

Having a "Firm but Flexible" Gameplan

Paraphrasing the poet Robert Burns, we are all familiar with the experience that the best laid plans of mice and men often go awry (Hirsch, Kett, & Trefil, 2002). Despite our best efforts to stick to an intended purpose and recruit members who can help us do so, things can and do go wrong in focus groups. Scripts developed to guide questions and discussions can quickly seem irrelevant, interactions among members may take directions we never anticipated, or our carefully constructed opening lines could be met with stony silence.

Qualitative methods can adapt to some degree to the unexpected and are used in the first place to encourage group members to open up on topics that developers already recognize as unfocused or poorly understood. Still, this flexibility should not be stretched beyond reasonable limits. These include remembering the primary objectives of the group and making sure they don't get lost in the ensuing discussion. Objectives for a scaling project might include:

- Hearing how members define a vague construct
- "Road-testing" language commonly used in other settings for its relevance to members' own experiences
- Previewing scale structural components for acceptability and utility
- Getting feedback on proposed sampling and data collection strategies for the quantitative phase of scale validation.

Ethical Considerations

As with any aspect of formal data collection, protection of human subjects is paramount and calls for oversight by the appropriate institutional review boards. The more complex the project, the more such groups may become involved. Focus group members have a right to know what is being asked of them, to be informed of any identified risks or benefits, and to be given the opportunity to consent based on full and accurate disclosure.

In this context, considerations regarding incentives become important, particularly in settings where potential members are poor or otherwise disadvantaged and may be unduly coerced. As much as we may want (and believe we need) participation, it is critical not to tempt others to take risks that might expose them to harm. Similarly, we must take pains to ensure that those providing consent (or, in the case of children, assent) really understand what is being asked of them. Where the potential risks of a study have been determined to be reasonable in relation to the potential benefits (to the participants or to some larger purpose), members must still have an easy exit and referrals for support if they become distressed.

In focus groups, anonymity can obviously never be assured (because members meet each other face-to-face). Even confidentiality can be hard to protect, especially when groups are run in small communities where members' lives may overlap through extended families, work, or school.

Members should be reminded of these risks and strongly encouraged to respect one another's privacy, and group leaders should do their best to keep conversations within pre-approved bounds to minimize risks of wandering unprepared into controversial or provocative topics.

Don't Forget the Mechanics

The pros and cons of available settings should also be considered. Where meetings are held can make or break the process. Thought should be given to the accessibility of the location and whether physical features (e.g., too many stairs or curtainless windows) might inhibit attendance. Convenience is also a factor. How far is the setting from good transportation or settings familiar to the participants? Will the site support confidentiality of those attending, or will they need to enter through visible, public spaces? Ideally, there should be minimal environmental distractions (e.g., noises or intrusions) and reasonable assurance that people who might dampen free discussion (i.e., work supervisors) won't be around.

Again, the "best laid plans" can still come undone. In Grenada, organizers arranged a setting for the PLHA group thinking that a private, discrete location would encourage otherwise shy members to keep their agreement to show up for a very sensitive session. In picking a site on the margins of a hospital being renovated, researchers ended up in a non-air-conditioned room where a bulldozer was knocking down walls just outside the window. Needless to say, transcribing the recorded session was a huge challenge.

Having the right hardware is also critical. Digital recorders can save situations like those described earlier, as sound editing software "cleans" unwanted material from target content and salvages otherwise inaudible conversations. Redundancy is always a good idea. Where budgets permit, bring back-up equipment and extra batteries. Once the group breaks up, it may never be possible to reassemble them or to recreate the dynamism of a "first conversation" that sheds lots of light on an important subject.

Assign and Maintain Clearly Defined Roles

Considering the potentially complex objectives and processes involved in running a focus group, a good game plan depends on clear role definitions and assignments in advance. These include: facilitator(s), technician, accountant, transcriptionist, and analyst(s). The facilitator manages the script, tracking the sequence and flow of questions and encouraging usefully focused discussion. His or her job is to make sure the basic objectives are addressed and to introduce clarifications or follow-up questions as needed to take full advantage of the discussion. The technician makes sure that critical information is captured through recording or note-taking and is familiar with the primary and back-up hardware as required. Any funds involved (i.e., for incentives) are managed and distributed by the accountant, who may also be tracking consent forms as necessary.

After the fact, the transcriptionist and analysts become involved. Faithfully transferring audio content into a format suitable for analysis is a critical skill best handled by someone with proficiency and stamina. Transcriptions can be lengthy and, when infused with jargon unique to specific groups or communities, are best handled by someone with advanced knowledge of focus group members' culture and dialect.

Qualitative data analysis is another skill far beyond the scope of this text. Strauss and Corbin (1998) provide an excellent primer on the coding of resulting material and the search for meaning in the wide-ranging responses of group members.

Of course, these roles need not be handled by separate people. Failing to keep their functions distinct, however, can result in focus group snafus that are embarrassing, frustrating, and sometimes irreparable. When successfully conducted, focus groups can fill in gaps and build developers' confidence that they are, after all, on the right track. At this point, they are ready (as were those who more easily reached this goal with "only" a convincing literature review or their own considered sense of the meaning and relevance of a core construct) to move on to structural considerations for their proposed measure.

SCALE STRUCTURE AND FORMAT

Once conceptual issues are settled, developers can turn their attention to design components that consider the perspective from which questions or items will be developed, the accessibility of the language used, and the resulting burden of the measure. Each of these somewhat depends on the other, and all must be thoughtfully integrated if the new scale is to succeed. As we will demonstrate, purely pragmatic or even cosmetic considerations in scale design can influence the resulting reliability and validity.

Deciding Whether to Watch or Ask

Walter Hudson claimed that there were two, and only two, ways to know what was going on in the life of another: to watch or to ask (Springer, Abell, & Hudson, 2002). In the context of scaling, this simple maxim translates into two primary scale formats: *behavioral observation* or *self-reporting*. For our purposes, these will be distinguished primarily by the nature of the target construct and secondarily by the intended source of the reported information.

For observational scales, the target is often an overt behavior, defined as actions directly observable by others. This could include a health-care provider touching a PLHA during an office visit or a couple practicing communication skills in counseling. Such overt behaviors could be recorded directly by the subject (as with the provider keeping a log following each patient visit) or by another (as with a therapist charting each time clients demonstrated understanding of their partner's meaning in an exchange). The key with observations of overt behaviors is that the targets are measurable, meaning they can be expressed in discreet, mutually exclusive units and are countable.

Successful scaling requires clear definitions of the behaviors to be observed and provision of a metric in which they can be recorded. To "demonstrate an understanding of their client's meaning during an exchange" is highly abstract. If they are clearly defined as "accurately reflecting the content of the sender's message before reacting" and recorded as a straightforward "yes" or "no", then even complex behaviors can be usefully reported.

Often, measures of overt behaviors are reasonably simple. Counting frequencies of cigarettes smoked or tantrums thrown requires more patience and commitment than complex thought. When well-constructed, simple scales of these behaviors are reasonably obvious and require little second-guessing to establish their credibility. Some authors broaden the scope of observational measures to include *covert behaviors* as well (Fischer & Corcoran, 2007a). Here, thoughts and feelings are also viewed as measurable and countable. The distinction is that covert behaviors cannot be observed directly by others. For our purposes, this extension of behavioral observations is most useful when focused on thoughts or feelings that are taken primarily on face value (as when someone reports on the frequency of their urges to smoke, or the number of times they held back from touching a PLHA). Logs or recordings of such events can be charted just like overt behaviors and used to track change or progress over time.

In this text, we reserve the use of *self-reporting measures* for scales capturing experiences that are more complex, and we will devote most of our attention to developing such tools. The latent constructs of family responsibility or parental self-efficacy, as previously defined, are not so self-evident. In these cases, the nature of the construct being measured requires generation of a pool of observable indicators (scale items) that must be rigorously tested before claims that they collectively represent the target construct can be defended. The thoughts or feelings they express are abstractions that must be grounded in the lines of evidence necessary to validate such measures (American Educational Research Association et al., 1999). Furthermore, for most such constructs, the best—if not the only—credible informant is the person who has the experience. Although observable analogs can be proposed, for the most part, the only person who can say whether she believes she is capable of handling her own medical needs is the patient herself. For scale developers, then, initial decisions about scale format and structure are based on determining whether the target is overt or covert, and on who would be the best source of information about its occurrence.

Accessibility of the Proposed Measure

From a user's point of view, once a scale has been clearly focused and its credibility established (a topic we will devote much attention to in Chapters 4–6), deciding whether to use it largely depends on *utility*. Ideally, scales should be short and easy to understand, administer, score, and interpret (Bloom, Fischer, & Orme, 2006). Once designers have decided on self-reporting or observational formats, they must turn their attention to the desired "look and feel" of the scale as a prelude to writing the actual items.

Readability and Developmental Considerations

No matter how elegant its design and thorough its conceptual foundation, if a scale cannot be read and understood by its intended audience, it is useless. Developers must sometimes be "yanked back to reality" and caused to remember that the person taking the scale is the most crucial player in the process. Consequently, respondents' ages, educational levels, ethnic or cultural identification, and developmental ability must all be considered in the wording and layout of an instrument.

One basic consideration is the readability of the scale. Is the wording and sentence structure understandable for the target audience? Common software (i.e., Microsoft Office) includes built-in tools to assess these factors. The Flesch Reading Ease and Flesch–Kincaid Readability scores are both based on the average sentence length and number of syllables per word in a document. The former scales scores from 0 through 100, with higher scores reflecting easier reading, and the latter estimates difficulty based on U.S. school grade levels.

Although not captured in standard indices, idiosyncrasies of dialect and tone also contribute to the accessibility of scale language. Focus groups can be invaluable in getting an early sense of the appropriateness of item wording. Readability and language usage must also be considered in relation to the complexity of scale instructions and response options, as we discuss below.

Anticipating Scale Length and Burden

All things being equal, shorter scales are preferable to longer ones. Rapid assessment instruments (RAIs) have come into favor largely because efficiency is king in managed care contexts, attention spans and available time for assessment are shorter, and scale developers have gotten better at what they do. The pros of RAIs include their ease of use and increased availability, whereas the cons include potential psychometric weaknesses if too much is sacrificed for the sake of brevity (Fischer & Corcoran, 2007a).

Putting too much attention on low burden (i.e., short time for administration, ease of scoring and interpretation) can cause other desirable scale qualities to suffer. As we will see in Chapter 3, some of the associated RAI limitations can be anticipated in the design phase and buffered by modifications to scale structure and format.

One risk is that in shrinking the initial item pool, important content is abandoned and the definitional complexity of the construct is constrained. The resulting scale, even if psychometrically sound, may be unsatisfying to users who see critical aspects missing and feel the scale is too simplistic. As a consequence, the content validity of the measure may be weakened. Another risk is that too few items will lead to inadequate reliability. As we will see, the Spearman–Brown prophecy formula (c.f. Nunnally & Bernstein, 1994) provides a method for estimating the impact on internal consistency when the number of items is altered. To some degree, truncation of the item pool can be offset by the choice of response options, as more choices (i.e., selecting from a range of intensities rather than a simple "yes" or "no") increases respondents' ability to show how they really are and to have their scores track real changes as they occur.

In the end, the "ideal length" of a scale is determined by the projected burden of using it (including the capacities of the intended respondents and the preferences or constraints of administrators or investigators), the standards set for acceptable psychometric strengths, and the complexity of the target construct. The dimensional structure of the scale adds another important consideration to this list.

Dimensionality

The dimensional structure of a scale can be described as a quadrant, with items on one axis and *dimensions* on the other (*see* Fig. 2.3). For now, we can consider dimensions as essentially equivalent to *constructs* or *factors*. (These and other terms in psychometrics have evolved to have multiple uses over time. We'll do our best to keep them straight as we go.) The number of dimensions intended for a scale is determined by the range of topics the developer wishes to capture, and by the level(s) of underlying complexity associated with each.

As depicted in Figure 2.3, varying combinations of items and dimensions determine the conceptual structure of a scale. Scales having only one item and intended to capture only one construct (uni-item, unidimensional) are known as *individualized rating scales* (IRS) or, in their self-reporting formats, *self-anchored scales* (Fischer & Corcoran, 2007a). They provide a clear, unambiguous structure for respondents to indicate their experience of a single issue. "I know I can take care of myself when I need to" or "I'm sad more often than not" could reflect self-efficacy or depression, respectively, and provide a "quick take" on how a client is doing with a specified problem. Although these are generally considered *unstandardized* scales (meaning that they lack proven

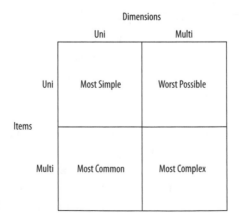

Figure 2.3 Scale dimensionality.

psychometric qualities), Nugent (1992) has argued that they can be reasonably robust.

The worst possible scale structure would be uni-item, multidimensional. Like the familiar "double-barreled" question students are warned to avoid in clinical training, these put the respondent in the position of having to answer two potentially conflicting questions at once. Asked to state whether "I am happy in my relationship with my partner and my child," the unlucky client who feels great about his child but is ready to break up with his lover is in an untenable bind. Although these contradictions in phrasing seem obvious when pointed out, they can sneak into an item pool and should be avoided at all costs.

Multi-item unidimensional scales are extremely common and in many ways the ideal expression of the RAI concept. They are focused, simple, and typically short. The FRS was developed to capture the broad construct of family stress in relation to parenting. As illustrated in Figure 2.1, items in the scale reflect feeling overburdened, unable to keep up, concerned about job performance, and constantly focused on doing things for others. However, these all tie back to the single overarching construct of family stress in relationship to parenting.

Even unidimensional scales can capture multifaceted constructs. The design decision when this structure is desired involves spreading the definitional content across the item pool so that critical components are included without any one aspect becoming dominant. This could be thought of as a form of dimensional sampling from definitional content. Like the proverbial loading of Noah's Ark, two of each creature are selected to create a sustainable representation of the whole. A depression measure created this way might include items on sad affect, withdrawal, and loss of energy, with no single component overshadowing another. When successful, respondents will find many aspects of their depression represented and feel satisfied that the scale really captured their experience.

Multi-item multidimensional scales are the most complex. In their most elaborate forms (i.e., the Minnesota Multiphasic Personality Inventory or the Achenbach Child Behavior Checklist), they capture a broad set of individual constructs that, when combined in scoring and interpretation, generate diagnostic profiles or complex behavioral summaries. Scales of this magnitude, with large sets of items and complex administration and interpretation requirements, fall outside the scope of RAIs. Still, many RAIs are multidimensional, and developers are wise to recognize when they are or are not the best format for their needs.

Typically, dimensionality of RAIs is determined by the underlying complexity of the target construct and by pragmatics. Because each factor in a multidimensional scale will require its own evidence of psychometric strength and, often, be tested for its cohesion with or distinction from other factors in the larger scale, the work required in validation increases accordingly. Sometimes the complexity of a target construct seems to leave little choice but to "go for it," juggling construct clarity and structural complexity throughout the development and validation process.

In designing the PSCS, concerns for HIV-positive parents' abilities to manage some of their own caregiving needs included a global construct of self-efficacy with three underlying dimensions of emotional, instrumental, and nursing self-care. These three were conceived as separate but related capacities that might vary as concerns from person to person. Their content was guided by a review of social support literature underscoring the importance of type, rather than source of support, and by consultation with HIV/AIDS case managers regarding the issues most often mentioned by PLHA. Consequently, it seemed best to frame them as distinct issues that could be scored separately and, potentially, collectively to yield a set of meaningful subscales as well as a global or total score. The overall length of the item pool should be sufficient to capture each dimension while not overburdening the respondents.

Creating Scale Items

After all of these issues have been thoroughly considered, developers are ready to move on to item generation. Creating an item pool can be both fun and frustrating, as it is the stage where the "rubber meets the road" as designers translate their abstract ideas into specific representations of the construct(s) they wish to capture. The familiar measurement notions of constructs being mutually exclusive, distinct, and exhaustive come into play as we test how well these sophisticated goals can be achieved in language that is familiar to (and on the reading level of) the most likely respondents to the new scale.

Domain Sampling Model

One of the best conceptualizations of this challenge is represented in Nunnally and Bernstein's (1994) notion of the *domain sampling model*. Using this approach, designers writing an item pool start from the premise that a construct can be best expressed through a process of brainstorming. In the abstract, this means generating items until the equivalent of *theoretical saturation* has been reached. For Strauss and Corbin, writing from the qualitative point of view, this means "reaching the point in the research where collecting additional data seems counterproductive; the 'new' that is uncovered does not add that much more" to the interpretation that already exists (1998, p. 136). For scale developers, it means generating items until it seems no more new content can be identified. In the context of scale development, capturing constructs in this way "assumes an infinite pool of possible items, but it works well as long as the pool of potential items is large" (Nunnally & Bernstein, 1994, p. 217).

In Figure 2.4, we see a depiction of the process as applied to the PSCS. First, we consider the definitions of target constructs to be captured, as each will become *domain boundaries* as items are developed. Because the scale is multidimensional, there are several: the separate constructs of emotional, instrumental, and nursing self-care, and the intended global construct of overall perceived self-efficacy. On the global level, designers wished to learn how sure HIV-positive parents were that they could care for themselves while still taking care of their families. Within that framework, they were more specifically concerned with three underlying dimensions of self-care: emotional (managing their feelings and moods), instrumental (taking care of concrete or personal household needs), and nursing (taking care of bodily and medical needs).

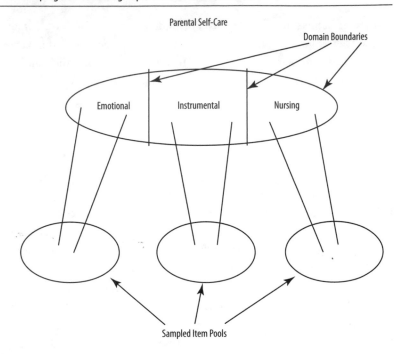

Figure 2.4 The domain sampling model.

Using these definitions as guidelines, the designers "taught to the test"; that is, they brainstormed items intended to represent each separate subscale in a *mutually exclusive* and *distinct* way. (As we will see in Chapter 6, this design decision will have implications later for selecting an approach to factor analysis.) Adding the feature of *exhaustive*, the hypothetical (although not literally practical) goal is to continue generating items that fall uniquely within each subscale domain boundary until all possible ways of expressing the construct have been included. Doing so will avoid *construct underrepresentation*, wherein a measure fails to include some important aspect of the target (American Educational Research Association et al., 1999)

In aiming for such theoretical saturation, a bit of redundancy is almost inevitable. As DeVellis (2003) notes, this is not necessarily a bad thing. So long as items are not literally identical, repetition of item content can have the effect of rotating a three-dimensional object to gain a view of it from all angles. Although some respondents may not "connect" with the statement "Emotional upset is not a problem for me," they may find that "I can handle being upset" gets it just right. Clark and Watson (2003) argue that to some extent, allowing this brainstorming to include a bit of marginal or ambiguous content might prevent unintentionally overlooking key definitional components and suggest that subsequent psychometric analyses will separate the good items from the bad. The trick is to explore the nuanced meaning of constructs through experimentation with phrasing suitable for the intended respondents, without straying too far outside the definitional boundaries of the domain.

In a larger sample, this varied representation of a common theme can enhance both the content validity and internal consistency of the scale. We will elaborate on these implications in Chapters 4 and 5. For now, returning to Figure 2.4, consider that the domains have been saturated by successfully brainstorming large initial item pools. (Examples of the items in each domain pool are shown in Fig. 2.2.) If a creative well has been tapped, then the designer will face an embarrassment of riches. There can, in fact, be too much of a good thing if the resulting item pool is not critically assessed to weed out excess duplication without sacrificing critical item content. This is where the "sampling" aspect of domain sampling comes into play. The designers might rely exclusively on their own sense of which items to trim from the initial pool or turn to experts for advice. Either way, the goal is to achieve an item pool that is larger than ultimately desired but small enough to be reasonable for administration in a large-sample validation.

Writing "Reversed" Items

Sometimes, scale developers will consider writing "reversed" items. These so-called "negative" items have wording that intentionally trends in the opposite direction of the "positive" items on a scale. Consider a measure of self-efficacy with Likert-type response options ranging from $1 =$ never to $7 =$ always, where high scores are meant to reflect more self-esteem. A "positively" worded item might state "I know I can do what it takes to get by," whereas a "negatively" worded item might state "I have a hard time doing what it takes when the going gets tough." The idea is to design some items as opposites and insert them randomly throughout the item pool.

When this is successful, "reversed" items may reduce what has variably been called acquiescence, affirmation, or agreement bias (DeVellis, 2003) or respondents' tendencies to drift into a form of "autopilot," where their answers are based less on item content and more on a pattern they have somehow slipped into. This may be intentional, reflecting a wish to appear in a certain way (i.e., social desirability), or unintentional, resulting from a simple lapse in attention while filling out a scale.

Hudson's widely distributed Computer Assisted Assessment Package (c.f. Bloom et al., 2006) includes a collection of his instruments developed with this feature and administers them with management of reversed items in mind. The scoring algorhythm identifies when response to an item is inconsistent with others in the larger item pool and prompts respondents to confirm that they really meant to answer as they did. This creates an opportunity to correct the unintentional lapses in attention noted above or to affirm that the respondent really does feel differently about a particular item. Once responses are confirmed, negatively worded items are reversed before being scored with others in their pool, yielding scale scores summing in the developer's desired direction.

As DeVellis (2003) has noted, the risks associated with writing such items may not be worth the intended benefits. Respondents may feel confused by items that seem contradictory, and developers may find that such items fail to perform as expected in psychometric analyses. Choosing whether to include them requires consideration of both the complications and potential benefits they introduce as well as a willingness to closely examine whether the desired effects are achieved.

Anticipating Face and Content Validity

As indicated in Chapter 1, psychometric methodology is in many ways nonlinear. We have already dropped several hints regarding how decisions in the construct conceptualization and item development phases have implications for scale reliability and factor structure. When designers are writing scale items, it's wise to also anticipate tests of *face* and *content validity*. We will have more to say about these features in Chapter 5. To prime the pump, however, it is important that designers make the connection between emerging scale items and the degrees to which the scale will look like a measure of what it claims to be (face validity) and have content that clearly conforms to the definitional boundaries of its domains (content validity).

As previously discussed, focus groups can serve many purposes, including confirmation of the social relevance of a target construct and identification of phrases and terms that might best express it for a particular population. The qualitative approach taken in working with focus groups can later be supplemented by a quantitative process asking experts to rate how successful item generation has been.

Expert Panels

Expert panels are usually small groups (6–10 members) composed so others who understand the designers' methods or objectives can provide feedback before the scale is subjected to a full-scale validation. Refining an over-large item pool at this stage can streamline the validation process and decrease the length and resulting burden of a data collection instrument. The experts selected may include academics with backgrounds in scale development or the theories or models used in construct definition, clinicians or administrators with experience working with target problems or groups, or members of the target groups themselves. Whatever their particular expertise, criteria and procedures for selecting them should be clearly described (American Educational Research Association et al., 1999), and all must be given clear instructions and encouraged to stay on task.

Two versions of the instructions given to expert panelists are shown in Figure 2.5. In the first, panelists are asked to indicate how well the construct of "outgroups" is represented by a set of scale items. Here, the term reflects one dimension of stigmatizing PLHA that designers wish

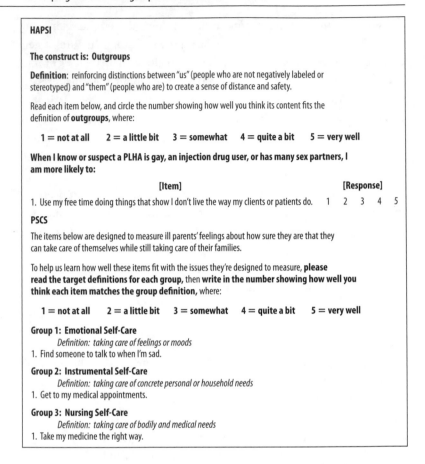

Figure 2.5 Expert panel content validation templates: HAPSI and PSCS.

to include in the HIV/AIDS Provider Stigma Inventory (HAPSI) (Abell, Rutledge, & Whyte, 2007). To guide the panelists, designers name the target construct, provide the definition they used to guide item generation, and insert instructions for rating the degree to which the content of each item matches that definition.

The second illustration shows how the same process could be applied to a multidimensional measure like the PSCS. In both cases, the resulting ratings provide an initial indication of how well the designers have achieved their goals. In addition, panelists can be invited to edit words or phrases they feel could be eliminated or improved, to suggest new items altogether, or to comment more broadly on the overall impression left by the set of items. Although this feedback can be invaluable, given the small sample sizes usually involved, it is best to view it as advisory rather than definitive. In Chapter 5 we will elaborate on considering expert panel responses in the larger context of retaining or removing potential scale items.

Item–Response Options

Although scale items provide the stimuli inviting respondents to reflect on their experiences with particular constructs, response options are their necessary counterpart. They provide the structural means for expressing and recording the specific nature of the respondents' experiences. The format chosen by designers is critical not only for its implications in scaling and eventual scoring and interpretation of responses but also because the "forced choice" answers it dictates will influence the phrasing of the items themselves.

Hudson identified four options for expressing the nature of experiences (Springer, Abell, & Hudson, 2002). Essentially, these are:

- switch: whether the problem exists or the issue is considered to be "true"
- Magnitude: intensity, ranging from very little to quite a lot
- Frequency: how often a problem occurs or is a concern
- Duration: in two forms:

  o Episodic: how long an event continues,
  o Historical: how long, over time, the issue has existed.

Although there are many response options available to capture these experiences, we concentrate here on the three most frequently used in RAIs: dichotomies, Likert-type category partitions, and semantic differentials (*see* Figure 2.6). Each has strengths and weaknesses and should be selected in part based on the perceived variability in possible responses

Dichotomy

Working with HIV+ patients or clients can be challenging. Please read each item below and circle the response indicating whether the statement is true or false for you.

1.   If I work with an HIV+ person, I will catch the virus from them.   T   F

Likert-Type Category Partition

The statements below are about the pressures you may feel in your family. There are no right or wrong answers. Please read each statement, and circle the number on the right which answers best for you.

1 = never
2 = hardly ever
3 = a little of the time
4 = sometimes
5 = a good part of the time
6 = most of the time
7 = all of the time

1. Taking care of my family is overwhelming.   1   2   3   4   5   6   7

Semantic Differential

Taking good care of yourself while being a parent can be a big job. Please read each item below, then write a number from 0 - 10 in the blank to the right to show **how sure you are that you can take care of yourself** in these ways **while still taking care of your family.**

   0   1   2   3   4   5   6   7   8   9   10
Cannot do at all   Probably can do   Sure I can do

1. Find someone to talk to when I'm sad.   _____

Figure 2.6   RAI response options.

and also on the importance of capturing subtle distinctions across a broad range versus simple classification.

Dichotomy

When the nature of the target problem can be usefully expressed as *switch* (i.e., present or absent), dichotomies can be useful. Common options are "yes" or "no," or "true" or "false." These are best selected when the problem is such that knowing its simple presence could lead to meaningful assessment or when subtle variations are considered unlikely or unimportant. For instance, simply knowing that a 6-year-old child has appeared in school with unhealed cigarette burns on her arm would be enough to trigger an investigation. How deeply she was burned might matter, but simply noting that "yes" she had been harmed would be meaningful.

On the other hand, asking whether working with an HIV-positive person will result in catching the virus and providing only dichotomous responses could lead to frustration. Lacking an opportunity to provide more detail, a respondent couldn't indicate how strongly they felt that way or how often they believed they were at risk. Helping a client show or tell how they really feel often requires greater levels of detail.

Likert-Type Category Partition

So-called "Likert scales" permit capture of much more detail in magnitude or frequency. Typically ranging from four to seven response options, their formal name reflects the structure partitioning a range of choices into "equal-appearing intervals," so named because each text label is associated with a number on the continuum. Whereas unnumbered choices including "hardly ever" and "a little of the time" reflect gradations in frequency, purely semantic interpretations would make it impossible to tell whether the distance between them was the same as the distance to the next step: "some of the time." Imposition of the numbers helps defend interpretations claiming that if respondents perceive the distance between two and three as equal to the distance between three and four, they will make the same associations regarding the text labels.

Designers selecting Likert-type response options hope that associating the labels with the numbers will help respondents express their true feelings or thoughts. By convention, the number of partitions rarely exceeds seven, as writing meaningfully different labels becomes very difficult beyond that point. As we will see in Chapters 4 and 6, choosing wider response ranges can enhance scale reliability (in part because having more options improves the sensitivity of the scale) and minimize concerns regarding treatment of data as continuous rather than categorical (Tate, 1998). Still, developmental and reading abilities may justify narrowing the options to avoid overwhelming children. "Ideal" psychometric characteristics are arguably meaningless if the structure of the scale makes it unusable for the intended population.

Finally, designers must consider whether to offer an odd or even number of response choices. Designers using an even number of choices often do so because they object to providing a neutral option, fearing that if too many people pick the middle choice, their data will be less revealing. Remembering our assertion that scales should provide clients every opportunity to express how they really are, we reject this notion as a false complaint. After all, if a respondent generally feels neutral about something, scales lacking that option will have missed the mark and, as we will see later, will have inflated the instrument's measurement error.

Semantic Differential

The third option in Figure 2.6 depicts the widest range of response options and hence, the greatest potential for sensitivity. By giving respondents even more choices, they are even less likely to feel that the scale lacks an option to show how they are. With a semantic differential, this wider range is achieved by abandoning the idea of linking written labels with every choice and simply labeling the poles. By placing opposites on either end (completely true—completely false; never—always) and sometimes a neutral anchor in the middle, designers give respondents lots of latitude. Sensitivity is maximized, and internal consistency is almost always enhanced.

As with many other things, however, there can be a point of diminishing returns. Designers are unlikely to improve scale performance much by providing more than 10 or 11 options. Often, pragmatics, including such issues as the "eye-appeal" of the scale based on page layout, or the sheer number of items deemed necessary to cover all of its conceptual goals must be factored in to design choices about response options. If there are many items to be included, designers may opt for a dichotomous response option, knowing that a large number of good items can offset the resulting impact on sensitivity. On the other extreme, where a very short RAI is essential, they may go for a semantic differential to compensate for the narrow range in item content. Consequently, response option decisions cannot be made independent of considerations of what to measure or for whom. In the end, scale structural components must be integrated with the complexity of the constructs being targeted, the characteristics of the intended respondents, and designers' preferences for the overall "look and feel" of the scale.

Minimizing Reactivity

Finally, scale developers should consider how their choices for item phrasing or response options might trigger reactivity, or the potential that simply taking the scale might change the respondents' experience (Fischer & Corcoran, 2007a) or their willingness to disclose it. We hasten to add that on its face, reactivity is neither good nor bad. The critical aspect is that designers do their best to anticipate its potential and to develop, administer, score, or interpret RAIs accordingly.

Hudson's *Partner Abuse Scale: Physical* (PASPH), for example, includes items like "my partner slaps me around my face and head", ". . . . beats me when he or she drinks", and ". . . . makes me afraid for my life" (Fischer & Corcoran, 2007a, p. 156). It is not difficult to imagine two very different scenarios. In the first, a woman who has endured several years of abuse finally decides she has had all she can take and seeks refuge in a shelter. On intake, when given this scale, she feels great relief ("they *know* what it's been like for me") and really opens up, first on the scale, and next in the counseling session that follows. In the second scenario, the same woman sees the scale items and is shocked ("I don't know these people. If he finds out I told them this, he'll kill me!"). She hides the truth of her experience and leaves the shelter at the first opportunity. In both cases, her reaction to the content of the instrument had very different effects, either of which would have been difficult to detect in advance. The designer of a scale using such strong language, regardless of the content, might build in cautions about these possibilities with scale instructions. Clinicians using it could then be on the lookout for strong responses and decide on their scoring interpretations and follow-up accordingly.

Taken together, these considerations in scale development can increase the likelihood that RAIs reflect their target constructs, respect the people who will eventually use and interpret the measures, and minimize the burden associated with administering and taking it. In Chapter 3, we turn to designing the large study necessary to determine whether its performance lives up to its promise.

3

Study Design

Having established the purpose and relevance of a proposed measure, drafted an item pool, and incorporated suggestions from expert panel review, RAI developers will be ready to move forward with an initial validation. Much of the rigor associated with sound research design applies to psychometric studies. Here we will emphasize those factors particular to assessment of new measures, flagging issues to be anticipated, identifying their implications, and proposing guidelines for addressing them.

Planning at this stage requires considering not only the basics of testing psychometric hypotheses but also the pragmatics and ethical questions associated with data collection, cleaning, coding, and analysis. Designers must make intentional decisions and consider how these can be described in written manuscripts with enough clarity to make them replicable. As all psychometric conclusions are explicitly *sample-dependent*, meaning directly applicable only to the sample from which they were derived, disclosure of the nature and mechanics of study design is critical. When handled well, readers can interpret results with appropriate cautions, and researchers can make design decisions for replication or modification based on accurate descriptions of method.

Psychometric studies are sometimes viewed as "cook-bookish" and straightforward. As we will see, there is a little truth in this. Still, underestimating their complexity can lead to big problems, especially when designers fail to appreciate the interlocking nature of the parts that make up the whole. In the sections that follow, we will consider conceptual, methodological, and statistical issues associated with sampling, the composition of a complete data collection instrument, issues to consider in data collection, and the importance of anticipating data analyses before the study gets off the ground.

SAMPLING CONSIDERATIONS

Sampling in scaling studies can be thought of in two broad categories: drawing items from a conceptual domain and selecting respondents from a population of interest (Nunnally & Bernstein, 1994). Although the former is crucial to any validation study, it has already been included in discussion of construct identification and the generation of item pools. Thoroughly considering the domain within which a construct falls and sampling items until theoretical saturation is achieved are good ways to increase the likelihood that the items will adequately represent the latent construct they are meant to express.

Selecting respondents for a validation study involves considering who *should* be included, who *can* be included, how they can be approached and recruited, and whether the extent to which they represent anyone other than themselves can be known. Although there are ideal answers to these questions, we will consider them in the context of "real-world" constraints sometimes faced by researchers in social and behavioral sciences. However samples are ultimately achieved, *The Standards* (American Educational Research Association et al., 1999) emphasize that procedures be thoroughly reported and, when appropriate, that samples be as representative as possible of the populations for which the measure is intended.

Respondent Characteristics

Regarding who *should* be sampled, respondents in a scaling study should, of course, be drawn from a population relevant to the construct being scaled. To learn how HIV-positive single-parent heads of household respond to statements about their confidence that they can manage their medical needs while caring for their families, people living with HIV/AIDS (PLHA) who are parents need to be recruited. Another set of questions involves whether or not such respondents *can* be sampled, how, and with what constraints. We will elaborate on these as we go, but for starters, designers of such a scale must think carefully about whom such parents might be and whether the circumstances of their lives or experiences make it feasible to approach them about participating in a study. If approaching a target population seems possible, then the next question will be "how." If approaching seems impossible, then the question will be whether useful progress can be made in developing the intended measure without them. Surprisingly, the answer to the second question is not always "no."

Clinical Samples

Clinical samples are so named because in therapeutic settings they are comprised of people diagnosed with or receiving treatment for a specific condition (i.e., depression or anxiety), and they include potential respondents known to fit a particular classification. For our purposes, they need not be limited to diagnostic categories. More broadly, they are groupings of people sharing a common characteristic associated with the scale developer's construct of interest.

Children who have been exposed to violent trauma, social service providers for geriatric patients, or health-care surrogates for loved ones in hospice might each represent a special interest of the scale developer because of their life experiences. Some will require more effort to sample than others. Because children are particularly vulnerable to coercion and manipulation, they will be protected by barriers requiring first consent of a parent or guardian, then their own assent. Providers of geriatric services may be easy to locate but guarded by administrative bureaucracy and burdened by caseloads and responsibilities. And health-care surrogates, approached during one of life's most difficult transitions, may either welcome the distraction or resent the intrusion of an invitation to complete a survey.

Scale designers need to be clear from the beginning how crucial responses from a clinical sample will be. If the nature of the construct is such that it can only be known by a person living the experience (as with an HIV-positive parent's report of self-efficacy), finding a way to draw a sample may make or break the proposed validation. On the other hand, if what we'd like to know from a health-care surrogate is the extent to which they feel obligated by family duty or motivated by altruism and love, then it may be possible to begin scale validation on a sample not currently experiencing such strain.

Nonclinical Samples

Student samples are sometimes maligned because they are assumed to be "captive audiences" coerced into study participation or not of "the real world." But coercion that is not fully disclosed and knowingly consented to is never appropriate, no matter whom the potential respondents are. And concluding that students, increasingly diverse by age, ethnicity, and family status, lack any authentic life experience is condescending, at least.

For scale developers, deciding whether to go with a sample of people not known to have the ideal experience or characteristics should be based on *(a)* the nature of the target construct, and *(b)* the feasibility of achieving a clinical sample. If the problem is one like HIV-positive parents' self-efficacy, that can only be known by asking such people, emerging difficulties in sampling them may result in compromising on the "ideal" clinical sample or abandoning the project altogether. If, on the other hand, the problem is determining motivations for caregiving, then it may be possible to make initial progress by conducting a pilot study on a nonclinical sample. This is easier to defend when the target construct is truly novel, and no one has yet attempted to capture it as proposed. Demonstrating that a new construct can be captured *somewhere* helps establish its conceptual legitimacy and may set the stage for clinical replication when sampling difficulties can be overcome.

Responses from people actually "living" the desired experiences are sometimes hard to get. Clinical samples can be infeasible when the ideal respondents cannot be identified or accessed, or when overcoming these obstacles is unaffordable. Although cost is the most difficult limitation to defend (we can always try harder to find money, right?), the first two obstacles are formidable. Because of social stigma and restrictions on accessing medical status, for instance, master lists of PLHA generally do not exist. When a substitute can be generated (i.e., through agency caseloads), persons included in a sampling frame must still have their identities protected and may not agree to be approached, much less participate.

Sometimes, sampling problems make planned analyses impossible or limit their subsequent interpretations in important ways. After determining how close to the lived experience respondents must be, designers must also consider whether those invited are likely to have a normally distributed range of experience with the target construct. Beyond *population relevance*, respondents must also be assessed for the likelihood that they will be *heterogeneous* with respect to the target construct. If their responses to items lack sufficient *variance* (i.e., distribution across a range from "high" to "low") or are excessively *skewed* (i.e., overloaded on one or the other side of the range), then critical assumptions of statistical testing may be violated, making specific analyses inappropriate. Even when techniques are *robust* to certain degrees of skewness, legitimate questions about the representativeness of the sample can be raised when many participants share a generally higher or lower average score on a measure than would be expected in a normal population. If the only people agreeing to be surveyed in a study of caregivers for PLHA report relatively low stress and a general willingness to continue with their responsibilities, then authors are obligated to acknowledge that the results may not apply to caregivers whose experiences are different (c.f. Abell, 2001).

We will have more to say about these topics in Chapters 4–6. For now, it is important to note that recognizing and reporting such limitations are a primary responsibility when presenting validation results. Being realistic in advance about the likelihood of achieving the necessary sample may be distressing in the short run. Careful planning and advance consideration of how much deviation from the ideal can be tolerated can ultimately save even greater frustration when overly optimistic plans fall short.

Vignettes

One approach to overcoming the absence of literal or immediate experience with a target problem is through the use of vignettes. Studies of health-care surrogates are almost never conducted during "real time" (i.e., the period when decisions about terminating life supports are being made, and the patient is still alive) (Buckey, 2007). Doing so might reveal uniquely potent feelings or thoughts from the surrogate but come at the cost of disrupting an ongoing, life-changing process. Through use of vignettes, researchers might create written prompts intended to put respondents who are not in the middle of such a trauma in a frame of mind that encourages them to reflect on their potential reactions if they were. The question is whether such hypothetical situations reasonably mimic the desired conditions and whether responses generated under such circumstances are ultimately meaningful.

Vignette development requires careful attention to content, and designers are cautioned to track how well their text captures the intended domain (i.e., an encounter with someone with mental illness, a particular sexual identity, or an expectation to perform a specific action). In a study of children's prosocial tendencies, children ages 10 through 17 years were asked to consider the likelihood that they would offer help to another (Abell, McDonnell, & Winters, 1992). Because theory indicated that such tendencies might vary with how well the helper knew the person in need, and how much they believed the need was justified, those factors were included in vignette content. Different versions were designed to reflect a close or distant relationship (Stranger/Friend) and whether or not there was a compelling external reason for being in need (External/No External). Figure 3.1 illustrates scale instructions and sample vignette content. Response options gauge whether the subject's reason for needing help was acceptable and the likelihood that help would be offered.

Expert panels, as described in Chapter 2, can be useful in performing vignette content validity checks, following some of the same principles

The stories below are examples of situations people may find themselves in. First, read each story and think about how good or bad you believe the person's reason was for doing what they did. Next, read the sentence after each story and think about how much you believe you would do the same thing that is suggested.

Friend/External Condition

A friend did not finish all of last night's homework. The friend told you, "I decided not to do the work because my little sister got really sick, and my Mom needed help taking care of her."

The friend's reason for not doing the homework was (circle one):

1 = *very good*   2 = *a little good*   3 = *a little bad*   4 = *very bad*

If this happened, I would help my friend finish the homework (circle one):

1 = *really would*   2 – *probably would*   3 = *probably would not*   4 = *really would not*

Stranger/No External Condition

Someone you just met did not bring any lunch to school. The person said, "I couldn't fix anything because I was late. I knew it was time to get up, but I decided to stay in bed anyway."

The person's reason for not bringing any lunch was (circle one):

1 = *very good*   2 = *a little good*   3 = *a little bad*   4 = *very bad*

If this happened, I would share the food I had with that person (circle one):

1 = *really would*   2 = *probably would*   3 = *probably would not*   4 = *really would not*

Figure 3.1 Vignettes assessing children's prosocial tendencies.

outlined in discussion of domain sampling for item generation. (See Springer, Abell, and Nugent [2002, pp. 206–209] for a detailed illustration.) The confidence placed in data obtained from vignette respondents will depend heavily on how convincingly the narrative captured the target content without straying into extraneous or conflicting material. Relevant context should support, rather than distract from, depicting the desired conditions.

Recruiting Respondents

Once RAI designers have decided who *should* and *can* be approached, the next issue is *how* to do so most efficiently and effectively. First, protection of human subjects must be carefully considered and factored into all aspects of sample recruitment, data collection and management, and reporting of results. During recruitment, developers have a responsibility to make sure informed consent and assent procedures are carefully considered and rigorously implemented. The language they choose to communicate details should balance formal institutional requirements (i.e., satisfying the lawyers) with accessibility and clarity for potential respondents.

Figure 3.2 displays portions of a consent letter used in a series of studies validating the Family Responsibility Scale (FRS) and Parental Self-Care Scale (PSCS) (Abell, Ryan, & Kamata, 2006; Abell, Ryan, Kamata & Citrolo, 2006). In this case, all families receiving services from the collaborating AIDS service organization received a cover letter asking them to give permission to be contacted regarding participation in a survey. The letter described the purpose of the study and emphasized that participation was anonymous and voluntary and that published results would never identify individual responses.

Decisions regarding incentives (whether to provide them, and if so, what to offer) should balance reasonable inducements against undue coercion. Cash is a powerful motivator, so much so that offering it could sometimes be considered unethical. In this case, the amount was determined to be enough to encourage participation without being so much that people in distressed circumstances would risk exposing themselves to a process they would otherwise avoid.

Designers should also consider whether signed consent forms are necessary and, if not, whether they can be replaced with a clear statement that completion of a survey instrument will represent respondents' agreement to be included in the study. Often, when studies do not include minors or others recognized as especially vulnerable to coercion (i.e., prisoners, pregnant women, employees), signatures are deemed unnecessary. When this is the case, designers save a step in data management and, potentially, remove a disincentive to participation. (Providing signatures may cause some to doubt assurances that their identities will be protected.) Ultimately, institutional review boards (IRBs) have the last word in making such decisions, providing an important check against

What is this about?

• The university and this agency are working together to evaluate the services you receive, as well as the daily challenges you face.

Who is participating?

• All families involved with this agency are being asked.

Is my participation required?

• No, it is completely voluntary.
• Filling in the survey means you agree to participate.

Will my participation affect the services I receive from this program?

• No, your choice will not affect the services you receive.

What does participation require?

• Filling in the survey and mailing it back in the stamped envelope we've provided.
• The agency will collect the envelopes without opening them and send them to the research team at the university.

Will my participation and the information collected be anonymous?

• Yes, no one will know who you are. (Do not put your name on the survey.)
• Your information will only be seen by the research staff.
• The results may be published, but no individual information can or will be identified.

How will my participation be beneficial?

• You will be able to share your opinion of the services you receive and improve our understanding of them.
• Your answers may help future clients of this program, as well as others struggling with this illness and its effects.
• You will be eligible to win a $25 gift certificate.

How can I win a $25 gift certificate?

• Attached to the survey is a 2-part raffle ticket. Take one part and leave the other attached. Once the deadline for completing the surveys have passed, 10 winners will be chosen from the returned tickets. The winning numbers will be announced in the newsletter and posted at the agency. If your number matches one of the winning numbers – you get a $25 gift certificate.

If you have any questions, please feel free to call your case manager or the research team at the numbers listed below.

Figure 3.2 Informed consent for the FRS and PSCS.

the risk that researchers will overlook potential problems in an effort to simplify recruiting a sample.

Sample Size

Sample size decisions are typically based on a host of factors, including the anticipated qualities of the intended respondents, the length and complexity of the scale being tested, the desired precision of estimation for statistical coefficients, and the pragmatics of actual data collection. Conventions guiding such decisions sometimes seem pulled from thin air when, more typically, they reflect the accumulated but inarticulate experience of seasoned researchers. Other times, they result from rigorous simulations applying Monte Carlo methodologies. There, hypothetical data sets are generated to possess specific characteristics and permit comparisons of the benefits and costs of varying sample sizes on the validity and generalizability of observed coefficients. As we will see, the results of these approaches are sometimes conflicting but fortunately trend toward support of some very general recommendations for scale developers.

A reasonable starting point may be to consider the range of research questions and hypotheses to be addressed in a psychometric study. As shown in Figure 3.3, these questions do not always lend themselves to familiar forms of power analysis used in other sample size calculations. Considering the range of techniques needed to examine qualities of a new scale, developers often default to the most statistically demanding test and match their sample size decisions to its requirements. As we will see in more detail in coming chapters, validating a factor structure and, where desired, examining item invariance usually override other sample size considerations.

Respondent Qualities

As we have already illustrated, respondents recruited for a validation study may or may not be broadly representative of a target condition or trait. If people with a wide, normally distributed range of stress in their roles as caregivers cannot be recruited, the study may be fatally

Scale Quality	Question/Hypothesis	Analysis
Reliability	Internally consistent?	Coefficient Alpha (standard error of measurement)
	Stable over time?	Correlation
Valid factor structure	Theorized constructs confirmed?	CFA
	Defensible constructs discovered?	EFA
Item invariance	Patterns comparable across relevant groups?	SEM with covariate DIF
Construct validity	Convergent	Correlation, ANOVA, t-test
	Discriminant	Correlation, ANOVA, t-test
	Concurrent Criterion	Correlation, ANOVA, t-test
	Predictive Criterion	Correlation, ANOVA, t-test

Figure 3.3 Primary psychometric questions and hypotheses.

flawed. On the other hand, skewed distributions of target constructs can become just another factor to consider when deciding the form of reliability to report (Maydeu-Olivares, Coffman, & Hartmann, 2007) or whether data should be transformed prior to analysis (Aroian & Norris, 2004). Where possible, of course, we'd prefer a probability sample drawn from a representative cross-section of our desired population. Failing that, a purposive sample with normally distributed representation on our construct of interest is the next best choice.

Scale Complexity and Precision of Estimation

Conventional recommendations for sample size in psychometric studies are often framed as the number of participants per parameter (NPPP) (Jackson, 2001) the ratio of the number of observations to parameters (N:q) (Jackson, 2003) or the ratio of the number of variables to the number of factors (p:r) (MacCallum, Widaman, Zhang, & Hong, 1999). Each considers an aspect of scale structure in relation to the requirements of factor analyses.

Guidelines associated with NPPP or N:q are most common and generally vary from 5 to 10 respondents per scale item in exploratory factor analyses (EFA) (c.f. Nunnally & Bernstein, 1994). This may expand to include additional coefficients (i.e., error terms) generated in confirmatory factor analyses (CFA) with structural equation modeling (Tate, 1998), where ratio recommendations may range as high as 20:1 (Kline, 2005). Recent studies (Jackson, 2001; MacCallum et al., 1999) have challenged the primacy of this ratio, observing that other factors, such as overall sample size and the reliability of individual item responses, generally are more influential than NPPP in determining the accuracy of factor analyses (Jackson, 2003; Russell, 2002). We will consider this in greater depth in Chapter 6, where recommendations for CFA fit indexes impacted by sample size will be addressed.

Although the criteria discussed thus far describe how sample size might be driven by the number of items in a scale, the *p:r* addresses the ratio of the number of observable indicators (i.e., individual items) to the number of latent variables (i.e., separately scorable factors or scales). In a sense, sample size is converted to consideration of how well the construct itself has been expressed through a representative sample of meaningful items and how many such items are desirable to maximize scale performance.

What we discussed in Chapter 2 as theoretical saturation of item domains is converted in this context to factor *overdetermination* (MacCallum et al., 1999), or the degree to which useful content associated with a latent trait has been introduced as a potential construct indicator. The better this is achieved, the fewer respondents will be required to justify a satisfactory test of scale qualities. For unidimensional scales, three items per factor is considered the minimum (Jackson, 2003), and four or more are desirable (Russell, 2002). For multidimensional measures, achieving a "highly overdetermined" scale requires that the number of items be several times the number of targeted factors (MacCallum et al., 1999, p. 90).

On the other side of this equation, of course, is the number of latent variables themselves. In the context of CFA, these are presumably known, or at least hypothesized. In EFA, they are by definition unknown and remain to be discovered. Ideally, developers are encouraged to think carefully about the complexity of their instruments and, when possible, err on the side of simplicity. Fewer target factors expressed through a modest set of items are more likely to succeed psychometrically than many factors that are underdetermined (expressed through too few or too poorly written items). And when it turns out that the items designed for factors associate strongly where they are intended to, again, fewer respondents are needed to demonstrate success.

Frustratingly, these recommendations ask that developers know (or can reasonably predict) in advance the answers to questions that can only be formally considered after the data are in! If we knew we had written "good" items, we would stop generating more and move on to data collection. Part of the fun of scale development is thinking through these considerations as carefully as possible during scale design, and then constructing a data collection instrument with the right components, gathering a sufficient sample, and putting it to the test.

Realities of Data Collection

As Comrey observed, "it seems that psychometricians always want sample sizes that are larger than clinicians are willing or able to provide" (1988, p. 758). Recommendations to achieve respondent-to-item ratios of 10:1 or higher have led to charges of "sample size overkill" and to conclusions that desirable sample sizes for factor analysis be no fewer than 50 and no more than 100 (Sapnas & Zeller, 2002). Studies with excessively large samples waste time and money, not to mention the labor associated with collecting and managing a data set. The issue for RAI developers comes down to how to balance conventional recommendations and practices with more empirically derived methods in determining sample size.

Although power analyses may be applicable to overall tests of model fit in specific applications of CFA (c.f. Kahn, 2006; MacCallum, Browne, & Sugawara, 1996), they are less common—although emerging—in other applications like estimation of internal consistency (Bonett, 2002). A growing body of Monte Carlo studies has reaffirmed conventional notions of sample size adequacy for assessing internal consistency and factor structure, with minimal estimates generally ranging from 100 (MacCallum et al., 1999) to 150 (Holbert & Stephenson, 2002). Less conservative authors have suggested that minimum sizes should trend toward 200 (Jackson, 2003), with suggestions for 300 "to be safe" for EFA (Kahn, 2006, p. 701). Asserting that measurement error is especially important when scales are assessed for individual clinical applications, Charter (2001) has argued that precise estimates of internal consistency (e.g., coefficient α and other indicators) require samples of 400 or more.

Readers are encouraged to examine some of the included references for more detailed discussion related to their particular needs. How long (and complex) is the intended scale? How much variability is likely to exist in the target population? How confident are you that the items to be included solidly represent their intended constructs? For those reluctant to put in the effort, we revert to the safety of conservative advice, and encourage a minimal sample of 200 to 300 respondents.

COMPOSING THE DATA COLLECTION PACKAGE

When a scale has been drafted, desirable respondent characteristics identified, and an estimated sample size determined, developers can move forward with composing the complete data collection instrument. This package typically includes a set of demographic items, all elements of the novel scale, additional items and standardized scales to be used in construct validation, and documents supporting informed consent. All of this must be assessed for comprehensive coverage of the validation needs of the developer, human subjects' protection assurances to participating and supervising institutions, and accessibility and readability for participants. And, of course, it must be packaged in a way that minimizes respondent burden and reactivity and encourages complete and thoughtful responses to all items. Sequencing and layout of instrument package components can be as critical as their content to the ultimate success of data collection.

Demographics

Accurate description of survey respondents serves numerous purposes, some related to reporting characteristics of interest in results and findings, some related specifically to the validation of the novel scale, and still others permitting *post hoc* analyses of *secondary* or *applied hypotheses*. Developers should think carefully about what to include, the format in which responses are collected, and the sequencing and placement of specific items.

In Figure 3.4, sample demographic questions from the PSCS and FRS validations illustrate how potentially sensitive information can be collected and recorded to capture key respondent characteristics while minimizing risks of errors in data entry. Some questions (i.e., education level, gender, race or ethnicity, employment status, and income) simply describe respondent qualities. Questions like these are generally included whether or not they are part of study hypotheses because they are conventional sample descriptors. Other descriptors, such as HIV status, having other health problems, or reports of the impact of illness on activities of daily living, were specific to the target population. These could become useful in analyses of so-called secondary or applied questions that, although interesting, were not considered critical to scale validation. Such questions address substantive issues of interest and are appropriately pursued only after the novel scale has been successfully validated.

Components Supporting Construct and Criterion Validity Analyses

The demographic items in the final set of Figure 3.4 can be called *single-item indicators*. Illustrated in the last two items, these include direct, straightforward definitions of the core constructs being validated. In this case, feeling overwhelmed by family caretaking captures the essence of family stress in the *Family Responsibility Scale*, whereas reported abilities to care for self while caring for others matches the notion of self-efficacy targeted in the *Parental Self-Care Scale*.

Although single-item indicators are less desirable than standardized scales (as we will see in Chapter 5), both measurement forms can provide tests of the convergent construct validity of RAIs. Developers may opt for single-item indicators when standardized instruments *(a)* do not exist,

| **What is your HIV status?** |
| ☐ HIV− ☐ HIV+ ☐ AIDS Diagnosis ☐ Don't Know |

| **If you are HIV+ or have an AIDS diagnosis, are you currently taking combination drug medications (also called 'drug cocktail')?** |
| ☐ Yes [If yes, how long? Years – (____); Months – (____)] ☐ No |

| **If you are HIV+ or have an AIDS diagnosis, how often does your HIV/AIDS limit your daily activity around the house?** |
| ☐ None ☐ Hardly Ever ☐ Sometimes ☐ Often ☐ Always |

| **Do you have health problems?** |
| ☐ No ☐ Yes – If yes, what is the condition? (_____) |

| **If you have other health problems, how often do they limit your daily activity around the house?** |
| ☐ None ☐ Hardly Ever ☐ Sometimes ☐ Often ☐ Always |

| **Highest Education Level** |
| ☐ Less than High School Graduate |
| ☐ High School Graduate or GED |
| ☐ Some College |
| ☐ College Graduate |

| **What gender are you?** |
| ☐ Male ☐ Female ☐ Transgendered |

| **What is your race or ethnicity?** |
| ☐ Black ☐ Hispanic ☐ Asian or Pacific Islander ☐ Caucasian |
| ☐ Alaskan Native or American Indian ☐ Other (_____) |

| **Do you work outside the home?** |
| ☐ No, not employed ☐ Part-time ☐ Full-time |

| **How much money does your family make from all sources each month?** |
| ($_____ /month) |

| **How often do you feel overwhelmed by taking care of our family** (circle one) |
| 1 2 3 4 5 6 7 |
| Never Sometimes All of the Time |

| **How much do you believe you can take care of yourself while also caring for your family?** (circle one) |
| 0 1 2 3 4 5 6 7 8 9 10 |
| Cannot do at all Probably can do Sure I can do |

Figure 3.4 Sample demographic questions.

(b) are mismatched to the target population in some important way, *(c)* have become outdated, *(d)* are too expensive, or *(e)* are too long. Careful literature reviews are essential to answering some of these questions, whereas others are settled by responses from focus groups or participants in small pilot studies prior to full-scale data collection. As we will demonstrate, each standardized scale limitation can provide some justification for defaulting to single-item indicators in construct validation.

Anticipating the analyses overviewed in Figure 3.3, developers must be sure the data collection instrument will capture the information necessary for each test. Relationships among variables can only be examined if they have first been captured in credible, unambiguous ways. Because developers must ultimately explain results that confirm *and* disconfirm their validation hypotheses, careful consideration of how respondents will provide key information is essential.

Precoding and Postcoding

Data entry errors can take at least two forms: mistaken or unclear answers provided by respondents and inaccurate transfer of information from its "raw" form on the data collection instrument to the data file created for analysis. Often, by the time a researcher recognizes that data provided on an instrument is uninterpretable, it is too late (or impossible) to go back to respondents for correction. And although researchers' data entry errors are often correctable, doing so is labor intensive. It is best to avoid them altogether. Careful coding of response options can minimize respondent errors and streamline data entry, enhancing accuracy in the process. Although our discussion here is intentionally brief, the topic should not be underestimated, and excellent resources are available for more detail (c.f. Groves et al., 2004).

Precoded responses are associated with closed-ended questions and typically make up the bulk of any psychometric instrument. In Figure 3.4, most items are precoded, meaning that distinct, mutually exclusive, and exhaustive options are associated with specific items. HIV status can accurately be classified as testing positive for HIV antibodies (HIV+), testing negative for them (HIV−), or having progressed to a level of immune system disorder classified as "full-blown" AIDS. Each of these represents a unique status, and provision of a "don't know" option reduces the potential for uncertain respondents to guess. The goal with precoding is for every meaningful response to be anticipated and included among the options.

Sometimes precoded options are imperfect or subject to evolution in social meaning or acceptability. Developers must stay current with language and labeling preferences and provide options that meet conventional research standards while respecting preferences of target populations. Reporting of race or ethnicity in Figure 3.4 illustrates the introduction of a *postcoded* option ("Other") in an open-ended format. In this case, researchers must log answers recorded in the blank and assign numerical values after the fact for data entry and analysis. Postcoded options give greater flexibility to respondents, add more labor for researchers, and should be kept to a minimum where quantitative analyses are anticipated. Every transposition required of someone entering data introduces an opportunity for inconsistency or error that must later be identified and corrected.

In some cases, researchers may decide that risks of data entry errors are "worth it," based in part on the level of measurement desired. When recording income, for instance, the format in Figure 3.4 invites a continuous level of measurement. Respondents can report any value and have their data recorded accordingly. Doing so imposes the fewest restrictions on the data obtained (as opposed to, for instance, precoded categories of monthly amounts). Researchers desiring continuous values for analyses will have the data they need and retain the ability to collapse it into ordinal or other categories later. If the data were originally collected in categories (as illustrated with highest education level), then it is not possible to deconstruct the answers into total years of education later.

Sequencing of Items and Elements

Several purposes are served by careful attention to the sequencing of items within an RAI and the sequencing of elements within a data collection package. In general, designers should remember the importance of gaining an adequate number of responses to support appropriate analysis of scale properties. This means that the RAI itself must be thoughtfully composed and embedded in a larger data collection instrument that guides and encourages respondents toward completion. Just as confusing items or response options can lead to uninterpretable data, carelessly constructed instruments can frustrate respondents and discourage them from finishing a survey they had consented to start.

Regarding RAI items, Comrey (1988) advises that the fairest tests of factor structure and internal consistency are achieved when items intended for a given scale or construct are separated (i.e., by randomizing their placement in a set of survey items). Doing so reduces the dependence of resulting responses. This enhances confidence that if patterns are found where originally intended (i.e., with responses to depression items clustering as designed), then the best explanation is shared construct, rather than method variance. That is, the observed responses clustered because they reflected a common latent construct, not because they were placed closely together in the instrument.

This is intuitively reasonable and follows a similar logic to randomizing "reversed" items throughout the item pool to break up unintended response patterns. A counterargument of sorts has been posed by Schwarz (1996, as cited in Dillman, 2007), who observed that a questionnaire should evolve like a conversation. There, constantly switching topics can give the impression that the questioner (or, in this case, the survey designer) is not "listening" to the respondent's answers. Failing to develop a coherent theme in item presentation can lead to disinterested or unfocused replies. Consequently, designers should try to avoid excessive "teaching to the test" (i.e., packing items of a common type together without interruption) while conveying enough consistency to reduce distraction or confusion for respondents.

In Chapter 2, we argued that RAIs should be straightforward and, barring some exceptional need, transparent to respondents. Although results from randomized items might be most convincing to a statistician, that presentation may be unnecessarily trying to a "regular" person hoping to make sense of a lengthy set of questions. Recall our earlier assertion that scales should ultimately maximize the opportunity for clients to express how they really are. This holds true in this stage of scale development as well. In this context, reasonable clustering of items on a common theme may be acceptable.

Similarly, the notion of an ordered, social conversation can guide the sequencing of elements within a data collection package. Here, the developer's goals include recognition that, as George Orwell wrote, "some animals are more equal than others" (1946, p. 112). Although we may want answers to everything in our instrument, some elements may be more critical to successful validation. Their placement in the mix of survey components may influence the likelihood of complete and accurate answers. Recalling the psychometric goals in Figure 3.3, confirming the factor structure may come first, with establishing reliability a close second. Accurate description of respondent characteristics is important, and establishing construct validity may be last. All are important, but science can "march on" to an extent if only the first questions are answered in an initial study.

Therefore, Dillman (2007) proposes that items with the most potential value to respondents be placed early in the package, the better to draw them in to the "conversation." The cover letter should have prepared them for general topics, and they should find that "good faith" is being maintained by getting down to business accordingly. Designers should avoid beginning with a series of disjointed demographic questions, particularly if some are of an overly sensitive nature and may provoke "motivated misreporting" (Groves et al., 2004, p. 224). After respondents have become engaged with the task and convinced of its value, they may be more willing to answer sensitive questions (e.g., relating to HIV status or income). Often, these are best placed near the end of the questionnaire.

Again, in the spirit of this orderly conversation, survey topics should be grouped according to logical patterns, where reflection on meaningful themes is encouraged. For instance, questions about HIV-related problems in daily living could be followed by questions on similar problems related to other illnesses. And finally, common response options should be grouped to minimize confusion in the mechanics of survey completion. Vacillating back and forth from Likert-type responses to dichotomies to fill-in-the-blanks can be taxing to respondents and invite carelessness or error.

Implications for Layout and Content Sequencing

In a sense, art meets science in the successful composition of a data collection instrument. Although the ordering of elements is critical, the graphic layout may be equally important to attracting and maintaining the respondents' interest. As we rely on Dillman (2007) for many of the most up-to-date recommendations, readers are encouraged to study his "do's and don'ts" of graphic design. Numerous studies have led to suggestions for best practices with text boxes, varying font sizes and intensities, "white space," and other elements meant to make it as easy as possible for respondents to get (and stay) on task.

Among the most important recommendations are making sure that instructions are clear, leaving no doubt as to what is requested or how responses should be provided. Having thought through all the content validation issues introduced in Chapter 2, RAI designers must avoid dropping the ball in late stages of instrument package development. Dillman (2007, p. 96) boils it down to three related steps:

1. Defining a "navigational path" for all information on every page.
2. Creating visual guides assisting respondents in staying on track.
3. (Where appropriate) Inserting additional visual guides interrupting established patterns and redirecting to new ones when attention should be shifted to something new.

Collectively, these illustrate the importance of guiding respondents in ways that enhance, rather than inhibit, provision of full and complete information.

Potential for Reactivity and Burden

Beyond considerations of sequencing and layout, overall burden and the potential for reactivity must also be considered when composing the data collection instrument. The first issue reflects concerns that the overall package is too long or too difficult for respondents to complete. Often, hard decisions are faced when RAI developers consider what is essential and what is expendable in the "wish list" of ideal package elements. We have already encouraged including more items than will ultimately be retained for the new RAI. In anticipating the full set of validation questions, we have also acknowledged the importance of including measures for testing convergent and discriminant hypotheses. The ideal number of elements needed for these obviously grows as the factor structure of a RAI becomes more complex. When demographics and variables for future applied hypotheses are added, the sheer volume of items can become overwhelming. If the constructs under investigation are more abstract or sensitive, require elaborate directions to follow, or are worded in language requiring a high reading level, then a sort of "critical mass" may be exceeded, blowing the likelihood that many (or most) respondents will stick with the process to completion. In short, if we aim for too much in putting the package together, then we may defeat ourselves in the process.

Similarly, the potential for reactivity, or changing something by the very act of measuring it (Fischer & Corcoran, 2007a), may cause respondents to back off or shut down in important ways. As introduced in Chapter 2 in the context of scale development, some of the content in Hudson's *Partner Abuse Scale: Physical*—where respondents may report whether their partner "physically forces me to have sex" or "tries to choke or strangle me" (Fischer & Corcoran, 2007a, p. 156)—can interrupt a respondent's willingness to complete a scale in unpredictable ways. Reactivity, in this sense, is neither good nor bad. However, it can lead to confounds either in data collection, interpretation, or clinical decision-making. RAI developers should carefully consider the potential that items they have developed for their new scale, or are incorporating from elsewhere as part of their validation package, may provoke strong reactions. If these are anticipated to be "deal-breakers" for respondents' completion of the data collection package (and this can sometimes be determined only through a good pilot study), then such elements should either be cut from the instrument or placed in sequence such that their potential impact may be minimized.

PLANNING FOR DATA COLLECTION

Substantial texts are devoted to the mechanics of data collection, attending to the range of issues from design and layout of the instrument through maximizing response rates (c.f. Dillman, 2007; Groves et al., 2004). In-depth discussion of these topics is beyond our scope, but we refer readers to these excellent texts for detailed guidance, including strategies for maximizing response rates and innovations in Web-based data collection.

Anticipating Costs

In our earlier discussion of sample size, the notion of "overkill" was introduced, highlighting the consequences of oversampling. When developers overestimate the number of respondents needed to achieve validation goals, they run the risk of taking on unnecessary costs in materials, labor, and time. Collectively, these may undermine enthusiasm for a project or even lead to its abandonment. Although many psychometric studies can be conducted with relatively little expense, failing to adequately anticipate them can cause otherwise avoidable setbacks.

Material expenses include costs of copying, distributing, and retrieving data collection instruments and may vary with the method employed. Incentives for potential respondents are material expenses, too. When data is collected face-to-face, material costs are minimized by eliminating the need for mailing. Response rates may also be increased as data is collected "on-the-spot" rather than requiring extra steps from respondents. If face-to-face collections are in group, rather than individual administrations, labor costs may also be lower, as multiple responses can be gathered in one session. Developers must consider the nature of their questions, the accessibility of their potential respondents, and their own flexibility in being available for administration when deciding how to balance cost control against efficient and effective response rates.

Another potential material cost is the purchase of copywritten instruments. RAI developers who include standardized scales to test their validation hypotheses must determine whether these are freely available or must be bought. In either case, they may also be concerned with whether the author permits reformatting or deconstruction of validated scales to match their layout and design preferences. Permission should always be obtained in advance and any expenses factored in to the total cost of the study.

The growing literature on Web-based administration and the emergence of improved survey software suggest that large samples can be effectively accessed with little or no paper-and-pencil expense, but these gains must be considered in light of the implications for sampling bias, respondent anonymity, and the researcher's confidence that people submitting online responses are members of the target population. Inclusion of previously standardized instruments in Web-based data collection should also be approved in advance by scale authors. If respondents with Internet access are suitable for the study, their identities can be reasonably protected, and their eligibility confirmed, then developers can save considerably on material and survey administration expenses.

Labor costs include production and duplication, distribution, and return processing of the data collection instrument or loading and monitoring for Web-based administration; staffing of data collection sessions or management of online procedures; coding, entering, and cleaning the data; and sometimes, data analysis. Web-based administration has the advantage of lessening the likelihood of respondent error in marking or coding the instrument, thus potentially lowering labor cost for entering and cleaning data. If respondents are offered incentives, translations are required for cross-cultural validation, or travel must be incurred to remote sites, then these may add to labor expenses as well.

Depending on available funding, developers will often find that there are multiple options for achieving acceptable, if not ideal, samples and make their decisions keeping pragmatics in mind. In this regard, expenses related to time are influenced by the desired sample size, accessibility of potential respondents, number of intermediaries (and intermediate steps) needed to identify respondents and gain permission to seek their consent, and the accuracy with which developers have anticipated all of the steps in the data collection process. Doing your homework on the mechanics of study design is almost as important as the clarity with which the RAI was conceptualized in the first place. The process truly is a continuum, and expertise across the board is an advantage in avoiding unnecessary delays and expenses and being able to shift gears to other acceptable options when things don't go as planned.

Recruiting and Training Associates

Although some psychometric studies are sufficiently "small-scale" that they can be managed by an individual investigator, more typically, they involve a team. When this is the case, responsibilities can be usefully distributed, but labor costs obviously rise as well. Each associate must be identified in human subjects' review applications, and their interactions with potential respondents and/or data specified. Research associates may have "behind-the-scenes" roles involving no contact with respondents or be directly involved with them. Their recruitment and training should be considered accordingly.

Research associates can be useful in production and distribution of data collection instruments, tracking expenses and receipts, supervising project staff, as well as entering, managing, and analyzing data. Although we cannot address each role in detail, one crucial consideration is assuring that associates understand the importance of fidelity to study procedures. Adequate training, and even literal scripting, is critical to assuring that data is collected consistently across all respondents and sites, that all aspects of informed consent are adhered to, and that any unanticipated or unusual events are immediately reported and processed.

After all the considerations raised thus far have been anticipated by the RAI developer and built into study design, attention to faithful execution of that plan is essential. Failure to do so can lead to consequences ranging from inability to explain response variability to disposal of poorly collected data to abandonment of the entire study. Our motto here is "designer beware." If you have carefully considered the design elements outlined here and factored them into your plan, then make certain that others involved in the study have the background and ability to understand both the steps they should take and the importance of following them. And, make sure that if they become stuck or confused, they know whom to contact and how. The most expensive cost of any study is the need to call it off because of failure to track the details.

NORMING STUDIES

A critical component of complete scale validation is the establishment of scale norms or reference scores by which responses obtained from an individual or group can be compared to some known standard. These should not be confused with being "normal," which implies a judgment on whether a trait or characteristic falls within some socially accepted standard or range. Rather, norms are empirically derived summations of how a specific population (e.g., clients receiving clinical care, or inmates in juvenile detention) scores on a particular instrument. They may be useful in diagnosis or assessment, where they guide determination of how serious an individual's problem might be.

For our purposes, these are studies of a second wave, generally possible only after initial validation has been established on a new scale. Once the reliability and validity of an instrument have been established, it then becomes possible to question whom it can usefully characterize and how as well as to design methods of data collection suited to that goal. To be convincing, these require large samples representing specific populations and typically require greater attention to probability sampling. They also place greater emphasis on establishing criterion validity and, consequently, identifying "cutting scores," indicating when responses fall beyond some critical threshold.

We will return to some of these issues in Chapter 5. For now, we hope this overview of design considerations provides a good foundation for transitioning from scale development to assessing the reliability and validity of the new instrument. In the coming chapters, we will outline the conceptual bases for fundamental scale qualities, describe methods for establishing them, and illustrate analytic techniques and their related interpretations. If data were gathered successfully following most of the principles outlined here, then those results should provide defensible answers to whether a novel scale has lived up to its promise.

4

Reliability

A tool is said to be reliable to the extent that it performs consistently over repeated use. In practical terms, a "measuring instrument is reliable to the extent that independent administrations of the same instrument (or a comparable instrument) consistently yield similar results" (Kyte & Bostwick, 1997, p. 173). Stated more precisely, *The Standards* frame reliability as the degree to which scale scores are free from errors of measurement (AERA, APA, & NCME, 1999).

Building upon this last view from *The Standards*, it becomes increasingly clear that scale developers must be mindful of the scale's reliability from the early stages of instrument design (*see* Chapter 2). What may seem conceptually clear to the scale developer can easily break down in attempts to "wrestle items to the ground" when constructing the instrument. This will certainly have negative ripple effects if poorly conceived items result in responses that are loosely related and inconsistent. *The Standards* unpack this line of thinking, identifying possible sources of measurement error:

> Different reliability coefficients and estimates of components of measurement error can be based on various types of evidence; each type of evidence suggests a different meaning. A reliability coefficient based on

the relation between alternate forms of a test administered on two separate occasions is affected by several sources of error, including random
response variability, changes in the individuals taking the tests, differences in the content of the forms, and differences in administration . . . .
It is essential, therefore, that the method used to estimate reliability takes
into account those sources of error of greatest concern for a particular
use and interpretation of a test. Not all sources of error are expected to
be relevant for a given test. (p. 19)

In short, differing scale structures (e.g., uni- or multidimensional, or
parallel forms) and methods of administration (e.g., self-reporting or
observational), correspond to varying forms of measurement error. The
skilled scale developer must possess the ability to project ahead and anticipate the potential impact of these variations in the earlier stages of scale
conceptualization and plan reliability analyses accordingly.

To illustrate key points from our theoretical overview of reliability,
we return to two scales familiar from previous discussions. The first is the
Family Responsibility Scale (FRS; Abell, Ryan, Kamata, & Citrolo, 2006).
The FRS (*see* Figure 2.1) is a unidimensional rapid assessment instrument that assesses family responsibility, or the feeling of overwhelm a
parent may experience as a result of fulfilling responsibilities as a head
of household with an HIV-infected child. The second is the multidimensional Parental Self-Care Scale (PSCS; Abell, Ryan, & Kamata, 2006),
which assesses HIV-positive parents' beliefs that they can care for themselves while maintaining their responsibilities as heads of households (*see*
Figure 2.2).

THEORY OF RELIABILITY

There are various ways to estimate the reliability of a measurement
instrument (c.f. Allen & Yen, 1979; Crocker & Algina, 1986; Cronbach,
1951; DeVellis, 2003; Nunnally & Bernstein, 1994; Springer, Abell, &
Hudson, 2002). As originally proposed by Spearman (1904), however,
reliability can be *conceptually* understood from the observed test score

as the composite of two unobserved components—a true score and an error score. Each person's observed score, O, consists of a "true" score, T, and a random error score, E. Random errors of measurement affect an individual's score because of purely chance happenings. Random errors reduce both the consistency and the usefulness of the scale scores. This relationship is depicted in the following equation:

$$O = T + E$$

This relationship is often referred to as the true-score model under the classical test theory, or the classical true-score model. T can be thought of as the score possible under "perfect" conditions, or it can be thought of as the average of the observed scores obtained over an infinite number of repeated administrations of the same instrument. Errors of measurement are always present. Classical test theory (e.g., Nunnally & Bernstein, 1994) assumes that if we knew the error scores and subtracted them from the observed scores, we would obtain the "true" scores. However, because the error is random and unobservable, we can never really know the actual error or true scores. It *is* possible to say that a true score is what the client is actually experiencing, and an error score is the gap between actual experience and what is observed as that experience.

Theoretically, reliability is defined as the squared correlation between observed scores and true scores among a population of examinees, r^2_{OT}, which is then expressed as the proportion of the true score variance to the observed score variance, $\frac{\sigma^2_T}{\sigma^2_O}$ (Lord & Novick, 1968), where σ^2_T is the variance of true scores and σ^2_O is the variance of observed scores. With the assumption that T and E are uncorrelated, σ^2_O is the sum of σ^2_T and the error variance σ^2_E—in effect, $\sigma^2_O = \sigma^2_T + \sigma^2_E$. Because the true score variance and the error score variance are reciprocal under the classical test theory, estimating the error variance can produce an estimate of reliability. Based on this reasoning, "reliability is defined through error" variances (Kerlinger, 1986, p. 408). Conceptually, error variance is the unexplained part of the true-score model. Thus, its proportion to the total data variation (observed score variance) is conceptualized as "unreliability." Likewise, true-score variance is the explained part of the model. Therefore, as stated earlier, its proportion to the observed score variance $\frac{\sigma_T^2}{\sigma_O^2}$ provides the "reliability" of observed test scores.

HOW TO ESTIMATE RELIABILITY

Several basic methods for estimating the reliability of RAIs will be covered here. Although numerous methods are discussed in the literature (e.g., parallel or alternate forms, reliability across raters, etc.), because of pragmatics regarding their use, our attention will be devoted briefly to consistency over raters (inter-rater or interobserver reliability) and to consistency over time, with a greater focus on internal consistency (across item responses). The conceptualization of reliability (and the computation of its estimates) varies with these definitions and purposes. Additionally, attention will be given to the standard error of measurement (*SEM*) and to recommendations for standards in judging the adequacy of RAI reliabilities.

Inter-Rater or Interobserver Reliability

Recall from Chapter 2 that there are two primary scale formats: *behavioral observation* or *self-reporting*. Observational measures generally consist of one set of items that capture a range of behaviors. To estimate the reliability of an observational measure, it is common to have two or more raters complete the instrument. The consistency of the observations over raters provides an estimation of the observational scale's reliability. In other words, inter-rater reliability "is a useful procedure for determining whether different users follow the same procedures, interpret the same responses in a similar way, and/or use techniques that elicit similar, relevant information. It is therefore an index of successful training in all of these areas" (Shaffer, Lucas, & Richters, 1999, pp. 10–11).

For example, suppose that you were interested in monitoring the impact of a cognitive-based intervention on participants' frequency of positive self-statements. To assess inter-rater reliability of this measure, you might train two raters who would observe and rate the frequency of positive self-statements made by participants receiving the cognitive-based intervention.

Recall in Chapter 2 that we explored the moving and interlocking pieces associated with instrument design. These components have relevance here as well, as considerations on the front end in designing an instrument may have positive (or negative) ripple effects later when attempting to establish evidence of a scale's degree of inter-rater reliability. For example, if scale items are not clearly developed and written (e.g., double-barreled questions), then their use and interpretation can be ambiguous to the raters. This, in turn, has great potential for increasing error. If settings vary across administrations of a scale, observed behaviors may vary too, resulting in misleading "consistency" scores across administrations. Finally, if raters are not equally trained or skilled or have varying relationships with the person being observed (i.e., parent or teacher), then even more error may be introduced.

If the two raters agree with one another about 80% of the time or more, then one might safely assert that the amount of random error in measurement was acceptable (cf. Harniss, Epstein, Ryser, & Pearson, 1999; Rubin, 2008). Early investigations of highly structured instruments such as the DISC (Costello, Edelbrock, Kalas, & Dulcan, 1984) went to great lengths to examine whether ratings obtained by clinicians and non-clinicians were systematically different. These studies were essentially asking whether clinicians and non-clinicians differed in their ability to read accurately and stick to the script, yet they did not differ (Shaffer, Fisher, & Lucas, 1999). In other words, to the extent that the scale developer can anticipate challenges such as these and incorporate corresponding preventative steps (i.e., clearly worded items embedded in a tightly structured scale administered by well-trained raters) into the design phase, the likelihood of being able to demonstrate evidence for inter-rater reliability will be enhanced.

Estimating Reliability Based on Consistency Over Time (Test–Retest)

We now shift our attention to estimating reliability for self-reporting scales. Test–retest entails giving the same scale to the same people twice with an intervening period of time. The correlation coefficient (e.g., Pearson's r, Spearman's Rho) between the two sets of scores (T_1, T_2), or the coefficient of stability, is used to measure this aspect of reliability. For example, if one were developing a new RAI to measure depression and wanted to establish test–retest reliability, he or she would administer the measurement package to the sample at one point in time. Then, the researcher would administer the measurement package again to the same sample, say, two weeks later. To the extent that both sets of responses on the new RAI correlated with one another, the test–retest reliability coefficient would be estimated.

The logic originates from the definition of the reliability mentioned earlier, the squared correlation between true scores and observed scores: r_{OT}^2. It has been shown that this definition can be re-expressed as the correlation coefficient between observed scores from two parallel forms of the scale, $r_{OO'}$ (Lord & Novick, 1968), under assumptions made in the classical test theory. Parallel test forms are defined as having the same true scores and the same error variances. In a test–retest reliability context, test scores in two test administrations are considered to be from two parallel test forms. They are in fact identical test forms, so our hope is that they retain characteristics of parallel forms—namely, the same true scores and error variances across two administrations.

However, the test developer should be cautioned about what the test–retest correlation coefficient may indicate in addition to what is reflected in reliability as defined by the true-score model. This happens when any changes affecting the true scores and error variances of the test exist. We consider this as a major reason that the test–retest correlation coefficient is appropriately referred to as the "coefficient of stability" to indicate more than reliability. For example, estimates related to time lapse between administrations of the scale leave room for errors, rather than random variability of responses, to occur. Too much time between administrations opens the door to occurrence of real change (i.e., respondents are actually more depressed on a second administration than they were on the first), whereas too little time raises the potential that second responses are based on memory of the first administration (i.e., the respondent not "tuning in" to how he or she really feels or behaves and just responding to items based on recall of how they were answered the first time). Both of these potentials lead to the possibility that obtained correlation coefficients will be misleading, because the correlation coefficient does not separate these different sources of error.

When we assess the reliability of scores from a scale, our interest is the random variability part of the error. Thus, we recommend the use of test–retest correlation coefficients in only two instances. First, where the trait being assessed is by nature predictably stable over time (e.g., acquisition of independent living skills, maintenance of "dry nights" following successful treatment of enuresis) or second, where some very credible alternate indicator of observed scores (T_1 and T_2, such as from an unbiased independent observer tracking an objectively verifiable behavior) can be used to confirm the "true" level of the characteristic being assessed. The bottom line is that test–retest is not as useful as sometimes implied, especially for the highly variable emotional and interpersonal traits that RAIs are designed to assess. Consequently, as Walter Hudson recommended, it should not be used unless the scale developer can demonstrate that she or he has minimized these problems (Springer, Abell, & Hudson, 2002).

Estimating Reliability Based on Internal Consistency (Coefficient α)

A reliability estimate based on the information about internal consistency is a more popular approach. Among several different methods, the coefficient α (Guttman, 1945; Cronbach, 1951) is the most frequently utilized method. Conceptually, it estimates how much the covariances between items account for the variance of the total test scores. Among its desirable qualities, coefficient α provides a direct estimate of the reliability of test scores under the condition, in which test items are "essentially τ-equivalent" to each other. When we say test items are essentially τ-equivalent to each other, it means that item-level true scores are only different by a constant for all examinees. An implication of this condition is that item-level true scores are correlated perfectly to each other. Practically, it means that item-true score differences all result from differences in item difficulties or, in the context of attitudes or affect, the severity of underlying traits that items capture. When this condition cannot be assumed, coefficient α estimates the lower bound of scale reliability, which means, from a practical perspective, that it is a conservative estimate of the reliability.

Coefficient α can be computed using one of several different formulas (we provide the general formula in the next section). One best known alternate formula is for a test with a dichotomous (e.g., true–false, yes–no) item-response format: the Kuder–Richardson 20 (KR20), derived by Kuder and Richardson (1937). However, because KR20 is equivalent to the coefficient α, and it indeed produces the same value as the coefficient α on the same data, we are not presenting the formula here. An interesting psychometric historical note is that the KR20 formula was derived before the more general coefficient α formula was first derived by Guttman (1945). (Another related historical note is that the coefficient α is often insufficiently attributed to only Cronbach [1951].) Another alternate formula worth mentioning is the formula for standardized item scores, simply known as the "standardized α" formula. The standardized α formula computes a coefficient α after item scores are transformed into z-scores; consequently, it is referred to as the standardized α. However, one needs to be alerted that a standardized α is not the same as a coefficient α. It indeed produces a different value from the coefficient α on the same data. In the past, it was popular to report a standardized α, but we do not recommend using it unless strong justification is provided. Our interpretation is that the standardized α was once popular because of simplified hand computations, where correlation coefficients between items provided sufficient information. However, we believe there is no other benefit from it, unless reported test scores are based on standardized item scores.

Indeed, the interplay between scale length and response options can certainly impact a scale's reliability properties. The scale developer must strike the right balance between the number of items and the range of response options. In Chapter 2, we gave a forward nod to how the Spearman–Brown prophecy formula (Nunnally & Bernstein, 1994) provides a method to estimate the impact on a scale's reliability when the number of items is altered. We return to this formula here, at least conceptually, but those interested are encouraged to consult other sources for a more detailed exposition (c.f. Crocker & Algina, 1986; Nunnally & Bernstein, 1994). For our purposes, suffice it to say that the Spearman–Brown prophecy reveals how a scale's reliability will be affected by shortening or lengthening the scale's number of items. For example, Crocker and Algina (1986) have demonstrated that doubling the length of a scale with a reliability of 0.60 will increase the reliability to 0.75, and tripling the length will increase the reliability to 0.81. Of course, "the Spearman–Brown projection is an accurate reflection of reliability only if the items added or removed are parallel in content and difficulty to items on the original test" (Crocker & Algina, 1986, p. 146).

Computing Coefficient α. Coefficient α generally provides a good estimate of reliability. The equation for the coefficient α is as follows (Nunnally & Bernstein, 1994):

$$\alpha = \frac{k}{k-1}\left[1 - \frac{\sum \sigma_i^2}{\sigma_C^2}\right],$$

where k equals the number of items, $\sum \sigma_i^2$ equals the sum of variances of scores on each ith item, and σ_C^2 equals the variance of the total score from the scale.

Here, we demonstrate how this formula can be used with a relatively small set of test items, using the computer simulated data that mimicks characteristics of the five-item finalized Instrumental subscale of the PSCS. A covariance matrix of the items provides sufficient information to use the formula. For the Instrumental subscale items, the covariance matrix is as follows.

$$
\begin{pmatrix}
5.801 & 1.537 & 1.398 & 1.266 & 1.524 \\
1.537 & 6.388 & 4.290 & 4.344 & 4.850 \\
1.398 & 4.290 & 6.421 & 4.585 & 5.014 \\
1.266 & 4.344 & 4.585 & 5.460 & 4.762 \\
1.524 & 4.850 & 5.014 & 4.762 & 5.803
\end{pmatrix}
$$

This is a 5×5 covariance matrix where the five diagonal elements are variances of the five items and the off-diagonal elements are covariances for a corresponding pair of items. For example, the variance of the third item is 6.421, and the covariance between the second and fourth items is 4.344. To obtain σ_C^2, one can compute the total test score and compute the variance of the total test score. Alternatively, the variance of the total test score can be obtained by summing all 25 elements in the covariance matrix, which gives us 97.013. On the other hand, $\sum \sigma_i^2$ is obtained by summing the five diagonal elements of the matrix, which gives us 29.873. It is obvious that $k = 5$, so by substituting these three quantities in the formula, the coefficient α is obtained as

$$
\alpha = \frac{k}{k-1}\left[1 - \frac{\sum \sigma_i^2}{\sigma_C^2}\right] = \frac{5}{5-1}\left[1 - \frac{29.873}{97.013}\right]
$$
$$
= 1.25(1 - 0.308) = 1.25(0.692) = 0.865 \ .
$$

To illustrate the computation of the coefficient α on a commonly available statistical software package, namely the Statistical Package for the Social Sciences (SPSS), we will use another computer simulated data set that mimics the characteristics of the FRS and the larger set of PSCS. We begin with the unidimensional FRS as the more parsimonious illustration and then move to the somewhat more complex PSCS to demonstrate the establishment of reliability for a multidimensional scale.

Unidimensional Estimates

The FRS (*see* Figure 2.1 in Chapter 2) initially consisted of 11 items. Once calculated on an original item pool, output from a reliability analysis can be used to guide retention and/or elimination of items from the final form of the scale. This process is illustrated in Table 4.1, which allows for the inspection of α coefficients in relation to α-if-item deleted data for the original and final versions of the FRS.

Using criteria for interpreting observed reliability coefficients that we will present later in this chapter, the coefficients for the FRS were "very good." For pragmatic reasons (i.e., ease of practitioner scoring and interpretation), we preferred a 10-item final scale structure. Table 4.1 reports the α-if-item-deleted values for the item pool of the FRS. Alpha-if-item-deleted data are extremely useful, as they display the effect on the total scale score reliability of removing any single item from the pool. The α-if-item deleted data indicated that reliability would be slightly increased, from 0.906 to 0.916, by removing Item 7. Caution should be given that this should not be the only criterion to decide the elimination of that item. Here, for illustration purposes, let us assume that we had other pieces of evidence to lead our decision on the elimination of that item

Table 4.1 FRS Internal Consistency Reliability

FRS item	α-if-item-deleted
1	0.899
2	0.907
3	0.891
4	0.889
5	0.889
6	0.889
7	0.916*
8	0.903
9	0.895
10	0.891
11	0.885
α	0.906
α if item 7 is deleted	0.916
SEM if item 7 is deleted	0.374

*Item removal would enhance subscale reliability.

from the scale. Accordingly, the "final α" reported in Table 4.1 would then be computed with Item 7 deleted.

Multidimensional Estimates: Subscale and "Global" Coefficients

The PSCS (*see* Figure 2.2 in Chapter 2) initially consisted of 30 items across its three domains.

Examination of the data in Table 4.2 allows for the inspection of α coefficients in relation to α-if-item deleted data for the original and final versions of the PSCS. Ultimately, we were aiming for a balance among three scale development goals: *(1)* strengthening internal consistency (by removing any "weak" items), *(2)* lowering instrument burden (by reducing scale length), and *(3)* easing scale scoring (by balancing the number of items in resulting subscales to facilitate hand calculations). In its simplest conceptualization, a multidimensional scale is a compilation of unidimensional scales. Thus, we had to determine the reliability for each subscale of the PSCS.

Targeting α coefficients greater than or equal to 0.90 using previously established standards (cf. DeVellis, 2003; Nunnally & Bernstein, 1994; Springer, Abell, & Nugent, 2002), the overall goal was to achieve compositions for each of the three PSCS subscales where additional item removals would not enhance resulting reliabilities. For Emotional self-care, coefficient α was computed as 0.915, and the original 10-item pool exceeded these standards. For the Instrumental subscale, three items indicated higher α-if-item-deleted values than the current coefficient α (0.731) for the subscale. These items (13, 18, and 19) were flagged for further investigation. If these items are actually removed from the subscale, coefficient α improves to 0.805. However, α-if-item-deleted values should not be the only criterion for item removal, as mentioned earlier, and such decisions are not made at this point. For the Nursing subscale, two items were flagged based on the α-if-item-deleted value (items 21 and 28). If these items are deleted, the coefficient α improves to 0.827.

It is sometimes of interest to sum up subscale scores from a multi-dimensional scale, yielding an intuitively meaningful "global" score. For

Table 4.2 PSCS Internal Consistency Reliability

PSCS item	α-if-item-deleted
(a) Emotional Subscale	
1	0.915
2	0.906
3	0.903
4	0.901
5	0.899
6	0.909
7	0.903
8	0.907
9	0.907
10	0.910
α	0.915
(b) Instrumental Subscale	
11	0.729
12	0.725
13	0.756*
14	0.661
15	0.662
16	0.659
17	0.653
18	0.735*
19	0.759*
20	0.730
α	0.731
(c) Nursing Subscale	
21	0.805*
22	0.742
23	0.738
24	0.778
25	0.780
26	0.747
27	0.775
28	0.795*
29	0.724
30	0.729
α	0.781

*Item removal would enhance subscale reliability.

the PSCS, item scores from the three subscales (Emotional, Instrumental, and Nursing) are summed and then divided by the total number of items to yield a global mean score. This is interpreted as an overall measure of parental capacity for self-care. The reliability of such scores can be computed by treating the entire scale as a unidimensional scale. For the PSCS, the coefficient α is computed based on the 20 finalized items. In fact, this provides us the estimate of reliability as 0.925. However, it is known that the reliability of a multidimensional scale tends to be underestimated by the α coefficient, and the degree of underestimation is larger for a scale with higher correlations between subscales (e.g., Osburn, 2000). One alternative reliability estimate is obtained by the stratified coefficient α (Cronbach, Shonenman, & McKie, 1965). The stratified α is obtained by the equation

$$\alpha_{stratified} = 1 - \frac{\sum_i \sigma_{O_i}^2 (1 - \alpha_i)}{\sigma_X^2},$$

where $\sigma_{O_i}^2$ is the variance of the total score for ith subscale, α_i is the coefficient α for the ith subscale, and σ_X^2 is the variance of the total score for the entire scale. For the PSCS data set, we have $\sigma_{O_i}^2$ and α_i for the three subscales as summarized in Table 4.3. In the table, the value of $\sigma_{O_i}^2 (1 - \alpha_i)$ is also computed for each subscale. As additional information, a covariance matrix for each subscale is presented in Figure 4.1. In addition, we have $\sigma_X^2 = 920.71$ as the variance of the summed total score of the 20-item scale. This quantity can be obtained by running a descriptive statistics procedure on statistical package software, such as SPSS. By substituting necessary quantities in the formula, we obtain the stratified coefficient α as

$$\alpha_{stratified} = 1 - \frac{36.137 + 13.095 + 4.945}{920.71} = 1 - .059 = .941.$$

In this particular case, the underestimation of reliability by the coefficient α is not that large, only by 0.016 compared to the stratified coefficient α. However, we recommend that developers always compute

Table 4.3 Quantities Required to Compute Stratified α for the PSCS

Subscale	$\sigma_{O_i}^2$	α_i	$\sigma_{O_i}^2(1 - \alpha_i)$
Emotional	425.14	0.915	$425.14(1 - 0.915) = 36.137$
Instrumental	97.00	0.865	$97.00(1 - 0.865) = 13.095$
Nursing	48.48	0.898	$48.48(1 - 0.898) = 4.945$

(a) Emotional Subscale

Inter-Item Covariance Matrix

	V1	V2	V3	V4	V5	V6	V7	V8	V9	V10
V1	6.532	2.386	3.169	3.569	3.022	2.548	3.159	2.497	2.802	2.263
V2	2.386	6.970	3.891	4.183	4.098	3.779	3.998	3.822	3.792	3.653
V3	3.169	3.891	7.045	4.714	4.592	4.017	4.179	4.436	3.463	4.053
V4	3.569	4.183	4.714	7.447	5.119	4.041	4.605	4.457	4.114	4.180
V5	3.022	4.098	4.592	5.119	6.989	4.300	4.757	4.930	4.342	4.616
V6	2.548	3.779	4.017	4.041	4.300	8.237	3.866	4.203	3.660	3.482
V7	3.159	3.998	4.179	4.605	4.757	3.866	7.188	4.389	3.735	4.190
V8	2.497	3.822	4.436	4.457	4.930	4.203	4.389	8.939	3.639	4.619
V9	2.802	3.792	3.463	4.114	4.342	3.660	3.735	3.639	6.972	3.657
V10	2.263	3.653	4.053	4.180	4.616	3.482	4.190	4.619	3.657	8.840

(b) Instrumental Subscale

Inter-Item Covariance Matrix

	V11	V12	V13	V14	V15	V16	V17	V18	V19	V20
V11	6.062	.444	−.059	1.771	1.119	1.426	1.538	.818	.334	1.050
V12	.444	5.801	.302	1.573	1.398	1.266	1.524	1.371	.138	1.042
V13	−.059	.302	11.094	1.660	1.678	1.167	1.441	.479	−.045	.527
V14	1.771	1.573	1.660	6.388	4.290	4.344	4.805	1.057	.516	1.517
V15	1.119	1.398	1.678	4.290	6.421	4.585	5.014	1.490	.678	1.222
V16	1.426	1.266	1.167	4.344	4.585	5.460	4.762	1.354	.969	1.326
V17	1.538	1.524	1.441	4.805	5.014	4.762	5.803	1.525	.620	1.304
V18	.818	1.371	.479	1.057	1.490	1.354	1.525	6.303	−.488	−.159
V19	.334	.138	−.045	.516	.678	.969	.620	−.488	8.134	.804
V20	1.050	1.042	.527	1.517	1.222	1.326	1.304	−.159	.804	6.548

(c) Nursing Subscale

Inter-Item Covariance Matrix

	V21	V22	V23	V24	V25	V26	V27	V28	V29	V30
V21	6.293	.868	.683	.616	.402	.487	.329	.301	.950	.708
V22	.868	3.642	1.679	.741	.697	1.609	.802	.615	1.910	1.968
V23	.683	1.679	2.404	.817	.894	1.360	.791	.487	1.845	1.722
V24	.616	.741	.817	3.738	.628	.722	.696	.371	.892	.845
V25	.402	.697	.894	.628	3.362	.481	.655	.130	.890	.881
V26	.487	1.609	1.360	.722	.481	2.814	.932	.663	1.666	1.618
V27	.329	.802	.791	.696	.655	.932	3.307	.310	.891	.853
V28	.301	.615	.487	.371	.130	.663	.310	4.160	.750	.660
V29	.950	1.910	1.845	.892	.890	1.666	.891	.750	2.353	2.034
V30	.708	1.968	1.722	.845	.881	1.618	.853	.660	2.034	2.442

Figure 4.1 Covariance matrices for the three subscales of PSCS data.

the stratified α if subscale scores are summed or averaged to obtain global scores.

Note that α and stratified α are not affected by linear transformations of the summed total subscale and global scores into their mean scores. In computation of stratified α, one can choose either the scale of the summed total scores or the mean scores to derive $\sigma_{O_i}^2$ and σ_X^2, and the end result of stratified α will be the same either way. In our illustration, we derived $\sigma_{O_i}^2$ and σ_X^2 based on the summed total scores, because $\sigma_{O_i}^2$ in the scale of summed total scores were readily available from the computations of α coefficients for the three subscales. When we choose to derive $\sigma_{O_i}^2$ from the scale of summed total scores, σ_X^2 must be derived from the scale of summed total scores too. On the other hand, if one chooses to derive $\sigma_{O_i}^2$ from the scale of average scores, σ_X^2 must be derived from the scale of average scores too. Finally, we would like to reiterate that the stratified α is the reliability estimate of global mean (or summed) scores. Therefore, the stratified α is meaningful only when we are interested in such global scale scores.

Reliability Standards

Because reliability estimates can range from 0.0 to 1.0, it is important to know how high this estimate must be for the scale developer to claim that he or she has developed a measurement tool that can generate reliable test scores. A satisfactory level of reliability depends on how a measure is to be used. This means that one can distinguish between reliability standards for use in scientific applications (i.e., to compare group means in nomothetic research) and reliability standards for use in making decisions about individuals (i.e., in direct practice). For large sample scientific work, a reliability coefficient of 0.60 or greater used to be considered acceptable (Hudson, 1982). Given the field's advancement in its ability to establish psychometrically sound scales in recent years, today we would not accept anything as credible for use in nomothetic research with a reliability coefficient below 0.70.

Furthermore, we believe that measurement tools that will be used to make decisions about a single individual should produce test scores with a minimum reliability coefficient of 0.80. Nunnally and Bernstein (1994) suggest that a reliability of 0.90 is even more appropriate. The only occasion where we believe lower reliability is acceptable is a case where individual scale scores are aggregated at the group level for data analysis with groups as units of analysis.

The reliability standards suggested here will likely serve quite well, but that depends in a great way on the importance of the decisions being made. In essence, the greater the seriousness of the problem being scaled (and the graver the risk in being wrong), the higher the standard should be held.

Standard Error of Measurement

Standard error of measurement (*SEM*) describes the expected variation of the true scores. Just as the total group of subjects has a standard deviation, theoretically, each subject's personal distribution of possible observed scores around the subject's true score has a standard deviation. When these individual standard deviations are averaged for the group, the result is the *SEM*.

The *SEM* is an estimate of the standard deviation of the errors of measurement (Lord & Novick, 1968) and is computed with the following formula (see Nunnally & Bernstein, 1994, for a technical discussion of the *SEM*):

$$SEM = \sigma_C\sqrt{1 - r_{tt'}},$$

where σ_C equals the standard deviation of observed test scores, and $r_{tt'}$ equals the estimate of reliability, such as coefficient α.

As the formula shows, *SEM* is directly related to reliability and can be seen as the unstandardized "unreliability" of test scores. (In this regard, the reliability coefficient can be seen as the standardized indicator for the degree of "nonerroneousness.") The *SEM* is practically useful for providing an interval estimate of how far the true score may lie from an observed score for a particular respondent, but there is no absolute guarantee that an individual's true score really falls in a confidence interval generated around the observed score.

Computing the Standard Error of Measurement for the Family Responsibility Scale. The *SEM* for the FRS was computed using the above formula, where $\sigma_C = 1.291$ and $r_{tt'} = 0.916$, resulting in *SEM* = 0.374. Note that σ_C is obtained by computing a total score based on the final item pool for the FRS and determining the standard deviation of those scores from the validation sample. The resulting *SEM* can be used to construct a confidence interval. For example, the confidence interval for a subject with a score of 5.3 is $5.3 \pm 2(.374) = [4.552, 6.048]$, indicating the probability that this interval captures the true score is 95%. The range of this 95% confidence interval is 0.784. If a scale has a low *SEM*, it will result in a narrower confidence interval, and the developer can argue that the scale has good measurement error characteristics. Springer, Abell, and Hudson (2002) developed and recommended a general rule stating that the *SEM* should be approximately 5% (or less) of the range of possible scores (as illustrated in Hudson, 1982, where scores range from 0 to 100). For the FRS example, the range of possible score is from 1 to 7. Therefore, the obtained *SEM* of 0.374 is 6.23% of the range, indicating a reasonably small *SEM*, which nevertheless slightly exceeds Hudson's recommended 5% or less rule. Generally speaking, a good measurement tool, from a measurement error point of view, is one that has a large coefficient of reliability and a small *SEM* in relation to the overall range of possible scores.

CONCLUSION

Reliability estimates established as a coefficient α are simple to calculate and, based on the standards originated elsewhere in the literature and updated here, relatively easy to characterize. When contextualized by accompanying *SEMs*, they provide the scale developer with a fairly solid foundation from which to begin judging the strength of a scale. As illustrated by the "moving target" of adequacy evolving in the literature over time, developers should remain mindful that no standards are absolute. Rather, they are simply the products of convention, with thresholds established as a function of what is generally viewed as achievable and acceptable in terms of measurement consistency. Still, as a primary principle in assessing the quality of scores from a scale, a solid reliability coefficient is indispensable, and must be established for each construct or factor when multidimensionality is claimed. In Chapter 5, we will build from this base of estimated scale consistency and consider strategies for accumulating evidence that scale scores are not only stable but also accurate reflections of their target constructs.

5

Establishing Evidence of Scale Score Validity

Determining the meaning of scale scores is the most demanding and, in many ways, the most interesting aspect of scale validation. And although validation is often applied to the whole process of establishing psychometric qualities, here we will begin to use it more precisely. The "lines of evidence" referenced in the *Standards* (1999, p. 5) reflect the view that *construct validation* has increasingly come to reference a composite of characteristics that can only be meaningfully interpreted as an integrated whole. At times, the abstractions being wrestled with have taken on an almost comical, theological tone.

Angoff identified a "monotheistic mode . . . of a unitary psychometric divinity" (1988, p. 25). Guion, in turn, objected to trends treating content, criterion-related, and construct validities as "something of a holy trinity representing three different roads to psychometric salvation" while asserting that there was some merit "in psychometric theology . . . (of speaking) of one validity, evidenced in three ways" (1980, p. 386). This "big picture" view was the basis for Messick's comprehensive conceptualization of construct validity as "nothing less than an evaluative summary of both the evidence for and the actual—as well as potential—consequences of score interpretation and use" (Messick, 2003, p. 243). No single aspect of validation was sufficient by itself. "Construct validity . . . exists when everything fits together, not when we have some small bit of evidence of a significant result in a particular direction" (Stickle & Weems, 2006, p. 217). Good theory must guide the testing of empirical hypotheses, and these must be interpreted with consideration for the context in which the target construct operates (Goldstein & Simpson, 2002). These must also converge in an integrated argument for the accurate interpretation of scale responses.

Although there is much to gain from thinking of validity in this way, starting from such a frame without first understanding the parts and pieces from which it is built can be intimidating, if not overwhelming. Guion's trinitarian view may sound a bit grandiose but is at least entertaining and reflects the seriousness (and complexity) developers must grapple with when evaluating new scales. In fact, the evolution of construct validity from Campbell and Fiske's (1959) early work on convergent and discriminant "types" into Messick's emphasis on the social relevance and meaning of scale scores was significantly influenced by the "law of unintended consequences" (McPhail, 2007, p. 4). McPhail describes the Civil Rights Act of 1964 and the subsequent creation of the Equal Employment Opportunity Commission as primary drivers to ensure that poorly interpreted or inadequately validated scale scores not become obstacles to the rights or opportunities of respondents.

In practice, several of the forms of validity evidence we hope to distinguish may be based on highly similar statistical techniques, where the primary differences between them boil down to the developer's intent (i.e., the nature of the questions or hypotheses) rather than the empirical values observed (DeVellis, 2003). Consequently, we'll do a little deconstruction first, breaking down the historical elements of scale score validity and weighing their relative merits. In the end, we'll attempt to put them back together, showing that although none are adequate in themselves to defend the accuracy of scale score interpretations, each contributes something to the ultimate assessment of how well a scale measures what it's intended to.

So far, we have concentrated on setting clear targets in RAI development: focusing on specific constructs, determining scale dimensionality, settling on a structure for stimulus and response, writing items, and gathering feedback on how well we have hit our mark. We have also detailed the importance of adequate sampling through meaningful representation of construct content in scale items and identification and recruitment of appropriate survey respondents. If successful, we will have seen reasonable content evidence of validity (to be detailed further below) and established the consistency or stability of our measure through examining its reliability.

All of this sets the stage for the next, most critical set of questions regarding whether our scale measures what we think it does. Claims that a set of scale responses can be interpreted to mean what RAI developers say they do go to the very heart of validation and, as Messick writes, can only be established on the basis of "serious attempts" to do so (1989, p. 36). By this, he means achieving adequate sample size and acceptable scale reliability. Lacking these, developers risk misinterpreting correlations among variables as too small or insignificant when, in fact, their unexpected performance could result from having too few respondents or inadequate stability of measurement. When minimum design criteria are met, the parts and pieces of scale psychometrics can begin to add up. Clear construct conceptualization and well-executed study design increase the odds that credible evidence will result in defensible conclusions about the new RAI.

In this chapter, we will elaborate on the sort of questions developers might ask regarding the meaning of scores on their new measure and illustrate techniques for analyzing and interpreting evidence. Fundamental questions are summarized in Figure 5.1, where we see the elements of evidence for scale score validity sequenced in the order in which they are often examined. Factor structure seems best treated in an expanded discussion, reserved for Chapter 6. All forms of validity evidence are inter-related, and as we consider their individual contributions, we will keep the big picture in mind, considering:

- the internal structure of the scale and its external relationships to other variables
- the meaning of empirical evidence, avoiding mechanical interpretations, and
- the degree to which such evidence permits supporting or refuting theory guiding expectations for scale performance.

Taken together, this information should help us gain increasing confidence in inferences based on a new scale and, as we'll see, make best use of both logical and empirical evidence.

Type of Evidence	Fundamental Questions
Face	Does the scale *appear* to measure what it claims to measure?
Content	Does item content reflect the construct definition?
Factorial	Does the scale measure the number of constructs it claims?
Construct	
Convergent	Do variables that should correlate with the scale score do so?
Discriminant	Do variables that should not correlate with the scale score not do so?
Criterion	
Concurrent Known-Groups	Do scale scores adequately categorize respondents with known characteristics?
Concurrent Known-Instruments	Do categorizations based on new scale scores adequately match those based on previously standardized measures?
Predictive	Do scale scores accurately predict future behaviors or attitudes of respondents?

Figure 5.1 Establishing evidence of scale score validity.

ESTABLISHING EVIDENCE OF VALIDITY

Face Validity Evidence

As introduced in Chapter 2, face validity evidence is established by determining whether a scale "looks like" it measures what it is intended to. As Charles Mosier concluded over 60 years ago, over-reliance on such evidence for establishing scale score validity is "dangerous because it is glib and comforting to those whose lack of time, resources, or competence prevent them from demonstrating validity (or invalidity) by any other method" (1947, p. 194). He added that resorting to face validation was tempting because it implies that the developer's

> knowledge and skill in the area of test construction is so great that he can unerringly design a test with the desired degree of effectiveness in . . . . evaluating defined personality characteristics and . . . . do this so accurately that any further empirical validation is unnecessary. So strong is this ego complex that if statistical verification is sought and found lacking, the data represent something to be explained away by appeal to sampling errors or some other convenient rationalization . . . (p. 194).

He concluded that this risk was so potentially damaging that the term should be "banished to outer darkness" (p. 191.)

Well, at least we've been warned!

Although we can hope Mosier's views directly influenced our more modern concerns with minimizing developers' bias in scale validation, the caution he raises remains true today. Bias and prior assumptions about scale qualities can cloud even well-intended analyses and lead to distortion of resulting evidence, particularly when "looks like it to me" is the only standard applied.

Still, some residual value may remain in his notion of face validity by *appearance* and respondents' impressions of it. Mosier observed that to some extent, it matters that a scale's appearance correctly advertises its intended use and promotes a sense of open communication between respondent and interpreter. There may be some gain in scale titles or construct labels that clearly state what they intend to measure and in scale items that, at a glance, appear consistent with that goal. Years later, Messick echoed these ideas, observing that

> whether a test is judged relevant to its objectives by respondents, users, or others can affect examinee cooperation and motivation as well as use and public acceptance of the results. Therefore. . . .face *in*validity should be avoided whenever possible — except, of course, when indirect or disguised measures are intended (1989, p. 19).

In fact, respondents may interact differently with an instrument depending on the clarity with which its purpose is revealed and their understanding of its intended use. In terms of scale utilization, the results could be interpreted as either positive or negative. Someone seeking protection from an abusive partner, for instance, may be eager to detail the nature and severity of the violence in a relationship. The perpetrator, on the other hand, recognizing that the truth, if revealed, may cost them visitation rights with a child or lead to a criminal record, may be just as eager to mask the truth. Both responses can be stimulated by the "first impression" created by a scale and the respondent's expectations regarding its meaning and use. The catch, as Mosier wrote, was for the developer to fully describe the *concept* the scale was originally meant to capture. When the intended meaning was explicitly stated, others could join in the assessment by cross-checking for any hidden bias.

Content Validity Evidence

In essence, content validity evidence has come to express what Mosier implied. Moving beyond a glancing or superficial assessment, it requires a logical process of judging, intuitively or subjectively, how well item content reflects the definition of the target construct. As such, it resides "not in the test, but in the judgment of experts about domain relevance and representativeness" (Messick, 1989, p. 41). Seen in this way, content validity evidence depends heavily on two components: the care with which items were originally constructed and the expertise and suitability of those selected as judges.

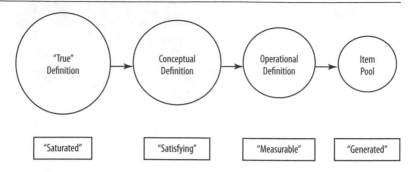

Figure 5.2 Reduction of construct definitions in scale development.

As seen in Figure 5.2, the challenge for scale developers begins in the process of selecting and defining the initial target construct(s). Here, we adapt Jane Gilgun's (2004) work, illustrating how RAI designers start from the broadest or "true" definition of a construct. As an abstraction, this reflects an idealized or "saturated" understanding of the construct that must be reduced to an acceptable conceptual idea whose components can be usefully described and discussed. These key components are then operationalized, or expressed in measurable terms. Finally, an item pool is developed and becomes the basis for psychometric analysis. Recalling the domain sampling model from Chapter 2, we know that items emerge from a brainstorming process where ideas about or experiences of the target construct are gradually shaped into an acceptable item pool. If the process is successful, then the resulting items are distinct, measurable representations of the original idea and should stand up well to expert scrutiny. Assuming that developers have given it their best shot, let's see how the content validation process might play out.

Identification of Expert Panelists. As indicated in Chapter 2, picking the right experts is crucial, as developers are beginning to test their biases about construct conceptualization against evidence. In this case, the evidence will be a blend of qualitative judgments and some very limited quantified responses. Experts must be selected based on (*a*) their knowledge of the substantive area and (*b*) their capacity to understand the psychometric task, stay focused, and carry it to completion. Their knowledge may be professional, personal, or both. Whether they are published scholars with demonstrated expertise or "lay" experts (Rubio, Berg-Weger, Tebb, Lee, & Rauch, 2003) whose main qualification is life experience, developers are informally hypothesizing that the items they have come up with will be seen by these reviewers as appropriate and clear.

Although there are no hard and fast rules for expert panel composition, it is a good idea to strike a balance between those who have come by their knowledge through study and those who have lived it directly. Both can add valuable insights to whether or not the items are "on track." Beyond that, their capacity to understand and follow directions is critical and will be determined to a large extent by the clarity of the instructions they receive. Typically, 6 to 10 panelists will be enough (Rubio et al., 2003), bearing in mind that the primary goal is sufficient representation of backgrounds and opinions. The feedback gained from panelists can be critical, but developers should remember that the goal is mainly cross-checking and revision *before* large-sample data is collected.

Specifying the Tasks. Basic instructions for expert panelists were introduced in Figure 2.5. There, we saw a framework for stimuli and responses to be provided by the panelists. Here, in Figure 5.3, more detailed instructions are shown from a study validating the HIV/AIDS Provider Stigma Inventory (HAPSI). As introduced in Chapter 2, the HAPSI is based on social cognitive theories of stigma and is conceptually complex. Consequently, our goal is to orient panelists to the big picture, while encouraging them to focus on a few specific tasks. Inviting critique of the constructs themselves or debate over competing plausible definitions is more appropriate for an earlier, focus group process and is not what is needed here. Considering our adaptation of Gilgun (2004) in Figure 5.2, at this stage we are assuming that the "true" and conceptual definitions have been settled and are now concerned with how well the item pool has operationalized those ideas.

As shown in Figure 5.3, panelists are provided with a conceptual context for the scale, a description of its structure, and a summary of

The HAPSI is intended to assess HIV/AIDS health care and social service providers' stigmatizing attitudes and tendencies towards PLHA. The primary domains are *awareness* and *acceptance*, with underlying constructs in each case reflecting tendencies to shame, blame, or create/maintain social distance, and addressing:

- labeling
- stereotyping
- identifying others as members of outgroups, and
- discriminating

The measure is intended to capture these constructs as they are associated with both instrumental and symbolic stigma (fears and reactions associated with viral acquisition and/or social censure), and with personal characteristics of patients or clients known or thought to be HIV+. Providers will be asked to respond to each item on scales from 1-7, where 1 = completely disagree or very unlikely, and 7 = completely agree or very likely (as appropriate for each content area).

Instructions to future respondents will read:

The statements below concern service providers' interactions with people they know or suspect to have HIV or AIDS (PLHA). While there are no right or wrong answers, the most useful responses come from looking deeply into your own experiences. Answer as honestly as you can, trying not to choose responses just because they would make you feel best about yourself, or look best to others.

As a member of our expert panel, we are asking you to help us learn how well these items fit the definitions of the constructs they're meant to represent. Please read each item carefully, then **circle the number showing how well you think each item matches the target definition**, where:

1 = not at all   2 = a little bit   3 = somewhat   4 = quite a bit   5 = very well

Please use the space beneath each item to suggest any changes you believe might improve the item. Also, note that some items are "positive", meaning they reflect "more of" the given tendency, and others [marked below as **R**] are "negative", meaning they reflect "less of". You need not be concerned with that aspect at this stage. Just concentrate on whether the item content matches the target definition.

Figure 5.3   Expert panelist instructions for the HAPSI.

the instructions to be used by future scale respondents. Then, they are guided to focus on the fit between item content and construct definitions (which follow in the larger instrument), and they are encouraged to write in any suggestions they may have for item revisions. At the end of the content validation evidence instrument (not shown here), they are further invited to add summary comments on their overall impressions of the scale. There, they might also be asked to address the clarity of instructions, overall readability of the scale, or the appropriateness of dialect or slang for future respondents. This feedback can be invaluable, but developers should be prepared for their carefully stated instructions to be misunderstood or ignored and to weigh the ultimate usefulness of panelists' feedback accordingly.

Figure 5.4 summarizes comments received when a set of 10 adult panelists critiqued the proposed "outgroups" items for the HAPSI. Although most panelists provided quantitative information on all items (circling the number reflecting their judgment of definition/content "fit"), only a few provided qualitative comments. These ranged from observations that the items were too tangential, might be influenced by many different factors, or were simply unlikely to be answered by most respondents. In some cases, options for rewording were suggested.

When working with children, developmental capacity is critical and must be considered in the presentation of content validation evidence instructions. In Figure 5.5, instructions for two different age groups (younger children: 6–8 years old; older children: 9–11) are illustrated from a study of the Trauma Resilience Scale for Children (TRS-C; Thompson, 2007). In this context, the developer was committed to understanding factors children believed could help them return to "normal" functioning following exposure to violent trauma. Accordingly, she designed a content validation evidence tool to be used in settings where tasks like those we have described could be handled in a structured group setting. Children participating were presented with sets of items (read to them as needed) and asked for their views on the quality of items (younger children) and their fit and clarity (older children).

Analyzing and Interpreting Responses.   For all the careful thought that goes into collecting content validation evidence, in the end, interpretation calls for making some fairly subjective judgments about the value and meaning of information gained. In Figure 5.4, Panelist #8 (P8) clearly had some reservations about a number of items, doubting health-care or social service providers would respond to them or believing that responses could be driven by factors other than stigma. These are thoughtful observations, and the panelist took the time to detail concerns. On the other hand, only two items (1 and 7) drew as many as three comments from a panel of 10 members. Beginning to count or quantify patterns, as we are doing here, is potentially helpful if it contributes to an emergent theme or even consensus about an item's characteristics. However, remembering the size of our sample and reflecting on

Definition: reinforcing distinctions between "us" (people who are not negatively labeled or stereotyped) and "them" (people who are) to create a sense of distance and safety. Read each item below, and circle the number showing how\well you think its content fits the definition of outgroups, where:

1 = not at all   2 = a little bit   3 = somewhat   4 = quite a bit   5 = very well

When I know or suspect a PLHA is gay, an injection drug user, or has many sex partners, I am more likely to do the following:

1) Use my free time doing things that show I don't live the way my clients or patients do	1 2 3 4 5

P1: Make sure I don't live the way my client's do. "Free time" narrows the focus of the question
P2: Seems kind of odd?
P8: I'd be very surprised if anyone endorsed this. Alternative: feel ashamed if I found myself behaving in ways my patients do

2) Make sure others know I think their behavior is unacceptable	1 2 3 4 5

P1: Clarify the target of "their"—let others know I think my client's behavior is unacceptable.

3) Remind myself that I'm not like them	1 2 3 4 5
4) Think of my life as different from theirs	1 2 3 4 5

P2: I like this

5) Remind myself that we're all the same	1 2 3 4 5
6) Make sure others know I understand the difference between right and wrong	1 2 3 4 5

P2: This seems too tangential

7) Make sure I don't seem too friendly with them	1 2 3 4 5

P1: Change to "avoid friendships or personal encounters with clients"
P2: This could be interpreted as maintaining professional boundaries
P8: To whom? Colleagues? Patients?

8) Think that my good decisions in life have protected me from having problems like theirs	1 2 3 4 5

P1: Change to "am grateful that my personal decisions and behaviors have protected me from..."
P2: Not sure this really measures outgroup

9) Be open with others about the kinds of people I work with	1 2 3 4 5

P8: Confounds perceived views of others. The others could think it wonderful to be working with HIV+ people.

10) Be open with others about the kind of work I do	1 2 3 4 5

P8: Same concern

11) Keep my work and personal lives separate	1 2 3 4 5

P2: I don't think this measures "us"/"them"
P8: Lots of reasons for this besides stigma

12) Keep quiet when others say hurtful or mean things about PLHA	1 2 3 4 5

P8: Could be other reasons besides stigma

13) Make sure I speak up when others treat PLHA badly	1 2 3 4 5

P8: Could be other reasons besides stigma

14) Avoid spending my free time around the kinds of people I work with	1 2 3 4 5

P1: Change—avoid socializing with clients

Figure 5.4 HAPSI expert panelists' qualitative comments: "outgroups."

When something really hard happens, what helps you the most?
We are asking kids about what helps them get over hard things.

Younger Children: Please tell us if each question is:

1 = Bad question   2 = Just okay question   3 = Great question

Older Children: Does this question talk about _____ (Domain name) well?

1 = Does not talk about _____ (Domain Name) well   2 = Talks about _____ okay
3 = Really talks about _____

Is this a clear question?

1 = Too hard to understand   2 = Kind of hard to understand   3 = Clear and easy to understand

Figure 5.5 Children's content validation instructions.

how confident we are that our "experts" truly deserved their titles or understood their tasks conditions the weight assigned to their views.

Qualitative input at this stage should obviously not be discounted. Why go to this much trouble only to dismiss the resulting feedback? Keeping it in perspective, however, often involves treating it as a sort of "conversation" with the developer, where everyone's opinion matters; however, lacking overwhelming agreement, the practical conclusion may be that items like 1 and 7 are modified or adjusted or even left "as is" rather than being excluded. Holding on to these initial impressions so that they can be reviewed later, when more item-level evidence has accumulated, is sometimes the best choice.

Quantitative analyses are a little more complex, and some authors have gone to great lengths to describe techniques for crunching the data. Among the options are the content validity index (CVI; DeVon et al., 2007), which can be calculated to report the proportion of panelists rating an item as acceptable, or the proportion of the total number of scale items deemed content valid. Inter-rater agreement (IRA; Rubio et al., 2003) computes agreement among panelists, expressed as the reliability of multiple raters' estimates of the fit between item content and construct definition. Finally, the multirater kappa (κ) coefficient samples the "proportion of interrater agreement remaining after chance agreement is removed (Schaefer, Schmidt, & Wynd, 2003, p. 511). Readers are directed to these sources for detailed discussions of the computation and interpretation of these coefficients.

Taking another perspective, our view is that the very small sample sizes and limited data typically collected in content validation argue against attempting to make more out of this information than can be reasonably defended. Assessments of statistical significance in these contexts are a bit risky, and some have observed that use of the CVI, for instance, may misrepresent the true level of agreement among raters (Schaefer et al., 2003). Instead, we illustrate an analysis that makes use of the quantitative data by stating intuitively reasonable rules of interpretation, then applying them to the responses obtained.

In Table 5.1, numerical ratings from 10 panelists responding to the HAPSI "outgroups" items are displayed as arranged by a standard spreadsheet. Their individual item responses are reported, along with sample means and standard deviations. Intuitively, with response options ranging from 1 = not at all to 5 = very well, anything above a midpoint of 3 would indicate some endorsement that the item content fit the target construct definition. To be a little more convincing, we set the most conservative target threshold as 3.5 or greater. Dark-shaded boxes in Table 5.1 mark the five items meeting or exceeding this standard. Setting a slightly more relaxed standard (i.e. one that is a little more liberal or easier to achieve, such as $\geq 3.0 < 3.5$) could still be argued as a positive assessment of content/definition fit. Lightly-shaded boxes show that an additional eight items met this standard. Using this approach, only one item (#11) was rated below the mid-point on the scale. Computing standard deviations on a sample of 10 adds an estimate of the range of respondents' ratings around a given mean and may add some marginal information to initial assessments about scale quality. In this illustration, the authors opted to retain all items except #11 for subsequent, large-sample data collection.

In sum, content validity evidence can be the basis for flagging items for modification or elimination from an item pool. Data such as those described and illustrated here can contribute to an "informed

Table 5.1   HAPSI Expert Panelists' Quantitative Ratings: "Outgroups"

Items						Panelists						
	1	2	3	4	5	6	7	8	9	10	Mean	SD
1	3	3	3	4	3	2	3	5	3	2	3.10	0.88
2	5	4	5	4	2	5	1	5	4	5	4.00	1.41
3	4	4	4	3	4	4	1	5	4	5	3.80	1.14
4	4	4	5	4	4	5	3	5	4	5	4.30	0.67
5	4	3	5	4	4	5	1	5	2	1	3.40	1.58
6	3	4	4	1	2	N/A	2	2	5	5	3.11	1.45
7	4	4	3	1	3	N/A	2	5	3	3	3.11	1.17
8	4	4	5	1	4	2	1	5	4	5	3.50	1.58
9	4	4	4	1	4	5	2	2	3	1	3.00	1.41
10	4	4	4	1	4	5	3	2	3	1	3.10	1.37
11	3	2	1	4	4	1	3	1	5	5	2.90	1.60
12	3	4	4	1	4	5	3	4	1	5	3.40	1.43
13	4	3	4	1	5	5	4	4	4	1	3.50	1.43
14	4	4	3	4	2	2	1	2	5	5	3.20	1.40

Panelists' ratings from 1 = Not at All through 5 = Very Well; N/A = rating not provided

impression" conditioned by the success with which expert panelists were identified and recruited, and their responses interpreted. These impressions are subject to being overridden by the RAI developer's counterarguments, and the resulting decisions are simply precursors to the subsequent large-sample, quantitative validation. Where unexpected or strong concerns emerge, developers may consider use of small-sample pilot data collection to confirm or disconfirm problems and make adjustments as needed before proceeding with a full-scale study.

Construct Validity Evidence

In the "parts and pieces" context we have emphasized so far, construct validity evidence centers mainly on two distinct notions: *convergent* and *discriminant* validation. Posed as two sides of the same coin (*see* Figure 5.1), they are based on conceptual arguments regarding expected relationships between scores on the new RAI and measures of other specified variables. Because the terms labeling these forms of validity evidence are sometimes interchanged with terms labeling other forms, we will aim for clear illustrations that minimize confusion. In the process, we will emphasize that the developer's stated intent in posing validation hypotheses can be the key factor distinguishing one type of validity evidence from another (DeVellis, 2003). Just as test validity evidence cannot rely on any one form, neither does it require any particular form, so long as "there is defensible convergent and discriminant evidence supporting score meaning" (Messick, 2003, p. 248).

To a large degree, convergent and discriminant construct validation can be thought of as processes of *approximation*. That is, developers theorize carefully regarding other variables that should or should not correlate with scores on their new measure, typically choosing variables that are indirect representations of, rather than proxies for, their new target construct (Cronbach & Meehl, 1955). In this sense, construct validation hypotheses are most critical (and useful) when attempting to measure something that has not been defensibly captured before.

Given the weight of these hypotheses (i.e., failing to support them means the developer must admit the scale may not measure what it was meant to), very careful consideration must be taken before conceptual bets are laid on the table. And even when such hypotheses are supported, Messick reminds us that the proper interpretation, attributed to Karl Popper and others, is that the validity of the scores from the scale is "not yet disconfirmed" (1989, p. 36).

Convergent Construct Validity Evidence. The notion of approximation plays out in convergent construct validity evidence similarly to the old saying: "If it *looks* like a duck, *walks* like a duck, and *quacks* like a duck, it must *be* a duck!" Here, the saying illustrates the integration of diverse forms of evidence, none of which fully expresses "duckness" by itself. Taken in combination, however, they sum to a reasonable argument that the creature has been correctly named. Beak, waddle, and tone, in this case, add up to the conclusion that we know what kind of bird we're dealing with. The RAI developer is claiming that if certain characteristics or qualities can be shown, then the conclusion is defensible, and if they can't, then it isn't.

More formally, regarding construct validity evidence, Cronbach and Meehl wrote that "numerous successful predictions dealing with phenotypically diverse 'criteria' give greater weight to the claim of construct validity than do . . . predictions involving very similar behavior" (1955, in Campbell & Fiske, 1959, p. 83). From this, we can see the importance of theorizing very carefully when stating convergent validation hypotheses. Coming up with one variable we are willing to bet will correlate strongly with scores on our new scale is challenging enough. Coming up with a set of such variables, each reflecting a slightly different, statistically and practically significant association with the target construct, is harder still.

As discussed in Chapter 3 (and illustrated in Figure 3.4), numerous convergent construct indicators were selected for validation of PSCS scores (Abell, Ryan, & Kamata, 2006). There, we drew on both standardized and unstandardized measures of variables theorized to be correlated with scores on parental self-care. As depicted in Table 5.2, we hypothesized a set of convergent relationships with PSCS scores, including *negative* associations with:

- HIV-related limitations in activities of daily living (HIV ADL)
- Other health condition limitations in such activities (Other ADL)
- Feelings of being overwhelmed by taking care of family (Overwhelmed)
- Reports of too much Family Responsibility Scale (FRS) and, finally,
- A *positive* association with reports of being able to take care of self while taking care of family (Self-Efficacy).

All variables but one were measured with single-item indicators (*see* Figure 3.4). HIV ADL and Other ADL ranged from 1 = none to 5 = always; Overwhelmed ranged from 1 = never to 7 = always; and Self-Efficacy ranged from 0 = can't do at all to 10 = sure I can do. Family responsibility was measured with the standardized FRS, ranging from 1 = never to 7 = always (Abell, Ryan, Kamata & Citrolo, 2006). In this case, pragmatic decisions regarding the overall burden of the data collection instrument were balanced against the benefits of using

Table 5.2 PSCS Construct Validity Evidence ($N = 161$)

	Sample Characteristics		PSCS Global Score	
	M	SD	r	r^2
Convergent				
HIV ADL	2.50	1.19	−0.41*	0.17
Other ADL	2.13	1.24	−0.47*	0.22
Overwhelmed	3.48	1.93	−0.29*	0.09
Self-efficacy	7.49	2.71	0.47*	0.22
FRS	3.73	1.54	−0.47*	0.22
Mean			0.42**	0.18
Discriminant				
Education	N/A	N/A	−0.14	0.02
Race/Ethnicity	N/A	N/A	−0.03	0.00
Income	$967	$653	−0.08	0.01
Mean			0.08**	0.01

* $p < 0.05$, ** absolute value; N/A = not applicable

standardized scales in making final decisions on construct validation measures.

As shown in Table 5.2, all hypothesized convergent relationships were tested by computing correlation coefficients (r) and were found to be reasonably large in magnitude and statistically significant. As predicted, HIV-positive parents reported greater confidence in their abilities to care for themselves when their illnesses caused fewer limitations in daily activities, when they were less overwhelmed, and when they reported less pressure from family responsibilities. Higher reports of self-efficacy on a single-item indicator were also correlated with higher Parental Self-Care Scale (PSCS) scores. Taken as a set, these convergent construct indicators can be expressed as a *mean validity coefficient* (V), reported in Table 5.2 as 0.42. This estimates, on average, the proportion of the variance in PSCS scores that is associated with the convergent construct evidence indicators.

Interpretation of these results requires consideration of both their statistical and practical significance. As indicated, the observed correlations are, independently and collectively, larger than would be expected by chance alone. But how large is large enough? As DeVellis (2003) states, there are no standard criteria for judging the adequacy of the magnitude of correlation coefficients as evidence of construct validity. Often one can only hope to set lower and upper bounds on such "loadings" (Cronbach & Meehl, 1955, p. 289). Developers should be mindful that whatever the magnitude of the correlations, they likely include not only the variance attributable to shared construct meaning and definition but also variance associated with similarities in measurement method, such as the patterns in response options or the manner in which data were collected. The multitrait–multimethod matrix (MTMD) devised by Campbell and Fiske (1959) details the possible confounds. (*See* DeVellis, 2003, and Messick, 1989, for further discussion and suggested remedies.)

Ultimately, the validity coefficients will always have an upper limit defined by the square root of the rapid assessment instrument (RAI)'s relevant reliability coefficient:

$$v \leq \sqrt{r_{tt'}}$$

In this case, the reliability of the global PSCS (reported in Chapter 4 as $\alpha_{stratified} = 0.941$) sets a ceiling for validity coefficients at 0.97. Given the improbability of ever observing relationships that large, some more readily interpretable guidelines are needed. Consequently, Table 5.2 also reports the r^2 coefficient. As an "index of goodness of prediction" (LeCroy & Krysik, 2007, p. 245), this expresses the proportion of variation in one score that is attributable to variation in another. As with all estimates of practical significance, meaning varies with the known context of the observed relationship (i.e., how much variance has been explained in existing literature) and the subjective or intuitive judgment of the reader. In this case, we judged the squared mean validity coefficient for convergent indicators ($V^2 = 0.18$) to be supportive evidence that the factors predicted to converge with PSCS scores did so to a meaningful degree.

Discriminant Construct Validity Evidence.   As the counterpart to convergence, evidence of discriminant construct validity is found when measures that should not correlate meaningfully with new scale scores are found not to do so. In this sense, it contributes evidence to the critically important question of "what a measure *does not* do" (Stickle & Weems, 2006, p. 216, emphasis added). Together with convergent evidence, these relationships help form an interlocking series of observable and theoretical relationships known as a *nomological net* (Cronbach & Meehl, 1955), grounding the understanding of the new scale score in both practical and conceptual contexts.

As Campbell and Fiske conceived discriminant relationships, "tests can be invalidated by too high correlations with other tests from which they were intended to differ" (1959, p. 81). Consequently, to establish evidence of discriminance, developers are challenged to hypothesize the absence of relationships between their new target constructs and other variables of interest. This is not as easy as it might seem, because "when a construct is fairly new, there may be few verifiable associations by which to pin (it) down. . ..As research proceeds, the construct sends out roots in many directions, which attach it to more and more facts or other constructs" (Cronbach & Meehl, 1955, p. 291).

Success ultimately depends on finding such relationships (or their absence) convincingly established or proposed in empirical or conceptual literature and in the latter case, trusting that such conjecture is correct. Lacking clear guidance, developers must do their best to logically consider what factors should not be related to scores on their new scale and then, essentially, place their bets. And beyond trusting, there must be evidence, because "rationalization is not a claim to construct validation" (1955, p. 291).

These decisions are not trivial, as finding significant relationships where none were expected undermines whatever reasoning was offered to support convergent construct hypotheses. If and when the evidence for convergence or discriminance does not line up, the developer must conclude that (*a*) RAI scores cannot be interpreted as intended (i.e., they haven't been shown to mean what the developer thought); (*b*) the bases for the convergent and/or discriminant hypotheses were incorrect; or (*c*) the validation study itself failed to provide an adequate test (Cronbach & Meehl, 1955). Coming to any of these conclusions can be painful considering the effort that precedes such tests, so developers must think things through carefully in the design phase, include instruments to capture the data needed to test the validation hypotheses, and then, if possible, enjoy the ride. Although disconfirmation isn't as fun as confirmation, either way we are adding to what was previously known about an attempt to measure a novel construct.

Seeking discriminant evidence for the PSCS, we were faced with the novelty of studying HIV-positive parents' views on their capacities to take care of their medical needs while maintaining their single-head-of-household responsibilities to their children. Admittedly, this was a narrow focus and a topic about which not much was known. Suspecting that potential respondents would already be stressed and potentially overwhelmed, we were also concerned that if the burden of completing the survey instrument was too great, we risked high rates of refusal or unusable returns.

Lacking much guidance from theory, we considered the demographic information needed to characterize the sample and how those qualities might be related to parental self-care. Finding no empirical evidence to the contrary, we developed a set of discriminant hypotheses predicting that no significant relationships would be found between the PSCS global score and a set of descriptors including education level, race/ethnicity, and income. Essentially, we proposed that none of these characteristics would meaningfully predict variation in reported abilities to care for oneself (Abell, Ryan, & Kamata, 2006).

In the original validation sample ($N = 161$), 39% had not graduated from high school, 26% had, 22% had some college, and 11% reported college degrees. The mean monthly household income was $967 ($SD = $653, range: 0–$4400); 23% were Black, 58% were Hispanic, and 13% were White. As shown in Table 5.2, none of the observed relationships were statistically significant, with a mean validity coefficient of 0.08. As a gauge of observed effect size, the squared coefficient was 0.01.

By themselves, these findings add some small measure of confidence that PSCS scores could not be predicted by factors proposed to be unrelated. Paraphrasing Campbell and Fiske's interpretation of evidence for discriminance, the scale could not be *invalidated* by finding correlations where they were not expected. Linked to the findings for convergence, the combined results provide preliminary evidence that the global PSCS score does, in fact, reflect respondents' beliefs about their capacity for self-care.

Criterion Validity Evidence

Although construct validity evidence is broadly guided by notions of approximation, evidence of criterion validity is based more generally on absolutes. Or at least that is the goal. As its name implies, such evidence is often established with correlations between scale scores and some external criteria. Because correlations provide only the most basic indication of significance in observed relationships and bring with them some potential risks in calculation and interpretation (DeVellis, 2003), measures of potency are sometimes sought as well. These estimate a "special type of effect size," describing how precisely scale scores identify the status of persons known to have (or not have) a particular diagnosis or characteristic (Kraemer et al., 1999, p. 258).

As indicated in Figure 5.1, developers may propose that their scale should substitute for another known measure, correspond to established diagnoses, or predict some future behavior (Cronbach & Meehl, 1955). The placement of these predictions in time, in the form of "concurrent" or "predictive" criterion validity, for instance, is not always clearly distinguished in psychometric literature. Goldstein and Simpson (2002) define concurrent as evidence of correlations "at the same point in time" and predictive as evidence "that can occur at three points in time: before, during, or after the instrument is used" (p. 152). As the time-bound nature is less important than the empirical strength of the observed relationship, the more neutral phrase "criterion-related validity" is generally preferred (DeVellis, 2003). Here, we will concentrate on evidence drawn from known groups and known instruments.

Often, the bases for these comparisons are so-called "gold standards"; established absolutes serving as external proxies against which the performance of scale scores can be examined (Derogatis & Lynn II, 2006). Whenever possible, these standards should be selected based on their conceptual relevance to the construct being scaled, adding to the nomo-logical net of evidence supporting the accuracy and relevance of scale score interpretation (Messick, 2003).

Known-Groups Concurrent Criterion Validity Evidence

Often referred to as discriminant validity, known groups' concurrent criterion evidence describes how well scale scores can establish respon-dents' group membership to match previously determined status. The use of one term to describe different forms of evidence is unfortunate, as it risks adding confusion to a vocabulary that is already abstract and complex. Compounding the problem, "discriminant" may actually make more intuitive sense if applied to known groups or instruments, because it implies an ability to discriminate based on respondents' established characteristics. Still, as traditionalists, we're sticking to Campbell and Fiske's (1959) original terminology and retaining discriminance as an essential component of the construct validity evidence described above. Developers must be aware that the terms have multiple meanings and closely examine the data, hypotheses, and techniques involved if they want to keep the varying forms of evidence straight.

In this context, one form of criterion-related validity evidence is established when scale scores are shown to correlate with some known status (Cronbach & Meehl, 1955). The idea is that respondents' associ-ation with a specific classification (or placement along a continuum of experience with a particular problem) can be first established through observations of their behavior or the diagnostic judgment of experts. It turns out that some distinctions are easier to confirm than others, leading to doubts about the "gold standard" or "absolute" character of criterion-related evidence.

With psychiatric diagnoses, for instance, reliability is notoriously sus-pect (c.f. Kutchins & Kirk, 1997), challenging the confidence placed in so-called "expert" decisions. Such disorders are themselves often hypo-thetical constructs with few confirmed signs or symptoms and only vaguely discernable origins (Derogatis & Lynn II, 2006). Doctors treat-ing medical patients newly diagnosed with a chronic or terminal illness, for example, "can often misperceive true clinical depressions . . . as reactive states of demoralization that are a natural part of the illness" (2006, p. 117). As we will see in discussion of diagnostic screening below, the risk of miscategorizing respondents as either having or not having the disorder in question has led to innovations going well beyond more fundamental evidence decisions based on correlations or their functional equivalents.

To illustrate establishing evidence for known-groups validity, the Adolescent Concerns Evaluation (ACE; Springer, 1998) will be used. The ACE is a 40-item multidimensional instrument developed to measure the extent to which youth ages 11 to 18 years are at risk of running away. The four domains include:

- Family: youth's perception of family relations and functioning
- School: youth's self-esteem as related to school
- Peer: youth's self-esteem as related to peers
- Individual: youth's level of depression.

Responses are measured on a five-point Likert scale ranging from 1 = *strongly disagree* to 5 = *strongly agree*. Higher scores indicate better family relations, better school and peer self-esteem, and more problems with depression. Respondents' ($N = 227$) status as being (or not being) at risk for running away was first established by considering their placement in community. Adolescents housed at a runaway shelter or detained at a juvenile assessment center were categorized as at-risk ($N = 110$), whereas those sampled from grades 6 through 12 at a high school were not ($N = 117$).

As expected, the sample with which a youth was affiliated predicted the likelihood of that youth being a runaway or throwaway. In the nonclinical sample, only one participant reported ever having run away (for 1 day) and none reported ever being a throwaway. By contrast, the clinical sample contained 76 runaways (69.1%) and 54 throwaways (49.1%), with some identifying as both a runaway and a throwaway.

Known groups' validity was conducted on each domain of the ACE, treating the group status (clinical or nonclinical) as the independent variable and each domain score as a dependent variable. Because the independent variable was nominal and dichotomous, a one-way analysis of variance (ANOVA) was conducted for each domain, using the eta (η) statistic produced by ANOVA as the known groups' validity coefficient. The eta^2 (η^2) effect size was also computed, which is analogous to r^2; it is the proportion of variance in the dependent variable (the domain scores) that is associated with differences among groups.

It is important to note that normally distributed observations on the dependent variable in both groups and equal population variances for both groups are assumptions of ANOVA (Stevens, 1996) and should be tested prior to conducting ANOVA. Thus, prior to conducting ANOVA, both the Two-Independent-Samples Kolmogorov–Smirnov Z Test and the Levene Test for Homogeneity-of-Variance were conducted for each of the ACE domains. The Kolmogorov–Smirnov Z Test is typically used to assess univariate normality, whereas the Levene Test is conducted to test whether equal population variances exist between two groups.

The results of the Kolmogorov–Smirnov Z Test revealed nonsignificant findings at the 0.05 level for each ACE domain, indicating that the two groups were univariate normal. Additionally, a graphical examination of univariate normality was conducted, which entailed examining the stem-and-leaf plot for each domain. The Levene Test was conducted to test that equal population variances between the two groups (clinical and nonclinical) existed. As long as the group sizes are approximately equal (as was the case here), the F statistic is robust to violations of this assumption (Stevens, 1996). The analysis produced a nonsignificant Levene statistic for all four ACE domains at the 0.05 level, providing evidence for equal population variances.

Computing the η in ANOVA revealed evidence of known groups' validity for all four of the ACE domains (Family: $[\eta] = 0.656$, $[\eta^2] = 0.431$; School: $[\eta] = 0.630$, $[\eta^2] = 0.397$; Peer: $[\eta] = 0.528$, $[\eta^2] = 0.279$; Individual: $[\eta] = 0.610$, $[\eta^2] = 0.372$), with all findings significant ($p \leq 0.05$) for the F statistic. As previously discussed, standards for judging the adequacy of correlations as validity coefficients are imprecise. As the η reported here are functional equivalents, their magnitudes are also subject to interpretation. We judged the proportions of variance explained (range: 28%–43%) to be encouraging evidence for the known groups' criterion-based validity of the four ACE domains.

Prediction of Group Membership. Although the ANOVA results above are encouraging, a discriminant function analysis was also computed for the ACE. The primary purpose of this analysis was to predict membership into the clinical or nonclinical groups using the domain scores of the ACE.

The first steps in this analysis were to test whether the observations on the dependent variables followed a multivariate normal distribution in each group (using the Wilks' Lambda statistic) and whether the population covariance matrices for the dependent variables were equal (using the Box's M test). The Wilks' Lambda revealed no significant findings ($p \leq 0.05$), indicating that the populations were multivariate normal. Similarly, the Box's M Test found no significant differences at the 0.05 level ($F = 5.71, p = 0.01$).

It is important to note that eight outlier items were dropped from this analysis based on Squared Mahalanobis Distance to Centroid (Mahalanobis D^2) and Cook's Distance (Cook's D) statistics. Any case with a Mahalanobis D^2 critical value (20.59, $\alpha = 0.05$) was considered for deletion from this particular analysis. To determine which outliers were influential, those cases with Cook's Distances greater than one were deleted from the analysis. Eight of 10 items with Mahalanobis D^2 critical values at the 0.05 level also had a Cook's D value greater than 1 and were deleted.

The results of the discriminant function are presented below, with the percentage of youth correctly (or incorrectly) classified indicated in Table 5.3. It is necessary to first point out one condition of this analysis. "If k is the number of groups and p is the number of dependent variables, then the number of possible discriminant functions is the minimum of p and $(k - 1)$" (Stevens, 1996, p. 263). Thus, because there were only

Table 5.3 Validity Coefficients in ACE Respondent Classification ($N = 219$)

	Known-Group Status	
	Non-Clinical (117)	Clinical (102)
ACE Scores		
Clinical (92)	False-positive a (9)	True-positive b (83)
Nonclinical (127)	True-negative c (108)	False-negative d (19)

Specificity = proportion of correctly identified nonclinicals, or true-negatives, expressed as a proportion of all nonclinicals $= c / a + c \times 100$

$108/117 \times 100 = 92.3$

Sensitivity = proportion of correctly identified clinicals, or true-positives, expressed as a proportion of all clinicals $= b / b + d \times 100$

$83/102 \times 100 = 81.4$

PPV = the proportion of adolescents scoring high on the ACE who actually were runaways or throwaways $= b / a + b \times 100$

$83/92 \times 100 = 90.2$

NPV = the proportion of adolescents scoring low on the ACE who actually were not runaways or throwaways $= c / c + d \times 100$

$108/127 \times 100 = 85.0$

two groups (clinical and nonclinical), it was only possible to have one discriminant function.

The Barlett's chi-square test was conducted to determine the number of significant discriminant functions. The eigenvalue (0.936, variance = 100%) for the one discriminant function yielded a significant value ($\chi^2[4] = 74.01$, $p = 0.01$) at the 0.01 level, revealing that there was significant overall association. A canonical correlation (0.695) was also produced at this time.

Discriminant function analysis determined the correct number of classifications (the hit rate) based on the discriminant function derived from the domain scores of the ACE. It was assumed that any given subject had an *a priori* probability of being in either the nonclinical or clinical group to which classifications would be made, and researchers have urged caution in using anything but equal *a priori* probabilities. The *a priori* probabilities for the nonclinical (0.526) and clinical (0.474) groups were approximately equal.

The correlations between the domains of the ACE and the discriminant function, presented here in descending order of absolute size of the correlation within the function, were family (0.719), school (0.717), individual (0.662), and peer (0.426). The correlations between the ACE's four domains and the discriminant function suggests that all of these domains can be interpreted as predictors that distinguish between runaway and non-runaway youth. Correlations in excess of 0.33 are generally considered interpretable (Tabachnick & Fidell, 1996). It is clear that the family domain primarily defines this function, but all domains contribute to the classification of youth.

Known Instruments Concurrent Criterion Validity

This form of evidence for criterion-related validity is established "when one test is proposed to substitute for another" (Cronbach & Meehl, 1955, p. 282). The basic idea is very similar to the logic for known groups. That is, if a new scale measures what it is intended to measure, scores on that scale should closely match scores on other scales known to measure the same construct. In this context, the existing, standardized scale is treated as the "gold standard" against which the new scale's performance is assessed. Considering this form of validation evidence also triggers questions about why, if existing scales are already available, a new one doing essentially the same thing is needed. Developers should be prepared to defend their efforts based, for instance, on new understandings about the target construct or adjustments made in its measurement to better fit the experiences of a new or emerging target groups.

As DeVellis wrote, "people often confuse construct and criterion-related validity because the exact same correlation can serve either purpose. The difference resides more in the investigator's intent than in the value obtained" (2003, p. 53). Keeping clear on that intent is critical to appropriate use of this technique and brings with it some particular risks. As Hudson indicated, when developers make an existing scale the gold standard against which their new scale is judged, they must assume the burden of whatever discrepancies emerge between the two (Springer, Abell, & Hudson, 2002). If the correlation is imperfect (e.g., 0.76), the developer must assume that the error is in the new scale and not the existing one. If the exact data resulted from a test of convergent construct validity evidence (where the test regarded the approximation, rather than absolute matching of scale scores), then the developer could proudly report that the resulting coefficient was quite high.

Bearing this in mind, developers should take great care in stating validation hypotheses and propose tests that fairly examine the performance of a new instrument without unnecessarily creating scenarios forcing less favorable interpretation of the results.

Screening, Sensitivity, and Specificity

Screening has been traditionally defined as "the ... identification of unrecognized disease or defect by ... tests, examinations, or other procedures ... applied rapidly to sort out apparently well persons who probably have a disease from those who probably do not" (Commission on Chronic Illness, 1957, in Derogatis & Lynn II, 2006, p. 119). If we substitute "trait or characteristic" for "disease or defect," we can see the foundation for credible estimates of criterion-related validity evidence in the social sciences. And, of course, the basis. If people whose status was not previously known are to be correctly identified using scores on a new scale, then meaningful precision is required.

This transposition of language across fields and eras characterizes the growing application of receiver operating characteristics (ROC) analyses to scale validation. Originating in assessments of electronic signal detection in radar, it has been adapted over time to differential diagnoses in medicine and diagnostic imaging modalities in radiology (Bridges & Goldberg, 1989; Pepe, 2002). In psychometrics, it has been applied to constructs ranging from post partum depression (Beck & Gable, 2001) to the gifted status of kindergarteners (Pfeiffer & Petscher, 2008). A full treatment of this topic is beyond the scope of our text. Here, we will concentrate on identifying the foundations and indicating their usefulness in advanced validation of scale scores.

Key terms, each of which may be referred to as validity coefficients (Bridges & Goldberg, 1989) include:

- *Sensitivity*: the capacity of the measure to correctly identify persons who have the target characteristic
- *Specificity*: the capacity of the measure to correctly identify persons who do not have the target characteristic
- *Positive Predictive Value (PPV)*: the likelihood that a person whose score indicates the presence of a characteristic actually has that characteristic
- *Negative Predictive Value (NPV)*: the likelihood that a person whose score indicates the absence of a characteristic actually does not have that characteristic (Glaros & Kline, 1988).

Sensitivity and specificity have values ranging from 0 to 1, with higher scores indicating better prediction (Gallop, Crits-Christoph, Muenz, & Tu, 2003). Both require consideration of the number of people classified by a given measure as a proportion of the total number of people actually having (or not having) the characteristic. The higher the sensitivity of a scale, the fewer "false-positives" (i.e., people who do not have the characteristic, although test scores indicate they do). Conversely, the higher the specificity of the scale, the fewer "false-negatives" (i.e., people who do have the characteristic, although test scores indicate they do not) (Bridges & Goldberg, 1989).

PPV and NPV vary with the setting of *cut-off scores*, or scale scores "determined to be that value that will maximize correct classification and minimize misclassification" based on the target characteristic (Derogatis & Lynn II, 2006, p. 126) and with the base rate or prevalence of the target characteristic in a given sample (Santor, 2005). Table 5.3 depicts the central relationships, illustrated with classifications derived from the ACE validation. Modifications to their computation (i.e., multiplying by 100) support reporting of results as proportions or probabilities ranging from 0 to 100. Cut-off scores ultimately determine the sensitivity and specificity of scales, because they are the basis for translating scale scores into the presumed presence or absence of a trait or quality. In this case, classification based on the ACE resulted from the discriminant function analysis described earlier in the chapter. As can be seen in Table 5.3, the ACE did an overall excellent job of classifying subjects correctly (i.e., predicting group membership). The proportion of youth correctly classified as nonclinicals, or true-negatives, was 92.3%. In other words, the ACE seldom identified a youth as being at risk of running away when, in fact, he or she was not at risk. The proportion of correctly identified clinical participants, or true-positives, was 81.4%. Together, these two findings provide evidence that the ACE maximizes specificity and sensitivity, respectively.

ROC curves enable the visualization of all possible relationships by charting the true-positive (i.e., sensitivity) and false-positive (i.e., 1 – sensitivity) rates based on a particular cut-off score or plausible set of such scores and comparing them on the basis of the *area under the curve* (AUC; *see* conceptual depiction in Fig. 5.6) (Bridges & Goldberg, 1989). This may be thought of as "a probability estimate that at each cutoff score a randomly chosen positive (or "case") will demonstrate a higher score than a randomly chosen negative" (Derogatis & Lynn II, 2006, p. 127). In an ideal circumstance, the ROC curve would reveal a high rate of true-positives and true-negatives, depicted as a line rising rapidly up the vertical axis, with a "shoulder" depicted high in the upper left corner (Gallop et al., 2003). Such a curve ("a" in Figure 5.6) would maximize the AUC toward its upper limit of 1.0. In the worst circumstance, the line would be depicted as a diagonal rising at a 45-degree angle from the lower left corner or origin "c" in Figure 5.6. In this case, the AUC is at its lower bound (0.50), indicating that the predictive capacity of the scale score is no better than chance.

To meaningfully establish and interpret cut-off scores, we must appreciate the context in which they originate. ROC analyses and the associated AUC coefficients can provide very useful comparisons of the reliability and validity of diagnostic methods (Hsiao, Bartko, & Potter, 1989). The level of agreement among raters using a particular method, as well as the accuracy with which that method captures specified

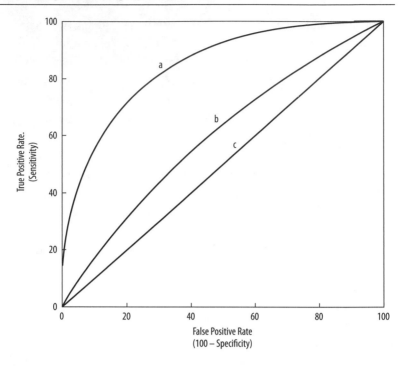

Figure 5.6 Hypothetical areas under the curve.

characteristics or traits, has a great deal to do with establishing the "gold standard" against which scale score performance is gauged. The ability to assess the relationship of true-positives (sensitivity) and true-negatives (specificity) resulting from varying cut-scores for a scale can result in a better understanding of the target problem itself and subsequently to improved diagnosis and related treatment planning.

One significant hitch is that such comparisons depend on the presence of diagnostic "gold standards" that, in the absence of unambiguous biological or behavioral markers, are notoriously difficult to establish. This is especially true for many subjectively defined problems (i.e., self-efficacy, parenting capacity, or perceived quality of life). Such problems are often of interest in social services. The implication is that meaningful application of this advanced statistical technique depends heavily on the conceptual clarity and available evidence underpinning the gold standard or its proxy. In short, we can't let the cart of statistical eloquence get before the horse of conceptual clarity as we apply ROC techniques to problems in psychosocial functioning.

When acceptably objective diagnostic criteria are identified, ROC techniques can be used to explore multiple optimal cut-off points for detecting risk or presence of specified outcomes. For example, use of The Alcohol Use Disorders Identification Test (AUDIT) to assess various medical and social consequences of excessive alcohol consumption revealed that a range of cut-off scores could be established to predict outcomes varying from medical disorders to physical trauma to social problems (Conigrave, Hall, & Saunders, 1995). Lab tests and responses to clinical interviews were used to establish the standards against which AUDIT cut-off scores were judged.

In this context, Conigrave, et al. (1995) observed that the trade-off in favoring detection of true-positives versus false-positives (balancing sensitivity and specificity) should be considered in relation to the costs of "getting it wrong." If sufficient resources exist in a clinical setting, for instance, then providers may be able to manage an initially higher rate of false-positives classified by a cut-off score if they have the time and energy to follow up with more detailed assessments. Confirming or disconfirming such diagnoses may ultimately be a benefit to public health (in the case of transmissible disease) or ultimate cost (where early prevention or treatment can head off bigger problems down the road).

As Conley (2005) observes in his application of ROC analyses to a set of alcohol problem-screening tools, the technique permits an objective determination of the optimal cut-point as the score "at which the test will result in the lowest possible overall number of misclassifications" (p. 144). This may be viewed as a useful foundation for other decision-driving factors. For instance, he observed that it proved difficult to find a balanced cut-off score for the AUDIT in his data, speculating that the measure's emphasis on harmful/hazardous drinking may have made a problematic match with the Diagnostic and Statistical Manual's (DSM-IV) criteria used as his standard for determining positive and negative cases. The DSM focuses more on the presence of an alcohol dependence syndrome that is not exactly synonymous with item content from the AUDIT.

Again, we see that use and interpretation of statistical techniques must always include attention to the conceptual foundations underlying any obtained scale score or summary rating of behaviors or events. As Conley (1995) points out, recognizing that a conceptual match or desired application is actually a poor basis for some conclusions does not mean the instruments employed were flawed. Rather, they were a poor fit for an ill-conceived comparison.

CONCLUSION

As we have seen, examining construct validity requires careful deconstruction and reintegration of multiple lines of evidence. To the extent that these tests are well-anticipated by scale developers, the relevant analyses will build toward conclusions supporting or refuting the accuracy of the measure. Both conceptual and empirical arguments can be meaningfully analyzed and defended.

Although achieving a holistic sense of this quality is the ultimate goal, we have tried to show how respect for each individual component is essential. Still, we have left one very large stone unturned: examining the factor structure of a measure. We take up that topic in Chapter 6, illustrating diverse (and sometimes contentious) conceptualizations and strategies. Although the topic clearly deserves at least a chapter of its own, readers should remember that, as depicted in Figure 5.1, establishing the underlying structure of an instrument must actually come before examination of specific forms of construct and criterion validity.

6

Factor Analysis

O ur goal for a psychological instrument is to measure respondent traits or states that are not directly observable, such as depression and aggression. Such qualities are referred to in measurement models as *latent traits,* simply because they are not directly observable to us. To represent a latent trait in a psychometric model, we typically use a variable that is called a *latent variable,* which is a representation of a latent trait, as noted in Chapter 2. Accordingly, a latent variable is a variable that is not directly observable. Because psychological measurement deals with the unobservable nature of psychological traits, a latent variable is almost always relevant. To best represent a latent variable, we typically use information from more than one observed variable. In other words, we utilize responses on multiple test or scale items that are a sample of attitudes, feelings, or behaviors relevant to the trait(s) we are interested in measuring. This situation in fact fits very well to a factor analytic model, in which observed variables are modeled as a function of underlying unobserved variable(s). For a psychological measurement, item responses on test or scale items are observed variables, and psychological trait(s) of interest are unobserved latent variable(s). Accordingly, item responses are modeled as a function of latent trait(s). In other words, observed item responses are predicted by latent trait(s).

A functional form of the factor analytic model depends on how many factors we assume in the model for what items. Given x_{ij} is the observed item score on the ith item by person j and ξ_j is the latent trait level for person j, the simplest form of a factor analytic model with only one factor can be written as

$$x_{ij} = \mu_i + \lambda_i \xi_j + \delta_{ij}.$$

This is essentially a regression model to predict x_{ij} by ξ_j. (ξ is a Greek letter that is pronounced "ksi.") The difference between the factor analytic model and the regression model is that the predictor is an unobservable latent variable for the factor analytic model, whereas the predictor is an observed variable for a regular regression model. Because a latent variable is not observed, it does not have any fixed scale inherent to the variable. In other words, there is no fixed mean or variance for the variable. Typically, the scale of a latent factor ξ_j is arbitrarily fixed, such as mean $= 0$ and variance $= 1$ without any loss of generality. In addition, the scale of x_{ij} is shifted such that the intercept will be 0. As a result, a functional form in practice becomes

$$x_{ij} = \lambda_i \xi_j + \delta_{ij}.$$

In the equation, λ_i is just like a regression slope to indicate the strength of the relationship between ξ_j and x_{ij}, and δ_{ij} is just like a residual term to indicate the unexplained part of the model. (λ and δ are Greek letters that are pronounced "lamda" and "delta," respectively.) δ_{ij}s are typically assumed to be independently distributed normally with mean $= 0$ and with unknown variance ψ_i^2. (ψ is a Greek letters that is pronounced "psi.") Note that there is no intercept in this equation. Of course it is still possible to retain the intercept in the model. Such a model is called a mean–structure factor analysis model. Accordingly, parameters to be estimated in this model are λ_i as many as the number of items, and ψ_i^2 as many as the number of items. For a 12-item test, for example, we will have 24 parameters to be estimated in all; 12 λ_is and 12 ψ_i^2s. As the number of factors increases, this regression equation form will have more predictors. For example, if three factors are modeled, like the PSCS scale, the equation will be expanded to

$$x_{ij} = \lambda_{i1}\xi_{j1} + \lambda_{i2}\xi_{j2} + \lambda_{i3}\xi_{j3} + \delta_{ij},$$

where λ_i and ξ_j are associated with additional subscript 1, 2, and 3 to indicate one of three latent factors. In addition to λ_i s and ψ_i^2 s, correlations between latent factor ξ_j can be parameters to be estimated. For a 12-item test with three 4-item subscales, for example, 51 parameters total are typically estimated (12 λ_is × 3 latent factors + 12 ψ_i^2 s + 3 correlations between ξ_js), assuming independence between δ_{ij}s. If dependency of δ_{ij}s is assumed, then covariances between δ_is will be additional parameters too. There are two different types of factor analytic procedures; exploratory factor analysis (EFA) and confirmatory factor analysis (CFA), as we will soon describe. The aforementioned models are general enough for both EFA and CFA. However, the numbers of parameters to be estimated are typically quite different between them. In EFA, we attempt to estimate all of these 51 parameters for the hypothetical 12-item three-factor example. On the other hand, because hypothesized relationships between latent and observed variables are modeled explicitly on theory or construct definitions, CFA typically constrains some λ_is to be zero. Also, error terms δ_{ij} are always assumed to be uncorrelated in EFA because the number of parameters to be estimated would otherwise exceed the number that actually could be estimated. In CFA, there is typically room for modeling some of their dependencies, although it is not a psychometrically desirable characteristic. Thus the number of parameters in CFA is usually much smaller.

EXPLORATORY FACTOR ANALYSIS

This type of a factor analysis is referred to as exploratory, because (a) the model formation (i.e., the number of latent variables) are explored, rather than specified by the intention or theory in the test/scale construction process and *(b)* factor structure is explored by modeling each item as a function of all common factors, rather than as a function of only a subset of the factors, to see which factor has strong relationship with the item and which factor does not. In a test/scale construction process, an EFA model could be useful in two aspects. First, it may identify test items that are not strongly correlated to an intended common factor. Second, it may uncover an unexpected factor structure of test items. Both of these aspects help us collect validity evidence of scores derived from a scale.

In this section, important concepts of EFA and its typical procedures in a test construction context are described by using the randomly generated PSCS data set. Recall that the original item pool for the scale is shown in Figure 2.2. Readers are cautioned that results presented in this chapter do not precisely reflect the characteristics and the quality of the actual PSCS, because the data set used here is simulated for demonstration purposes.

Choosing Variables

The first step in EFA is to choose variables to be analyzed. In a test construction context, we typically choose all items in the measurement scale to start with. Depending on the initial analysis results, we may decide to remove some of the items and rerun the analysis with a smaller set of items. In SPSS, for example, choose a procedure called *Factor Analysis* by choosing *Analyze* → *Data Reduction* → *Factor* from the menu. Then, in the dialog box, highlight the variables to be included in the analysis, and click on the arrow button to move the list of variables to the box in the right-hand side that is labeled *Variables*.

Deciding the Number of Factors

Another specification we need before running the analysis is the number of factors to be included in the model. We would like to emphasize that estimation of parameters is a separate process from deciding the number of factors. The estimation of model parameters is possible in

EFA only when the number of factors in the model is specified. There are at least three popular approaches for this decision-making: Kaiser criterion, scree plot interpretation, and parallel analysis.

Kaiser Criterion.   This approach determines the number of factors by the magnitudes of eigenvalues. Conceptually, an eigenvalue shows the amount of information represented by a common factor among a set of analyzed variables, where a higher value indicates more information. The number of eigenvalues that are 1.0 or greater is counted, and it is used as the number of factors to be included in the factor model as originally suggested by Guttman (1954). The rationale is that a meaningful factor should have a higher eigenvalue than the one would have been obtained from a single-indicator factor, which is 1.0. Also, important eigenvalues are associated with values higher than the expected value of it (average). Because the mathematical fact is that the mean of the eigenvalues is 1.0 for a correlation matrix, the number of eigenvalues with 1.0 or greater is considered as the number of important (above average) factors. However, we would like to emphasize that the value of 1.0 is still arbitrary. Kaiser criterion is the default method in the factor analysis procedure on SPSS. However, SPSS provides an option for the user to modify the Kaiser criterion by specifying a different criterion value, if one desires. For the illustrative data analysis of the PSCS, it turned out that three eigenvalues were larger than 1.0; thus, the number of factors to be extracted should be three based on the Kaiser criterion.

Scree Plot.   This method also uses magnitudes of eigenvalues for decision making. However, the decision is based on the pattern of the magnitudes of eigenvalues, rather than a specific value as a criterion. As originally proposed by Cattell (1966), rank-ordered eigenvalues are plotted on a graph. Then, we examine its decreasing pattern and find out where a diminishing return happens (*see* Figure 6.1 for the scree plot of the illustrative analysis). On SPSS, this plot can be requested in the *Factor Analysis: Extraction* dialogue box by checking the *Scree plot* box. It is typical that most of eigenvalues are small and similar to each

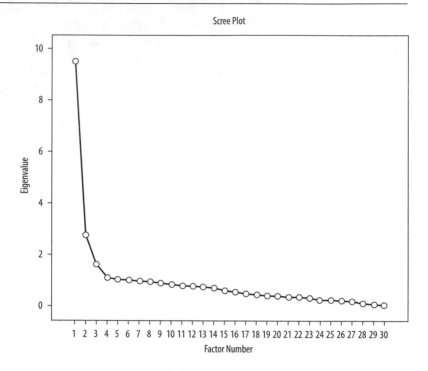

Figure 6.1 Scree plot for the illustrative PSCS data.

other, except a few distinctively large eigenvalues. This method attempts to graphically identify how many are among the "few" eigenvalues that are distinctively higher than the rest. Then, the count of those eigenvalues is used as the number of factors in the model. For the illustrative data analysis of the PSCS, it can be determined that three eigenvalues are distinctively larger than other eigenvalues, as the rest display a decreasing pattern in a near "flat" straight line.

Parallel Analysis.   This approach was originally proposed by Horn (1965), and its utility has been demonstrated by some authors, such as Humphreys and Montanelli (1975). This procedure is based on the principle that a factor to be extracted should account for more variance than it is expected by chance. Therefore, the procedure randomly re-orders observations within each variable and eigenvalues are recomputed from such a randomly re-ordered data set many times. Then, rank-ordered eigenvalues are averaged across replications. Finally, the rank-ordered eigenvalues from the original data set are compared to the averaged rank-ordered eigenvalues from randomly re-ordered data sets. Then, factors with larger eigenvalues than random eigenvalues are selected to be extracted. Unfortunately, none of standard statistical package to date offers this procedure readily available. To implement this method, one needs to utilize some resource outside of standard statistical package, such as publicly available SPSS and SAS syntax (e.g., O'Connor, 2000, 2001).

Subjective Judgment. The number of factors can be also determined subjectively *a priori* or *host hoc* to data analysis. It is reasonable to decide based on the theory that was used for test/scale construction. For the illustrative data analysis with PSCS data, we could make a decision to extract three factors in the model, because the test is intended to measure three subscales (Emotional, Instrumental, and Nursing subscales).

For the illustrative data analysis of the PSCS, because both Kaiser criterion and scree plot indicated that three factors should be extracted, our decision was to proceed in our analysis with three factors.

Factor Extraction Methods (Parameter Estimation Methods)

There are several different ways to estimate parameters for an EFA model. For example, SPSS allows us to specify such a choice as *Factor Extraction Method*, by clicking the *Extraction* button in the *Factor Analysis* main dialogue box. A new dialogue box labeled *Factor Analysis: Extraction* opens, and from the pull-down menu, one has a choice from several methods, such as maximum likelihood, principal axis, and least square methods. The method called *Principal Component* determines parameters such that the explained variances to predict latent variables by observed variables are maximized. It is indeed a principal component analysis, where each latent factor (a component, to be more precise) is a linear combination of a set of observed variables. Therefore, measurement errors are not modeled for observed variables, which is quite different from what we assume for a factor analytic model. Although it is a default choice by SPSS, we strongly recommend not utilizing this method unless there is a good reason for it. Initial data explorations may be where a principal component analysis may be useful; however, reported results should be from another method, such as maximum likelihood and principle axis factoring. For the illustrative data analysis, we chose maximum likelihood.

Maximum Likelihood. This method comes up with a set of parameter estimates, such that it maximizes the likelihood of observing the data. This method is probably the most popular choice in today's factor analytic practice because it allows us to test a goodness of fit of the model to the data.

Principal Axis Factoring. This method extracts factors such that the communality is maximized. Communality is the proportion of variance of each observed variable (treated as an outcome variable) explained by a factor or a set of factors as predictors. Examples of communality output from SPSS based on the computer-generated PSCS data are shown in Figure 6.2. The one on the right is from the output based on the Maximum Likelihood and the one on the left is from the output based on the Principal Axis Factoring. As can be seen, communalities are different between the two extraction methods. However, they are similar to each other.

Least Squares. The basic principle of least squares is to find a set of parameters that minimizes the observed data and predicted values of the data based on the estimated parameters. In the context of a factor analysis, this method determines parameter estimates such that the difference between the data covariance matrix (*see* Chapters 2 and 4 for the basic concept of a covariance matrix) and the implied covariance matrix (predicted covariance matrix by parameter estimates) is minimized. There is a variation of this method by weighting the covariance matrix by

	Communalities			Communalities	
	Initial	Extraction		Initial	Extraction
V1	.366	.364	V1	.366	.356
V2	.514	.522	V2	.514	.525
V3	.603	.621	V3	.603	.625
V4	.657	.703	V4	.657	.701
V5	.683	.729	V5	.683	.728
V6	.458	.461	V6	.458	.464
V7	.578	.595	V7	.578	.593
V8	.442	.453	V8	.442	.454
V9	.478	.481	V9	.478	.483
V10	.381	.372	V10	.381	.370
V11	.156	.100	V11	.156	.105
V12	.173	.120	V12	.173	.130
V13	.113	.062	V13	.113	.064
V14	.653	.666	V14	.653	.649
V15	.712	.736	V15	.712	.733
V16	.790	.821	V16	.790	.821
V17	.836	.906	V17	.836	.908
V18	.131	.109	V18	.131	.112
V19	.083	.055	V19	.083	.053
V20	.118	.071	V20	.118	.070
V21	.127	.062	V21	.127	.063
V22	.499	.487	V22	.499	.496
V23	.602	.619	V23	.602	.606
V24	.125	.074	V24	.125	.080
V25	.155	.111	V25	.155	.111
V26	.457	.453	V26	.457	.465
V27	.162	.129	V27	.162	.139
V28	.138	.112	V28	.138	.111
V29	.803	.895	V29	.803	.885
V30	.734	.783	V30	.734	.782

Extraction Method: Maximum Likelihood.   Extraction Method: Principal Axis Factoring.

Figure 6.2 Communality output from SPSS for the simulated PSCS data for maximum likelihood and principal axis factoring.

the error covariance matrix: weighted least square and generalized least square. Weighted least square assumes unequal error variances and zero correlations between errors, whereas generalized least square assumes unequal error variances and correlated errors.

Rotation of Factor Axes

Once parameters in the factor analytic model are estimated, our interest should be examining factor loadings, which depict the magnitudes of relationships between items and extracted factors. We should hope that we find some meaningful patterns for factor loading magnitudes, specifically reflections of subscales. To achieve such an interpretation, it is recommended to rotate factor axes before factor loadings are interpreted. When parameters are estimated, it is typical that one factor dominates in terms of the proportion of item score variances for which each factor accounts. Therefore, it is not unusual at all that all items are most highly related to the dominant factor, and other factors are weakly related to a majority of items. In such a situation, it is almost impossible (or very difficult, at the least) to distinguish items that are related to a common factor from items that are not.

When axes are rotated, it is conceptually a redistribution of explained variances to extracted factors. Therefore, nondominant factors' contributions will be amplified, whereas the contribution of the dominant factor will be suppressed to some extent. This is an acceptable procedure because it retains the communalities for all items unchanged. This way, it magnifies distinctions of groups of items that are related to a specific common factor and helps interpretation of extracted factors.

There are two distinct classes of rotation methods. One is called *orthogonal rotation*, where the axes are kept uncorrelated. This can be a reflection of no relationship between factors. Geometrically, orthogonal axes represent zero correlation between them. Note that when parameters are estimated initially in the EFA, one required constraint is zero correlations between factors. One widely used orthogonal rotation method is the *varimax rotation* (Kaiser, 1958), where the variation of factor loadings is maximized for all factors simultaneously. Another class of rotation is called *oblique rotations* (Hendrickson & White, 1964), where the axes are allowed not to be orthogonal to each other. In other words, oblique rotations will eventually estimate the degree of intersections between axes, which are representations of correlations between the factors. One widely utilized oblique rotation is the *promax rotation*, which is an extension of varimax rotation to further attempt to achieve a simple structure of factor loadings by allowing nonorthogonal axes. Simple structure is achieved when each item displays near-zero relationships with all but one factor. In a scale construction context, a simple structure is almost always desirable, because items are typically designed to measure only one subscale. Therefore, we strongly recommend oblique rotations for an EFA analysis in a scale construction context.

For the illustrative data analysis with PSCS data, promax rotation was chosen. On SPSS, this can be achieved by clicking on the *Rotation* button in the main *Factor Analysis* dialogue box and checking the *Promax* option in the *Factor Analysis: Rotation* dialogue box. By leaving the *Unrotated factor solution* option in the *Factor Analysis: Extraction* dialogue box checked, SPSS will also report initial solutions of factor loadings.

Interpretations of Results

For the illustrative data analysis with the simulated PSCS data, estimates of factor loadings before the rotation of axes are reported in the table labeled *Factor Matrix* (Fig. 6.3a). As mentioned in the previous section, interpretation of results will be difficult without rotations of axes, and these unrotated results are not going to be used directly for evaluation of results. However, the output is presented here only to display the fact that it would be difficult to distinguish items that are commonly related to each of the three common factors.

Rotated solutions to factor loadings are summarized in the table labeled *Pattern Matrix*. See Figure 6.3b for the PSCS analysis results. Now, factor loadings provide a much clearer picture. The first 10 items, which are intended to measure the Emotional subscale, have higher factor loadings for the first factor than for the other two factors, where loadings are near-zero. This is a good indication that the Emotional subscale is well-constructed by the 10 items. As a guideline, some authors suggest using 0.30 as a cut-off criterion. This is based on the idea that the proportion of variance explained should be about 10% or more for an item to be considered as a meaningful predictor for a latent factor. However, we would like to emphasize it is a rather arbitrary criteria. It should be used as a tool to flag items for further investigations, not as the sole criteria to remove items from the scale.

(a) Factor Matrix				(b) Pattern Matrix				(c) Structure Matrix		

Table (a): Factor Matrix[a]

	\multicolumn{3}{c}{Factor}	
	1	2	3
V1	.468	.345	.163
V2	.561	.387	.240
V3	.645	.354	.281
V4	.633	.449	.319
V5	.621	.429	.399
V6	.536	.331	.253
V7	.632	.352	.267
V8	.491	.361	.284
V9	.481	.409	.287
V10	.457	.312	.256
V11	.296	.066	−.093
V12	.314	.045	−.140
V13	.244	−.004	.054
V14	.763	.007	−.291
V15	.764	.069	−.384
V16	.830	.093	−.351
V17	.859	.074	−.403
V18	.265	−.010	−.198
V19	.215	−.036	.088
V20	.259	.033	−.054
V21	.241	−.044	.047
V22	.604	−.322	.135
V23	.647	−.411	.176
V24	.269	−.017	.038
V25	.275	−.182	.052
V26	.561	−.353	.119
V27	.358	−.034	.018
V28	.334	.030	.002
V29	.784	−.461	.260
V30	.735	−.436	.229

Extraction Method: Maximum Likelihood.
[a.] 3 factors extracted. 5 iterations required.

Table (b): Pattern Matrix[a]

	\multicolumn{3}{c}{Factor}	
	1	2	3
V1	.575	−.071	.102
V2	.702	−.029	.059
V3	.730	.064	.042
V4	.841	−.016	.009
V5	.883	.050	−.101
V6	.655	.027	.018
V7	.713	.053	.052
V8	.693	−.003	−.035
V9	.735	−.055	−.034
V10	.617	.018	−.028
V11	.073	−.008	.275
V12	.023	−.008	.339
V13	.112	.135	.051
V14	.002	.118	.739
V15	−.016	−.004	.869
V16	.051	.018	.866
V17	.002	.017	.940
V18	−.087	−.006	.375
V19	.102	.179	−.013
V20	.063	.036	.201
V21	.070	.171	.050
V22	−.001	.663	.056
V23	−.035	.799	.005
V24	.095	.150	.080
V25	−.039	.333	.030
V26	−.054	.668	.048
V27	.091	.191	.144
V28	.128	.105	.167
V29	.028	.959	−.044
V30	.011	.893	−.024

Extraction Method: Maximum Likelihood.
Rotation Method: Promox with Kaiser Normalization.
[a.] Rotation converged in 5 iterations.

Table (c): Structure Matrix

	\multicolumn{3}{c}{Factor}	
	1	2	3
V1	.599	.261	.379
V2	.721	.337	.433
V3	.784	.433	.488
V4	.838	.385	.468
V5	.851	.405	.422
V6	.678	.346	.400
V7	.767	.420	.482
V8	.672	.301	.349
V9	.691	.270	.342
V10	.610	.291	.326
V11	.223	.193	.311
V12	.208	.207	.346
V13	.204	.219	.195
V14	.469	.565	.811
V15	.467	.513	.858
V16	.542	.565	.905
V17	.534	.585	.951
V18	.119	.179	.323
V19	.178	.219	.151
V20	.192	.187	.258
V21	.178	.234	.192
V22	.342	.696	.456
V23	.343	.786	.468
V24	.210	.243	.224
V25	.134	.332	.209
V26	.287	.672	.421
V27	.261	.320	.310
V28	.270	.265	.301
V29	.454	.945	.550
V30	.418	.884	.522

Extraction Method: Maximum Likelihood.
Rotation Method: Promox with Kaiser Normalization.

Figure 6.3 Factor loading estimates and correlation estimates from SPSS.

On the other hand, items that are intended to measure the Instrumental subscale (items 11 through 20) display mixed results. By examining which factor these items load on the highest, a majority of items have the highest loadings for the third factor. Therefore, it can be interpreted that the third factor is the factor related to the Instrumental subscale. Exceptions are Items 13 and 19, which loaded more highly on the second factor. Items 11, 12, 18, and 20 are associated with the highest factor loadings for the third factor among the three factors; however, the magnitudes of their loadings were not as high as other items. Therefore, these six items are flagged for possible removable from the final scale.

For the items that are intended to measure the Nursing subscale (items 21 through 30), results were also mixed. All 10 items, with the exception of item 28, loaded the highest on the second factor, indicating that the second factor is a good representation of the Nursing subscale. However, items 21, 24, 25, and 27 did not display strong relationships to the second factor. In addition, the factor loading for item 28 was not only low for the second factor but also higher on the third factor. Therefore, these five items can be considered as candidates for possible removal from the final scale.

When factors (namely, axes) are orthogonal, factor loadings are the same as the correlation coefficients to factors. This applies to Factor Matrix in Figure 6.3a, as well as a case in which axis rotation is conducted by one of orthogonal rotation methods, such as the varimax rotation. However, when factors are correlated, factor loadings are not the same as correlation coefficients anymore. They become quantities analogous to semi-partial correlation coefficients, in which the correlations among factors are taken into account. To this regard, factor loadings in the Pattern Matrix represent unique contributions of each factor to the relationships between items and factors. On the other hand, correlation coefficients in the Structure Matrix (*see* Fig. 6.3c for the illustrative analysis) are unconditional bivariate correlation coefficients between items and factors. The distinction between the Pattern Matrix and Structure Matrix is analogous to the distinction between multiple regression slope coefficients and bivariate correlation coefficients between predictors and the dependent variable. A multiple regression coefficient represents the relationship between a particular predictor and the dependent variable, accounting for the relationship between all predictors, just like coefficients in Pattern Matrix. On the other hand, a bivariate correlation coefficient represents the relationship between a particular predictor and the dependent variable, without taking the relationship between predictors into consideration, just like coefficients in Structure Matrix.

In this illustrative analysis, it turned out that the intended factor structure was quite clearly extracted. However, it may not be the case in other analyses; results may indicate that a mixture of items that are designed to measure different subscales load strongly together on a common factor. If it happens, then we will have to carefully interpret factors based on the contents of items that commonly load on the same factor, which may in fact invalidate the scale.

Some Cautions for Exploratory Factor Analysis

First, we have to be mindful that EFA does not "magically" reveal hidden information about the data. In fact, results of EFA can drastically change by adding or removing just a few items. Also, factor loadings will be different depending on what rotation methods are used. As mentioned earlier, there is also no magic formula to determine the "correct" number of latent factors. Scale developers using EFA should be aware that many elements are arbitrary, including the number of factors and the rotation of axes. Thus, many decisions have to be made carefully by the user in the process of EFA to reach the final reporting model and its parameter estimates. However, a danger is that software package defaults can make all the decisions based on their arbitrary default criteria. Developers of scales should be careful not to assume that default criteria represent undisputed conclusions about the best steps to follow. Also, we need to be aware that the EFA model is a linear model. Therefore, an EFA does not capture any nonlinear relationships between latent factors and observed items, such as scores measured by an unfolding-type scale. Required sample size is always a concern. It seems that there is a belief among factor analysts that 10 to 20 observations per item are necessary. Gorsuch (1983) indicated either 100 observations total or 5 observations per item, whichever was larger, is an absolute minimum. However, these recommendations are based on experienced factor analysts' intuitions and can easily be either too liberal or too conservative. Systematic investigations (e.g., Guadagnoli & Velicer, 1988; MacCallum et al., 1999) have shown that required sample size is a function of the magnitudes of correlations between items and latent factors and the magnitudes of communalities, in addition to the number of items. According to these studies, EFA should work well (i.e., extract the correct number of factors and estimate parameters well) with a total sample size as low as 60 under ideal conditions. However, it is still difficult to reach a simple recommendation, because it almost always "depends." (See our related discussion in Chapter 3.) Regarding rotation, we would like to emphasize that it is primarily a method for deriving a simple structure in a scale development context. In this regard, oblique rotation is more useful especially for scale constructions when a scale instrument is designed to derive subscale scores. However, it may limit our geometrical understanding of an oblique coordinate when the correlations between factors are very high, because spaces between axes will geometrically become extremely uneven. This will be reflected in larger discrepancies between pattern and structure matrices with no particular patterns, which also make our interpretations difficult. An orthogonal coordinate is much easier to understand, although it is not as useful as an oblique coordinate when deriving a simple structure. Orthogonal rotation can be still useful for a test/scale battery, where we have a set of more than one independently constructed test/scale and can assume only weakly correlated factors, whereas oblique rotation should be preferred for a multidimensional scale, like PSCS, in which we expect subscales are interrelated.

CONFIRMATORY FACTOR ANALYSIS

Model Specification

The basic functional form for a CFA is the same as for an EFA. However, a CFA functional form is different from one for EFA in a way that not all modeled latent variables are predictors for each item. Predictors for an item are only a selected subset of hypothesized latent variables. In the instrument development context, it is typical that only one latent variable is a predictor for each item, reflecting an instrument structure in which each item only measures one subscale. As mentioned earlier, this is a representation of a simple structure.

The initial step in a CFA analysis is to specify the number of factors. At this point, one should have a good justification regarding how many factors the data have in common. In the scale development context, it is typically the number of subscales, where each factor is a representation of each subscale as a latent trait. If there are no subscales (i.e., the measure is presumed to be unidimensional), then the number of factors should be 1. Then, we specify which items are commonly predicted by the same latent variable. In other words, we specify which items load on which factor.

For example, let's consider the PSCS scale (*see* Fig. 2.2), where items 1 through 10 are designed to measure Emotional subscale of self-efficacy, items 11 through 20 are designed to measure Instrumental subscale of self-efficacy, and items 21 through 30 are designed to measure Nursing subscale of self-efficacy. Here our attempt will be fitting a three-factor structure, where items 1 through 10 are commonly predicted by one factor, items 11 through 20 are commonly predicted by another factor, and items 21 through 30 are commonly predicted by the third factor. We can write the functional form as follows:

Items 1–10:

$$x_{ij} = \lambda_{1i}\xi_{1j} + 0\xi_{2j} + 0\xi_{3j} + \delta_{ij}$$
$$= \lambda_{1i}\xi_{1j} + \delta_{ij}$$

Items 11–20:

$$x_{ij} = 0\xi_{1j} + \lambda_{2i}\xi_{2j} + 0\xi_{3j} + \delta_{ij}$$
$$= \lambda_{2i}\xi_{2j} + \delta_{ij}$$

Items 21–31:

$$x_{ij} = 0\xi_{1j} + 0\xi_{2j} + \lambda_{3i}\xi_{3j} + \delta_{ij}$$
$$= \lambda_{3i}\xi_{3j} + \delta_{ij}$$

In other words, the factor loadings are explicitly constrained to be zero for the factors that do not predict the item score. As a result, the number of parameters to be estimated is greatly reduced. With the above functional forms, in which all intercepts in the functional forms are zero, there are 63 parameters to be estimated (30 factor loadings, 30 error variances, and 3 factor correlations).

This model is graphically depicted in Figure 6.4. Squares labeled x_1 through x_{30} represent 30 observed items in the scale. Notice that straight lines point to these 30 items, indicating that the 30 items are outcome variables in the model. Circles represent unobserved variables. Ones with labels ξ_1, ξ_2, and ξ_3 are latent factors that represent trait levels for the three subscales. Straight lines that point to items represent factor loadings (λ_{11}, λ_{12}, etc.). On the other hand, circles with labels δ_1 through δ_{30} represent errors. (Errors are unobserved variables and, thus, latent variables, too.) Furthermore, curved lines that point to themselves indicate variances, representing error variances in the figure. Also, curved lines that connect two latent variables indicate covariances (i.e., correlation for standardized factors). Note that the three-factor EFA model in the previous section had 120 parameters (90 factor loadings and 30 error variances) before rotation. In CFA, it is also possible to retain

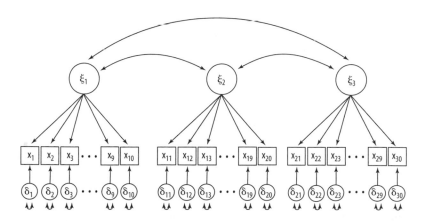

Figure 6.4 Graphical representation of the three-factor CFA model for PSCS data.

the scale of item scores, including the means and variances, accordingly to estimate intercepts in the functional form, in addition to factor loadings. Such a set up is referred to as the *mean structure* analysis. We are not going to discuss the utilities of the mean structure analysis in this book. Interested readers are referred to other resources (e.g., Brown, 2006).

Model Identification

For the model parameters to be estimated, our data have to provide sufficient information for the model we specify. When data provide enough information to estimate all parameters in the model, we say the model is *identified*. Sometimes, we distinguish a *just-identified* model, in which data provide just enough information to estimate all parameters and *overidentified* model, in which data provide more than enough information, because the model needs to be overidentified to assess its model fit. If data do not provide enough information to estimate all parameters in the model, then we refer the model to be *not identified* or *underidentified*. There are at least two requirements in a model set up for CFA regarding model identification. One is called the *t*-rule, which restricts the maximum number of parameters one can estimate in a model. According to this rule, we cannot estimate more parameters than the number of unique elements of the covariance matrix. (Note that the counts do not include intercepts for a mean–structure model, because intercepts are estimated from a different source of information than the covariance matrix—namely, a vector of means.) The number of unique elements in a covariance matrix is the sum of the number of variances (i.e., the number of variables) and the number of covariances (i.e., the number of all unique pairs of variables), which can be obtained by $\frac{k(k+1)}{2}$, where k is the number of variables in the covariance matrix. For the PSCS data, because $k = 30$, the number of unique components is $\frac{30(30+1)}{2} = 465$. Therefore, our three-factor CFA set up for the PSCS data with 92 parameters is a way below this number and will not have a problem regarding the *t*-rule. Note that *t*-rule provides only a necessary condition for an identified model but not a sufficient condition.

Another requirement specifies the minimum number of items required for a CFA model. A one-factor model, the simplest CFA structure, requires three items in the model to be identified, thus referred to as the *three-indicator rule*. If there are only two items in a one-factor model, the model would have four parameters (two factor loadings and two error variances, *see* Fig. 6.5a, whereas there are only three unique covariance matrix components with two variances and one covariance). Therefore, the model is not identified. If there are three variables, the number of parameters would be six (three factor loadings and three error variances, *see* Fig. 6.5b), while having six unique covariance matrix components (three variances and three covariances). Therefore, the model is just identified. For a one-factor model to be overidentified, we need four or more items. For the Family Responsibility Scale (FRS) example data, we have 11 items (indicators) with one factor. Therefore, it is obvious that the three-indicator rule is satisfied, and the model will be overidentified.

For a multifactor model with more than one factor, requirements regarding the number of items are far more complicated. One useful rule is the *two-indicator rule* under a model with no correlations between errors and the complexity of factors equals 1. When we say the complexity of factors equals 1, it essentially refers a strict simple

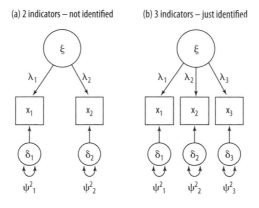

(a) 2 indicators – not identified   (b) 3 indicators – just identified

Figure 6.5   Examinations of the three-indicator rule for one-factor CFA model.

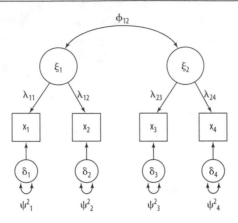

Figure 6.6 Illustration of the two-indicator rule.

structure, where each item is predicted by only one of the factors. Under this condition, a multifactor model would be identified if the model has two or more items for each factor. Note that both the two- and three-indicator rules are a sufficient condition, rather than a necessary condition for a model to be identified. For example, assume a two-factor model with a strict simple structure, where each factor is associated with two variables (items). Furthermore, we assume a correlation between the two factors but no correlations between errors. See Figure 6.6 for a graphical representation of this hypothetical model. In this model, there are nine parameters (four factor loadings; λ_{11}, λ_{12}, λ_{23}, and λ_{24}, four error variances; ψ_1^2, ψ_2^2, ψ_3^2, and ψ_4^2, and one correlation between factors; ϕ_{12}). Because there are 10 unique elements in the covariance matrix of the 4 variables ($\frac{4 \times (4+1)}{2} = 10$), the degrees of freedom is $10 - 9 = 1$, and the model is still overidentified. For the Parental Self-Care Scale (PSCS) data, because there are 10 items (indicators) per factor, the three-indicator rule will not be an issue.

Parameter Estimation

Although many different estimation approaches are possible, *maximum likelihood estimation* is most widely utilized for CFA with continuous variables. In principle, maximum likelihood estimation derives a set of parameters that maximizes the probability of observing the data, as mentioned earlier in the section for EFA. Similarly to EFA, such a solution must be obtained with an intensive iterative numerical procedure on a computer, rather than by hand computations. For a CFA model, we typically utilize specialized structural equation modeling (SEM) software to estimate parameters, rather than a general statistical "package" software. A "full" SEM, or simply SEM, is a model that contains structural relationships between variables, including latent factors. If a measurement part of a full SEM, which defines how a latent factor is measured by observed indicators, becomes a stand-alone model, then it is a CFA model. Thus, a CFA model is in fact a special case of SEM. There are many structural equation modeling software to choose from, such as AMOS (Arbuckle, 2006), EQS (Bentler & Wu, 1995), and LISREL (Jöreskog & Sörbom, 1996). In this book, we demonstrate the use of Mplus (Muthen & Muthen, 2007) as an example. However, it should be emphasized that the choice of software is just a matter of preference, and all CFA analysis procedures presented in this book can be executed by other SEM software. Also, their results should be very similar, if not exactly identical, as far as the same estimation methods are used. Any observed variations should be very small, as they result from subtle differences in some computational methods.

Statistical inferences for CFA parameters rely largely on a multivariate normal distribution of variables (item scores as variables) in the population data. However, it is often not feasible to evaluate an extremely high-dimensional multivariate normality, such as for 20 or 30 items. Therefore, it is advisable to test for evidence of violations of the assumption by evaluating univariate normality of each variable in data, including skewness and kurtosis. According to Kline (2005), a variable with the absolute value of skewness index greater than 3.0 is an indication of serious departure from normality, whereas the absolute value of kurtosis index greater than 10.0 should flag a variable. Because univariate normality of each variable in a set of multiple variables is a necessary condition for their multivariate normality, we would know that multivariate normality is violated when at least one of univariate

```
TITLE:     Basic 3-factor model for English group
DATA:      FILE IS PSCS_English.dat;
VARIABLE:  NAMES ARE x1-x30;
MODEL:     ksi1 BY x1*  x2-x10;
           ksi2 BY x11* x12-x20;
           ksi3 BY x21* x22-x30;
           ksi1@1.0;
           ksi2@1.0;
           ksi3@1.0;
OUTPUT:    STDYX;
           MODINDICES;
```

Figure 6.7 Mplus syntax for the three-factor model for PSCS data.

normality is violated. However, when we do not have evidence for violation of univariate normality for any of the items, it does not guarantee a multivariate normality.

Here, an Mplus syntax to fit the three-factor CFA model is presented in Figure 6.7. To run Mplus, one needs to prepare two files. One is a syntax file, and the other is a data file. Both files need to be plain text files. Typically, the syntax file is crafted on the Mplus program's syntax editing window, although a stand alone text editor such as Notepad works perfectly fine. Regarding data files, one easy way to prepare a data file is to "save as" a tab-delimited format from a proprietary format for a program that is more convenient for data management, such as SPSS and Excel. Also, Mplus offers an option to use a covariance matrix or a correlation matrix (with or without a variance vector and/or a mean vector) as a data source.

This Mplus syntax assumes that the data file has been saved as PSCS_English.dat in tab-delimited text format. To create this data file, we used SPSS to save the original PSCS SPSS data file as a tab-delimited format file with no variable names included. If the syntax is saved in the same directory as the data file, then there is no need to specify a full path. The line with VARIABLE statement specifies variable names. In this syntax, 30 variables (items) are labeled as x1 through x30. The lines with MODEL statement specify the model to fit the data. Here, three latent factors ξ_1, ξ_2, and ξ_3 are represented as ksi1, ksi2, and ksi3. For each latent factor, observed variables that are predicted by the latent factor are listed followed by the BY keyword. By default, Mplus assumes that latent factors are correlated, and errors are not correlated. There-fore, these three lines in the MODEL statement describe the three-factor model described in Figure 6.4. Note that Mplus will constrain the factor loading of the first item for each factor to be 1.0 by default. Here, it is stated ksi1 BY x1* x2-x10 instead of ksi1 x1-x10, as might have been expected. This specification overrides the Mplus default to constrain the factor loading for the first item to 1.0 by attaching an aster-isk to the first item as x1*. Thus, the factor loading for the first item is also estimated. Instead, the variance of the latent factor is constrained to 1.0 by ksi1@1.0. The same specifications are applied for the sec-ond and third latent factors. The last two lines with OUTPUT statement request additional output. One is the STDYX keyword to request fully standardized parameter estimates, and the other is the MODINDICES keyword to request modification indices. Modification indices will be explained later in this chapter.

Parameter Interpretation

As mentioned earlier, there is no fixed scale for the unobserved latent factor. Consequently, the scale of factor loadings is arbitrary, too. There-fore, it is recommended to evaluate fully standardized factor loadings. Fully standardized factor loadings are convenient in many applications, because they can be interpreted just like correlation coefficients for a model with a strict simple structure. In some SEM software program, fully standardized parameter estimates are part of a default output, whereas some others, including Mplus, require an additional specifica-tion to obtain fully standardized results.

Another caution related to this scale indeterminacy characteristic of CFA models is that all factor loadings are estimable because the scales of unobserved latent factors are arbitrarily fixed, such as mean $= 0$ and $SD = 1$. This is in fact just one type of constraint that a CFA model can assume, and other types of constraints are also possible. Alternatively, it is also possible to constrain one of the factor loadings for each factor to some arbitrary fixed value, such as 1.0. For example, in the hypothetical two-factor model with two items per factor presented earlier (Fig. 6.6),

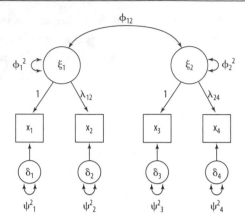

Figure 6.8 Alternative parameter constraints in hypothetical two-factor CFA model.

we can alternatively estimate the variances of each latent factor (ϕ_1^2 and ϕ_2^2). Instead, two factor loadings λ_{11} and λ_{23} should be constrained, such as to 1.0 (*see* Fig. 6.8), which in fact the default for Mplus as indicated earlier. These two different ways to scale parameters will result in completely different values of parameter estimates. However, these two are in fact based on "exactly" the same model, and the interpretation of the parameters should be ultimately the same. In fact, when parameter estimates are fully standardized, we should see exactly the same set of parameter estimate values between the two. Now the question is probably, "Which approach shall we take?" Ultimately, it is a matter of preference and whichever choice we make should not influence our interpretations. It seems that a preference of many factor analysts is the second approach, in which one of the factor loadings is constrained to 1.0, like it is a default setting for many SEM software programs, including Mplus.

Parameter estimation results from Mplus after fitting a three-factor CFA model to the PSCS data are presented in Figure 6.9. Again, readers are prompted that the data were simulated data, and the results do not reflect the characteristics and quality of the actual PSCS. Here, only fully standardized results are presented. In Mplus output, fully standardized results are labeled STDYX Standardization, indicating both dependent variables (Y) and predictors (X) are standardized. The first

	Estimate	S.E.	Est./S.E.	Two-Tailed P-Value
KSI1 BY				
X1	0.557	0.046	12.057	0.000
X2	0.710	0.034	20.880	0.000
X3	0.781	0.028	28.373	0.000
X4	0.817	0.024	34.084	0.000
X5	0.856	0.020	42.631	0.000
X6	0.663	0.038	17.441	0.000
X7	0.780	0.027	28.385	0.000
X8	0.701	0.035	20.155	0.000
X9	0.696	0.035	19.773	0.000
X10	0.661	0.038	17.299	0.000
KSI2 BY				
X11	0.273	0.060	4.541	0.000
X12	0.280	0.060	4.680	0.000
X13	0.202	0.062	3.251	0.001
X14	0.824	0.022	37.066	0.000
X15	0.855	0.019	44.981	0.000
X16	0.892	0.015	57.779	0.000
X17	0.952	0.010	95.891	0.000
X18	0.252	0.061	4.147	0.000
X19	0.122	0.064	1.900	0.057
X20	0.242	0.061	3.960	0.000
KSI3 BY				
X21	0.241	0.061	3.929	0.000
X22	0.707	0.034	20.878	0.000
X23	0.808	0.024	33.529	0.000
X24	0.327	0.058	5.601	0.000
X25	0.338	0.058	5.832	0.000
X26	0.685	0.036	19.234	0.000
X27	0.352	0.057	6.149	0.000
X28	0.247	0.061	4.037	0.000
X29	0.946	0.011	84.735	0.000
X30	0.894	0.016	57.467	0.000

Figure 6.9 Completely standardized Mplus output for factor loadings.

part of the output presents the estimates of factor loadings. They are reported in the column labeled Estimate. Because they are fully standardized parameter estimates in a strict simple structure model, they can be interpreted as correlation coefficients between each item and the corresponding latent factor. Note that standardized factor loadings will be no longer equivalent to correlation coefficients if they are not based on a simple structure model. In fact, they will be equivalent to semi-partial correlation coefficients, under a nonsimple structure model. The column labeled S.E. reports standard error of each estimate. The column labeled Est/S.E. reports the ratio of estimate to its standard error. This quantity is asymptotically treated as a t-statistic. If the value is larger than 1.96, it indicates evidence for significantly different effect from 0. The actual p-value for this hypothesis testing is reported in the last column. By examining factor loadings, there are some items with considerably lower loadings than others. Those include loadings for items 11, 12, 13, 18, 19, and 20 for the second latent factor and loadings for items 21, 24, 25, 27, and 28 for the third latent factor. According to these results, they are candidates to be removed from the scale, although this should not be the sole criteria.

Next, the part of output that reports error variances is presented in Figure 6.10. Again, they are fully standardized. Under the fully standardized scale, an error variance indicates the proportion of unexplained variation of the outcome variable. For example, for item 1, 69% of the variance of item scores is unexplained by the first latent factor. Under the strict simple structure with fully standardized scale, like this example, error variance and factor loading have a direct relationship $\psi^2 = 1 - \lambda^2$, stating that the error variance is 1 minus the square of corresponding factor loading. Therefore, for items with low factor loadings resulted in high error variances. For example, item 1 has $\lambda = 0.557$ (*see* Fig. 6.9). Thus, $\psi^2 = 1 - (0.557)^2 = 0.690$, and this value matches the value in Figure 6.10.

Covariances between latent factors and variances of are presented in Figure 6.11. As mentioned earlier, under the fully standardized scale, covariances are the same as correlations. The results here indicate similar levels of correlations between the three latent factors, at about 0.4 to 0.6. Note that variances of latent factors have been scaled to 1.0, because the results have been fully standardized.

Model Fit Evaluation

One of our interests when we apply a CFA model is how well the model fits the data. If the model fits the data well, it is an indication that our

	Estimate	S.E.	Est./S.E.	Two-Tailed P-Value
Residual Variances				
X1	0.690	0.051	13.432	0.000
X2	0.496	0.034	10.282	0.000
X3	0.391	0.043	9.099	0.000
X4	0.333	0.039	8.510	0.000
X5	0.267	0.034	7.774	0.000
X6	0.561	0.050	11.132	0.000
X7	0.391	0.043	9.115	0.000
X8	0.509	0.049	10.436	0.000
X9	0.515	0.049	10.519	0.000
X10	0.564	0.050	11.172	0.000
X11	0.925	0.033	28.173	0.000
X12	0.921	0.034	27.449	0.000
X13	0.959	0.025	38.034	0.000
X14	0.321	0.037	8.767	0.000
X15	0.269	0.033	8.277	0.000
X16	0.204	0.028	7.399	0.000
X17	0.093	0.019	4.924	0.000
X18	0.936	0.031	30.513	0.000
X19	0.985	0.016	63.288	0.000
X20	0.941	0.030	31.748	0.000
X21	0.942	0.030	31.781	0.000
X22	0.501	0.048	10.466	0.000
X23	0.347	0.039	8.919	0.000
X24	0.893	0.038	23.430	0.000
X25	0.886	0.039	22.676	0.000
X26	0.531	0.049	10.903	0.000
X27	0.876	0.040	21.713	0.000
X28	0.939	0.030	31.042	0.000
X29	0.105	0.021	4.972	0.000
X30	0.200	0.028	7.184	0.000

Figure 6.10 Completely standardized Mplus output for error variances.

theoretical factor structure is "confirmed." On the other hand, if the model does not fit the data well, it is an indication that respondents' responses to instrument items are not consistent with our theoretical factor structure of scale items, and it may be an indication of a need for possible revision of the scale instrument configurations, such as removal of some items, adding paths permitting them to be associated with other latent factors, or permitting error variances to correlate. Therefore, it is a "must" to evaluate the model fit for any CFA analysis.

There are several different ways to view model fit and numerous different indices and statistics. Covering a wide variety of those available

	Estimate	S.E.	Est./S.E.	Two-Tailed P-Value
KSI2 WITH				
KSI1	0.606	0.044	13.649	0.000
KSI3 WITH				
KSI1	0.437	0.056	7.847	0.000
KSI2	0.595	0.045	13.330	0.000
Variances				
KSI1	1.000	0.000	999.000	999.000
KSI2	1.000	0.000	999.000	999.000
KSI3	1.000	0.000	999.000	999.000

Figure 6.11   Completely standardized Mplus output for covariances between latent factors.

indices is beyond the scope of this book. In this book, we will present chi-square goodness-of-fit test statistic, Tucker Lewis Index (TLI), Comparative Fit Index (CFI), Root Mean Square Error of Approximation (RMSEA), and Standardized Root Mean Square Residual (SRMR), because they are reported in Mplus. Readers are referred to other sources, including Brown (2006), Kline (2005), Kahn (2006), and Hu and Bentler (1999) for more details and other available indices.

Chi-Square Goodness-of-Fit Statistic.   A chi-square goodness of fit statistic is derived to test a null hypothesis that says the data covariance matrix and reproduced covariance matrix are the same. By rejecting this null hypothesis, it indicates that there is enough evidence that the model does NOT fit the data; thus, our conclusion will be poor fit of the model to the data. However, it should be cautioned that the chi-square statistic is directly affected by the sample size. The chi-square statistic is a function of the sample size and the fitting function minimized by the maximum likelihood estimation. Therefore, keeping the sample size constant, the chi-square statistic will be smaller for a better fitted model. On the other hand, keeping the same magnitude of fitting function, the chi-square statistic will be larger for a larger sample size, indicating a worse fit. Therefore, when the sample size is large, we could often end up rejecting the null hypothesis with a quite small fitting function value. Therefore, it is also suggested to evaluate the ratio of chi-square statistic to its degrees of freedom. A small value indicates a good fit. Typically, a value less than 2 or 3 is considered acceptable, although there is no commonly accepted standard for this quantity.

Comparative Fit Index. This index is related to the difference between the chi-square statistic and its degrees of freedom for the proposed model and for the null model. Here, the null model is a model where all parameters are constrained to be zero, consequently analogous to the observed covariance matrix itself. The idea is that the fit of such a null model is the worst of all, and CFI is an indicator to measure the improvement of fit by the proposed model. The range of the index is artificially restricted to be between 0 and 1, with which a higher CFI indicates a better fit. A common standard is that a value above 0.95 is an excellent fit, and 0.90 is an acceptable fit (e.g., Hu & Bentler, 1999).

Tucker Lewis Index. It is also known as the Non-Normed Fit Index. It evaluates the ratio of chi-square statistic to its degrees of freedom in the proposed model, relative to the same quantity of the null model. Similarly to CFI, a higher value indicates more improvement from the null model, and its range is artificially restricted from 0 to 1. A value above 0.95 is considered as an excellent fit and 0.90 is considered as an acceptable fit (e.g., Hu & Bentler, 1999).

Root Mean Square Error of Approximation. This is a measure of model fit based on the degree of noncentrality of the chi-square statistic. Noncentrality is a quantity that indicates a degree of the deviation from the null hypothesis, where the null hypothesis in this context states that the data covariance matrix and reproduced covariance matrix are the same. If the model is perfectly fit the data, then the noncentrality parameter of the chi-square statistic will be 0, and RMSEA will be consequently 0. On the other hand, if the fit of the model is not perfect, then the noncentrality parameter will be a positive value, and the misfit of the model is represented by a non-zero positive RMSE value. Therefore, smaller values indicate better fit of the model to the data. It is suggested to obtain 0.05 or smaller RMSEA to claim a good fit. Also, 0.08 is considered as a cut-point for an acceptable fit (e.g., Hu & Bentler, 1999). A sampling distribution of RMSEA has been derived, and it is consequently possible to evaluate a confidence interval of RMSEA. In Mplus, a 90% confidence interval around the estimated RMSEA is reported. It is suggested that we evaluate whether the lower bound of the interval is very close to zero, whether zero is not included, and whether the upper bound of the interval is not too high, ideally lower than 0.08.

Standardized Root Mean Square Residual.   This is a standardized measure of discrepancy between the data covariance matrix and the reproduced covariance matrix based on estimated parameter values. It is suggested to obtain 0.10 or smaller SRMR to claim a good fit (e.g., Kline, 2005).

Example Mplus Output of Fit Indices.   Output of fit indices from fitting the three-factor CFA model to the PSCS data generated for our illustrations is provided in Figure 6.12. The chi-square statistic is reported as 487.454 with degrees of freedom $df = 402$. This statistic turned out to be significant, indicating not to support a good fit. However, this should not be interpreted as "bad" fit, especially if the sample size is reasonably large. In fact, when we evaluate the ratio of the chi-square statistic to its degrees of freedom, it is $487.454/402 = 1.21$, indicating a small and good value. Next, the chi-square statistic for a null model (labeled as the "baseline model" in Mplus output) is reported. It is 3899.644 with $df = 435$. This statistic is not directly related to the fit of the proposed model, but it is used for computations of the CFI and TLI, which are 0.975 and 0.973, respectively. These values indeed indicate excellent fit based on the standards provided earlier.

Next, a log-likelihood value is reported in the output. This value is again not directly interpretable, but it is reported because it is used for

```
TESTS OF MODEL FIT

Chi-Square Test of Model Fit

    Value                                        487.454
    Degrees of Freedom                               402
    P-Value                                       0.0022

Chi-Square Test of Model Fit for the Baseline Model

    Value                                       3899.644
    Degrees of Freedom                               435
    P-Value                                       0.0000

CFI/TLI                                          CFI/TLI

    CFI                                            0.975
    TLI                                            0.973

Loglikelihood

    H0 Value                                   − 15297.494
    H1 Value                                   − 15053.767

Information Criteria

    Number of Free Parameters                         93
    Akaike (AIC)                                30780.988
    Bayesian (BIC)                              31108.484
    Sample-Size Adjusted BIC                    30813.666
    (n* = (n + 2) / 24)

RMSEA (Root Mean Square Error Of Approximation)

    Estimate                                       0.029
    90 Percent C.I.                          0.018 0.038
    Probability RMSEA ≦ .05                        1.000

SRMR (Standardized Root Mean Square Residual)

    Value                                          0.058
```

Figure 6.12 Mplus output of fit indices
from fitting three-factor CFA model to
30-item PSCS data.

computations of indices reported immediately follow—namely, Akaike's
information criterion (AIC), Bayesian information criterion (BIC), and
sample-size adjusted BIC (ABIC). These are also kinds of fit indices and
classified as "information criteria." However, they are not standardized

and not interpretable by themselves. They become useful when one's interest is a model selection, where multiple models are compared by their magnitudes of fit to the data. We will cover this aspect of model fit in the section of model comparisons later in this chapter.

Finally, RMSEA and SRMR are reported. RMSEA is 0.029 and smaller than the standard of good fit. Its 90% confidence interval is reported as (0.018, 0.038). The lower bound is very close to 0, and the upper bound does not exceed 0.08, which is an indication of an excellent fit. SRMR is reported to be 0.058. Again, it is smaller than the standard of good fit (0.10). Overall, we have evidence of good model fit to the 30-item data.

Modification Indices

At this point, a scale developer probably has a good sense of the qualities of items in the scale. Before making final decisions on changes for the scale, it is recommended to examine modification indices as well. Essentially, they are expected changes in the chi-square statistic when a particular parameter is added to the current model. When a multiple-factor model with a strict simple structure is considered for a typical scale construction scenario like our PSCS example, one of the focal points is on "cross-loading" possibilities. Also, potential correlated errors can be detected by examining modification indices.

To obtain modification indices from Mplus, for example, we needed to add a keyword MODINDICES under the OUTPUT statement in the syntax file (*see* Fig. 6.7). By default, Mplus provides output with additional parameters that will result in the reduction of chi-square statistic by 10.0 or higher. This value is rather an arbitrary criterion that a user can change to other values, if desirable. For example, 3.84, the critical value for a chi-square statistic with $df = 1$, may be a reasonable alternative. For our three-factor CFA model, the PSCS data analysis resulted in the Mplus output displayed in Figure 6.13. In this example, two additional parameters were identified for the model, based on the 10.0-or-higher criterion. One is labeled KSI3 BY X19, indicating a factor loading of x_{19} on ξ_3, which will result in the reduction of 12.423 in chi-square statistic. This indicates that if we allow item 19, which is designed to measure

	M.I.	E.P.C.	Std E.P.C.	StdYX E.P.C.
BY Statements				
KSI3 BY X19	12.423	1.374	0.830	0.292
WITH Statements				
X17 WITH X4	10.248	−0.346	−0.346	−0.300

Figure 6.13 Modification indices output from Mplus for the three-factor model with the initial 30-item PCSC data.

the Instrumental subscale, to correlate also with the latent factor that represents Nursing subscale, the model fit improvement will be 12.423 in the reduction of chi-square statistic, which is statistically significant. In addition to the chi-square statistic change, Mplus reports the expected parameter change (E.P.C.) index. The E.P.C. index indicates what the parameter estimates would be if it is freely estimated in the model. It also comes with the standardized estimates; one with standardized latent factor (Std E.P.C.) and the other with completely standardized estimate (StdYX E.P.C.). According to the output, StdYX E.P.C. for the suspected loading will be 0.292. Recall that this item had a low factor loading on $\xi_2 (0.122)$. However, we should not cross-load the item beyond the intended factor or change the associated factor, unless it is theoretically consistent. This typically requires re-evaluating the item content to judge whether it matches the alternative construct equally well, or better than the one for which it was originally intended. In this illustration, we judged that the item should not measure the Nursing subscale. Therefore, at this point we conclude that this item needs to be removed from the scale.

The other flagged parameter is labeled X17 with X4, indicating the error covariance (i.e., correlation) between x_4 and x_{17}, which will result in the reduction of 10.248 in the chi-square statistic. Psychometrically, correlated errors indicate that the items are not locally independent, which means that items are correlated beyond what they are hypothesized to measure. One possible reason is that the items are so similar to each other and respondents could not distinguish the items. Another possible reason is that the items are commonly correlated with the third latent factor. If this is the case, however, modification indices should detect such a relationship. Some other reasons are also possible, such as scale administration conditions, item ordering effect, and so forth. Whatever the reason, if correlated errors are happening within the same subscale, they are absolutely not a desirable psychometric property to have in a scale. If it is the case, we should think that one or both of the items should be removed from the scale. On the other hand, if correlated errors are for between items that measure different subscale, like in our current illustrative PSCS data analysis, it may not be that problematic.

Model Comparisons

After model parameters, model fit indices, and modification indices are examined, one might decide to change the structure of the scale. One most probable modification is deletions of items that have been identified as not making a significant contribution to the scale or subscale. Other possible modifications include adding items from other subscales. As mentioned earlier, it typically requires re-evaluating the item content to judge whether it matches the alternative construct equally well, or better than the one for which it was originally intended. We typically avoid this type of modification, because items should have been carefully developed to measure a particular construct. Therefore, removing such items will be a more reasonable solution. In any scenario, it is always advised to evaluate the change of model fit of a revised model, compared to the model fit of the originally proposed model, before making a final decision of what factor structure we should use and what items should be removed from the scale.

Illustrative Analysis. For illustration purposes, we will go through a series of model comparisons using our simulated data for the PSCS to decide which items should be removed from the scale. At this point, our intention is to retain a strict simple structure. Therefore, we will not consider any of the items loading on more than one latent factor.

Table 6.1 Model Fit and Modification Results: Comparisons Between the Original
Model with the Model after Removing Six Items

	Original model	Model with six items removed
CFI	0.976	0.987
TLI	0.973	0.986
RMSEA	0.029	0.026
SRMR	0.058	0.046
Detected modifications	KSI3 BY X19 X17 WITH X4	X17 WITH X4

First, we examined how the model fit would change after removing
items with low factor loadings. Items 13, 18, 19, 21, and 28 were chosen
to be removed because their factor loadings were low, and the reliability
analysis also flagged these items based on the α-item-if-deleted values
(*see* Table 4.2 in Chapter 4). In addition, item 20 was also selected to be
removed, because it had lower factor loadings than item 18, which has
been chosen to be removed. The results are summarized in Table 6.1.
Although model fit was already excellent before removing the six items,
afterward the model fit was further improved. Regarding the detected
modifications, KSI3 BY X19 became no longer an issue, because item
19 was removed from the scale. However, X17 WITH X4 remained as a
potential problem.

Second, we considered whether items 4 and/or 17 should be removed
from the scale. We fitted two strictly simple structure three-factor CFA
models, one without item 4 and another without item 17. Results are
summarized in Table 6.2. Both improved model fit just slightly from the
previous model with six items removed. From the model fit perspective,
it seems that there is essentially no difference between removing items 4
and 17. Furthermore, respecified models run on both possibilities did not
detect any additional modifications. Therefore, we first concluded that
there was no need to remove both items. After all, our decision was not
to remove either items, because *(a)* they are both distinctively and highly
correlated with separate factors (0.817 for item 4 and Emotion factor
and 0.952 for item 17 and Instrumental factor); *(b)* they are not flagged
by any other analysis; and *(c)* model fit indices were already excellent

Table 6.2 Model Fit and Modification Results after Removing Two Items That Are Suspected To Have Correlated Errors

	Model without item 4	Model without item 17
CFI	0.989	0.989
TLI	0.988	0.988
RMSEA	0.024	0.023
SRMR	0.046	0.046
Detected modifications	None	None

without removal of the items. However, if they were measuring the same subscale, then our decision would have been to remove one or both of these items, depending on their contents.

We further examined the magnitudes of factor loadings and results from EFA to identify additional candidates for removals. For the Instrumental subscale, items 11 and 12 were flagged because they had weak loadings on the intended factor. It is also true for the CFA results after the initial removals of six items (0.271 and 0.277, see Table 6.3). For the Nursing subscale, items 24, 25, and 27 further display low factor loadings (0.326, 0.338, and 0.353, respectively, after the removal of the 6 items; see Table 6.3), and the same was observed for the EFA. However, we judged that it is also important to maintain a pragmatic value of the scale by retaining 20 items in the scale, rather than 19 items, and by having the same number of items in each of Instrumental and Nursing subscales. Therefore, we have decided to further remove only one item from the Instrumental subscale and an additional three items from the Nursing subscale. As a result, all 10 items were retained for the Emotion subscale, 5 items (items 12, 14, 15, 16, and 17) were retained for the Instrumental subscale, and 5 items (items 22, 23, 26, 29, and 30) were retained for the Nursing subscale. Table 6.3 provides the summary of factor loading estimates and some model fit indices for the initial 30-item model, the model with 6 items removed, and the final 20-item model. Once again, we would like to remind readers that the series of analyses is based on simulated data to mimic the structure of the PSCS data, and the results do not reflect the characteristics and quality of actual PSCS and its items.

Table 6.3 Factor Loading Estimates from the Three Models

	Initial 30-item model	Model with 6 items removed	Final 20-item model
Emotional			
Item 1	0.557	0.557	0.557
Item 2	0.710	0.710	0.710
Item 3	0.781	0.781	0.781
Item 4	0.817	0.817	0.817
Item 5	0.856	0.856	0.856
Item 6	0.663	0.663	0.663
Item 7	0.780	0.780	0.780
Item 8	0.701	0.701	0.701
Item 9	0.696	0.696	0.696
Item 10	0.661	0.661	0.661
Instrumental			
Item 11	0.273	0.271	
Item 12	0.280	0.277	0.277
Item 13	0.202		
Item 14	0.824	0.823	0.822
Item 15	0.855	0.854	0.855
Item 16	0.892	0.891	0.891
Item 17	0.952	0.954	0.954
Item 18	0.252		
Item 19	0.122		
Item 20	0.242		
Nursing			
Item 21	0.241		
Item 22	0.707	0.707	0.709
Item 23	0.808	0.809	0.808
Item 24	0.327	0.326	
Item 25	0.338	0.338	
Item 26	0.685	0.685	0.685
Item 27	0.352	0.353	
Item 28	0.247		
Item 29	0.946	0.944	0.946
Item 30	0.894	0.896	0.897
Model Fit Indices			
CFI	0.975	0.987	0.993
TLI	0.973	0.986	0.992
RMSEA	0.029	0.026	0.024
SRMR	0.058	0.046	0.033

Nested Vs. Non-Nested Models. Some readers may wonder why we did not conduct a chi-square difference test to evaluate the improvement of model fit in the process of removing some items from the scale. The reason was that the models we evaluated were not nested to each other. The chi-square difference test is only valid for comparison between nested models. Two nested models have different sets of parameters to be estimated, but a set of parameters from one model has to be a subset of parameters from the other model. To achieve this condition, two models must have the same set of observed indicators and unobserved latent factors. For example, assume the initial PSCS three-factor model with 30 items in Figure 6.4. In this model, we can add another parameter that represents a covariance between δ_4 and δ_{17}, indicating correlated errors between these items, as suggested by modification indices generated in our original analysis. This alternative model and the original model in Figure 6.4 are nested models, because the set of parameters in the original model is a subset of parameters in the modified model, while having the same set of observed indicators and latent factors for both models. In this case, we could utilize the chi-square difference test to evaluate the change in model fit. On the other hand, if some items are removed from the model, the modified model and the model in Figure 6.4 are not nested model, because they do not have the same set of observed variables. In this case, we cannot use the chi-square difference test and have to rely on standardized fit indices, such as CFI, TLI, RMSEA, and SRMR.

If one of two models is not nested to the other, but if the two models have the same set of observed variables, we could also utilize information criteria, such as AIC, BIC, and AIBC, to evaluate model fit. As mentioned earlier, these information criterion values are not standardized and not directly interpretable. However, we can compare the values of each criterion between models. Simply, a smaller value indicates a better fit. For illustration, we hypothetically compare the final three-factor model with 20 PSCS items with a one-factor model with the same set of items. Note that the one-factor model can be considered as nested to the three-factor model by treating the one-factor model as a special case of three-factor model where all correlations between three factors are fixed to 1.0. Therefore, we could use a chi-square difference test in this case; however, the

Table 6.4 Summary of Information Criterion Values and Other Fit Indices for 3-Factor and 1-Factor Models with the Final 19 PSCS Items

	Three-factor model with 20 items	One-factor model with 20 items
AIC	19558	20760
BIC	19780	20971
ABIC	19580	20781
CFI	0.993	0.620
TLI	0.992	0.576
RMSEA	0.024	0.170
SRMR	0.033	0.120

use of information criteria is still valid, and we use the information criteria for demonstration purposes here. Information criteria for the two models are obtained as indicated in Table 6.4. In this case, it is quite clear that the three-factor model is a much better choice than the alternative one-factor model, displaying much smaller AIC, BIC, and ABIC values. Also, a much better model fit for the three-factor model is supported by other fit indices. As a byproduct, this can be interpreted as discriminant evidence of the three subscales; consequently, additional construct evidence of the validity of the subscale scores.

Measurement Invariance

Once a measurement model is established, one might be interested in studying measurement invariance between subpopulations of respondents. Examples include invariance between males and females and between racial groups. For the purposes of illustration, we will use a context, in which the validation of bilingual (English and Spanish) versions of the PSCS is of interest. Two extended CFA techniques that are useful in measurement invariance studies are illustrated: CFA with covariate, and multiple-group CFA. Issues related to bilingual validation are also described in Chapter 7.

Confirmatory Factor Analysis With Covariates. A CFA model can be extended to a model with one or more observed respondent characteristic variables. Such extension is referred to as CFA with covariates, or multiple indicators multiple causes (MIMIC) modeling. The framework of CFA with covariates or MIMIC is useful in a measurement invariance study, where one's interest is in investigating invariance of the scale at the item level. Such item-level investigation of measurement invariance is referred to as *differential item functioning* (DIF). By definition, we say that DIF exists for an item if the expected score of the item is different between two or more subpopulations of respondents, given the same level of trait. Use of MIMIC for DIF detection is described in other literature, including Finch (2005). Typically, descriptions of DIF detection procedures assume item scores are categorical variables; however, the same modeling principles can be applied to cases where item scores are treated as continuous variables, especially for MIMIC and multiple-group CFA approaches. DIF can be estimated by additionally regressing the latent factors and items on a grouping variable. Graphically, this setup can be depicted in a path diagram in Figure 6.14. The diagram shows a hypothetical two-factor strictly simple structure with three indicators for each latent factor. In addition to the basic measurement model, a person-level variable G has been added to the model. For simplicity, let's assume the variable G is a dichotomous group indicator variable, such as two language groups. In this model, all items and latent factors are regressed on the group indicator variable. As illustrated in Figure 6.14, each item is regressed on the group indicator variable *and* a latent factor. Conceptually, this is just like a multiple regression, where item scores are predicted by the latent factor and the group indicator variable. In this context, the coefficient for the group indicator variable is interpreted as the performance difference between groups on the item, given the same level of latent trait. This is exactly how a DIF is defined as mentioned earlier; thus, dashed lines that connect G and x indicate DIF. On the other hand, dotted lines that connect G and ξ indicate mean difference between groups on latent factors, which is often referred to as "impact" in DIF literature to be distinguished from DIF.

Practically, it is not possible to simultaneously estimate parameters for all dotted lines and dashed lines, because of scale indeterminacy.

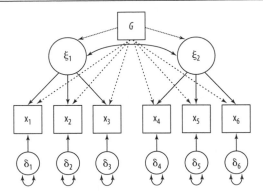

Figure 6.14 Graphical representation of DIF analysis model by MIMIC modeling.

In other words, data do not provide enough information to determine the scale of these parameters. One suggested approach is as follows:

- First, set up a full MIMIC DIF mode as depicted in Figure 6.14, but constrain all DIF parameters (the effects of the group indicator variable on all items) to be 0. When the analysis is executed, request modification indices.
- Second, examine reported modification indices values to determine if any of the DIF parameters have been flagged. Because all DIF effects have been constrained to 0, being flagged means that they are likely non-zero.
- Third, rerun the model by removing the 0 constraints for items with flagged DIF effects to estimate DIF parameters for the flagged items.

Note that modification indices are considered for parameters that exist in the model but constrained to be zero in Mplus. In the basic CFA model, such as the one illustrated in Figure 6.4, error covariances and factor loadings on unintended factors exist in the model, but they are constrained to be zero in the process of parameter estimation. That is why modification indices for error covariances and factor loadings for unintended factors are automatically considered. However, in a MIMIC model, coefficients of a grouping variable for items do not exist unless they are specified. Therefore, they need to be explicitly specified in the model by the user and constrained to zero for them to be considered for modification indices.

For illustrative purposes, we analyzed the simulated PSCS data with English and Spanish samples combined where Language is the group indicator variable. Mplus syntax for this illustrative analysis is provided in Appendix A–1 & 2. Here, English speakers were coded to 1, and Spanish speakers were coded to 2. Therefore, a positive DIF effect indicates a tendency of Spanish speakers to score higher on specific items than English speakers, given the same trait level (i.e., perceived self-efficacy). As a result, two items (items 2 and 5) were flagged by the modification indices (see Figure 6.15). By examining the signs of E.P.C. values, the Spanish group had tendencies to score lower on item 2 and higher on item 5 than the English group, given the same level of the trait (perceived emotional self-efficacy).

Next, the respecified model was fit to the data by removing the constraint of DIF = 0 for items 2 and 5. As a result, the DIF parameters were estimated to be −0.456 and 0.470 for items 2 and 5, respectively. These DIF parameter estimates are in the original scale of the variables (for both items and the group indicator), which is more interpretable because they indicate the expected difference between the two groups in the scale of original item scores (0 to 10). We need to eventually make a decision whether to retain those items flagged as displaying DIF. One way is to evaluate the practical impact of retaining these items compared to the magnitude of the standard error of measurement (*SEM*). See Abell, Ryan, Kamata, and Citrolo (2006) as well as Abell, Ryan, and Kamata

		M.I.	E.P.C.	Std E.P.C.	StdYX E.P.C.
ON Statements					
X2	ON GROUP	10.346	−0.538	−0.538	−0.104
X5	ON GROUP	13.277	0.528	0.528	0.097

Figure 6.15 Modification indices output from Mplus for the DIF detection MIMIC model with the final 20-item PCSC data.

(2006) for the detailed procedure for this approach. For this example, the impact of retaining both items will not be large, given the magnitude of DIF (-0.456 and 0.470), which is less than 1 point.

Multiple-Group Confirmatory Factor Analysis. Multiple-group CFA modeling approaches an invariance study on CFA parameters directly, specifically on factor loadings. Therefore, an aspect of invariance that a multiple-group CFA invariance study typically looks at is referred to as *factorial invariance.* Essentially, multiple-group CFA fits the same CFA model for multiple groups simultaneously. By imposing constraints on some parts of the model to reflect variant parameters across groups, the procedure will detect what part of the CFA model is not invariant between groups.

Typically, a series of analyses are conducted and model fits are evaluated for each model. First, a completely invariant model that assumes exactly the same parameter values between groups is fit. This model represents factorial invariance. Also, a factor-loading variant model, where factor loadings are different between groups, is fit. This model represents lack of factorial invariance. Then, model fit of these two models are compared. If the factor-loading variant model does not display substantially better fit than the completely invariant model, factorial invariance between groups is supported. In this case, the analysis will stop here. On the other hand, if the factor-loading variant model shows substantially better fit, factorial invariance is not supported. In this case, analysis will continue, and models with locally variant factor loadings will be examined to explore where variant loadings exist.

For example, we examine factorial invariance between English and Spanish language groups in the simulated PSCS data by the multiple-group CFA approach. As described earlier, two multiple-group CFA models are fit to the data: a completely invariant model and a factor-loading variant model. Here, we assume a three-factor structure with the final 20 PSCS items for the simulated PSCS data. Mplus syntax for the two models are provided in Appendix A–3 & 4. Model fit results from Mplus are summarized in Table 6.5. Unlike the model comparisons we described earlier to decide which items might be removed from the

Table 6.5 Model Fit Results Examining Factorial Invariance with Multiple-Group CFA

	Completely invariant model	Factor-loading variant model
Chi-square	481.993	452.994
df for chi-square	371	351
CFI	0.983	0.984
TLI	0.982	0.983
AIC	38821	38832
BIC	39196	39291
ABIC	38914	38946
RMSEA	0.035	0.034
SRMR	0.058	0.037

scale, these two models are nested models, because they are based on the same set of observed variables (20 items) and latent factors (3 factors). Therefore, we can utilize a chi-square difference test and information criteria for model comparison, in addition to standardized indices. The chi-square statistic difference is $481.993 - 452.994 = 28.999$, with df of $371 - 351 = 20$. The critical value of the chi-square statistic with $df = 20$ is 31.410 at the α-level of 0.05. Readers may obtain a critical chi-square value from a chi-square distribution table available in most introductory statistics textbooks. Because the chi-square difference is smaller than this critical value, we do not have evidence for a better fit of the factor-loading variant model. Therefore, factorial invariance is supported based on the chi-square difference test. The same conclusion is obtained by evaluating the three information criteria (AIC, BIC, and ABIC): the values are smaller for the completely invariant model, indicating a better fit of the completely invariant model. Values for CFI, TLI, and RMSEA are almost identical between the two models, indicating no evidence for a better fit of the factor-loading variant model. SRMR is the only index that showed substantial improvement for the factor-loading variant model. Therefore, our final conclusion is that the factorial invariance is supported between English and Spanish language groups.

As mentioned earlier, our analysis regarding factorial invariance should stop here, because we did not find evidence for a better fit of the factor-loading variant model. However, we provide an outline of how we *would* proceed with our analysis if we indeed *had* found evidence for a lack of factorial invariance. The next step would be to impose variant loadings on each of the factors separately. In other words, we would set up three separate models: first with variant factor loadings for items only on the first factor, second with variant factor loadings for items only on the second factor, and third with variant factor loadings for items only on the third factor. Then, the model fit of each of these three models will be compared to the completely invariant model. This way, we will be able to reach more specific conclusions about a lack of factorial invariance by noting which factor is associated with variant factor loadings. As an example, Mplus syntax for the model with variant factor loadings only in the first latent factor is presented in Appendix A–5.

Note that the two invariance studies based on the MIMIC model and multiple-group CFA resulted in different conclusions. However, it is not surprising because the two approaches evaluated two different aspects of invariance—namely, DIF and factorial invariance. Furthermore, the demonstrations were based strictly on statistical inference regarding model fit. In other words, the magnitude of the DIF or factorial invariance was not assessed rigorously. It is recommended to evaluate such magnitude in practice before making any decision about variant characteristics of the scale or scale items. Note that it is still possible to investigate DIF through a multiple-group "mean–structure" CFA, by testing invariance of intercepts in the model. Also, there are many other ways to investigate invariance and DIF. Readers are referred to other resources for more details and other issues related to DIF and invariance study (e.g., Kamata & Vaughn, 2004; Marsh et al., 2005; Tersi, 2006).

NEEDS FOR ITEM RESPONSE THEORY MODELS

So far, many data analysis methods have been described in this book. However, one needs to be aware that they all assumed that item response data are continuous variables. In other words, in the classical categorization of levels of measurement, item data were treated as interval-scale variables. Precisely speaking, this is unfortunately not a correct treatment of the data for a majority of test/scale items, although in many applications, this fortunately does not become an issue. However, we also need to be aware that in some applications, we have to depart from this interpretation and treat items truly as categorical variables. When we do so, we may rely on a class of psychometric modeling referred to as item response theory (IRT) modeling.

Typically, responses to items are represented in response categories. In the case of true–false or yes–no response items, they are dichotomous variables that are represented by only two values, such as 0 and 1. In the case of Likert-type scale items, we will have more response categories, but they are still categorical variables. Technically, we should not treat any categorical variable as continuous. However, it is not uncommon to do so in many applications. For example, we often see researchers compute means of item scores on Likert-type items. Such a practice may not be drastically bad when we have many response categories with evidence that item responses are not severely skewed. However, in extreme cases (i.e., when items have very few response categories, such as two), treating the variables as continuous is strongly discouraged. In such a case we must treat items as dichotomously scored categorical variables.

This distinction between continuous and categorical variables is analogous to the use of the regular regression model versus the use of the logistic or ordinal logistic regression model. Many of us know that it is unacceptable to use a regular multiple regression when we have a dichotomous outcome variable. The most obvious problem that such a modeling will encounter is a possibility of out-of-range predicted values. There are several other critical issues of which we have to be aware. See Long (1997) for an example of detailed discussions on this problem. The same is true for factor analysis. When we have dichotomously scored items (which are outcome variables), we should not use a factor analysis model that assumes they are continuous variables—we have to use a factor analysis model for categorical variables. In addition, because Pearson product–moment correlations for dichotomous variables are largely affected by the proportions of respondents who endorsed items (called "P-value" in psychometric literature), results of factor analysis may be unexpectedly affected by the P-values. Therefore, if we treat dichotomous items as continuous variables in a factor analysis, described factor structure can be unexpectedly a reflection of similarities in P-values of items, rather than relationships between items based on content similarities. On the other hand, when we have more than two ordered categories, the decision to use an ordinal logistic regression or a regular multiple regression will depend on factors, including the number of response categories, the shapes of data distributions, and sample size. To justify the use of a regular regression model, having more categories and symmetrically distributed variables would be more desirable. On the other hand, a categorical variable treatment does not require many response categories (in fact, fewer categories are easier to deal with), and it does not require symmetric data distributions. However, categorical data analysis requires a larger sample. The same logic applies to the context of factor analysis. For dichotomous response items, there is no question that we must use a factor analysis for categorical variables. For items with three or more response categories, we are advised to evaluate our data to make a decision whether to stay with a regular factor analysis or a factor analysis for categorical variables.

A factor analysis model with categorical variables (items) is a distinctive class of modeling, although it is quite similar to the regular factor analysis in many aspects. In traditional psychometric literature, such a modeling framework is referred to as IRT modeling. In a more modern structural equation modeling framework, such distinction need not to be explicit, because IRT and CFA with categorical indicators are under the same modeling framework. See Kamata and Bauer (2008) for more detailed discussion about the relationship between the two.

Here, we present only one type of item response model—namely, a two-parameter logistic (2-PL) IRT model for dichotomous items, which is equivalent to a one-factor factor analysis model with categorical indicators. The 2-PL IRT model can be written as

$$p_{ij} = \frac{\exp\left[\lambda_i \xi_j + \tau_i\right]}{1 + \exp\left[\lambda_i \xi_j + \tau_i\right]},$$

where p_{ij} is the probability to endorse item i by respondent j. ξ_j is the trait level of a respondent j, λ_i is the discrimination power of item i, and τ_i is the threshold of item i. ([τ is a Greek letter that is pronounced "tau."] As mentioned earlier, λ and ξ are pronounced "lamda" and "ksi," respectively. Also, "exp" is a mathematical exponential function.) In many IRT applications, the threshold is transformed into the difficulty parameter β_i by $\beta_i = -\tau_i/\lambda_i$, such that the inside of the exponential function has a form of $\lambda_i(\xi_j - \beta_i)$. The metric of ξ_j and β_i are typically scaled in a standardized scale, with a SD of 1. Conceptually, item discrimination λ_i, is analogous to factor loading, and threshold τ_i is analogous to intercept in the regular factor analytic model with continuous indicators. Thus, the 2PL IRT model is essentially the dichotomous item version of the one-factor CFA model. Note that this basic 2PL IRT model can be extended to models with multiple factors as well as for more than two response categories. In IRT literature, a model with multiple factors is referred to as a multidimensional IRT model, while a model with more than two response category items is referred to as a polytomous IRT model. Also, a multidimensional polytomous IRT model is possible.

Practically, it takes minimal effort to implement IRT modeling if we approach it from the CFA perspective. For example, in Mplus, all one needs to do is specify that items are categorical variables in the syntax by adding CATEGORICAL ARE keyword under the VARIABLE statement. Let's assume a hypothetical example where we have a 10-item scale with only one factor, where respondents are asked to answer yes or no to the statement in each item. To fit the 2PL IRT model to this data set, Mplus syntax should look like in Figure 6.16. It shows that this is essentially the same as what a regular one-factor CFA model specification would be, with the exception of an additional line CATEGORICAL ARE x1-x10 under the VARIABLE statement. Results of data analysis on computer-simulated responses from hypothetical 500 respondents on a unidimensional scale with 10 dichotomously scored items are presented in Table 6.6. With the specification shown in the syntax in Figure 6.16, parameter estimates are actually already fully standardized. Therefore, factor loadings (or item discrimination parameters in IRT terminology)

Table 6.6 Results of Illustrative IRT Analysis on 10-Item Dichotomously
Scored Items

Item	Discrimination	Threshold (Difficulty)
1	0.480	0.473(0.985)
2	0.412	−0.542(−1.316)
3	0.430	0.197(0.457)
4	0.514	0.233(0.452)
5	0.494	−0.126(−0.255)
6	0.155	−0.121(−0.777)
7	0.528	−0.369(−0.699)
8	0.503	−0.217(−0.432)
9	0.501	−0.548(−1.094)
10	0.401	0.462(1.153)

```
TITLE:     Hypothetical IRT model setup
DATA:      FILE IS exampleIRT.dat;
VARIABLE: NAMES ARE x1-x10;
           CATEGORICAL ARE x1-x10;
MODEL:     ksi BY x1* x2-x10;
           ksi@1.0;
```

Figure 6.16 Mplus syntax for a hypothetical 10-item
scale with dichotomously scored items.

can be interpreted as a correlation coefficient between the latent factor
and the item directly out of the standard output without further transformations. Note that this interpretation is true because of the explicit
specification in the syntax in Figure 6.16. The scale of parameters can
be quite different depending on how the model parameters and estimation method are specified. See Kamata and Bauer (2008) for more
detailed discussion on this matter. Results show that all items have similar magnitude of discriminations (ranging approximately 0.40–0.53 in
the scale of correlation), with the exception of item 6 with substantially lower correlation (0.155) than others. Therefore, from the scale
development point of view, we shall flag item 6 for a possible removal
from the scale. On the other hand, thresholds vary from item to item.

Thresholds are easier to interpret if they are transformed into difficulty. As mentioned earlier, difficulty is obtained by dividing the threshold by the corresponding discrimination. Note that Mplus estimates threshold in opposite sign; therefore, the transformation of a threshold into a difficulty is achieved simply by dividing a threshold by the corresponding factor loading without changing its sign (e.g., 0.480/0.473 = 0.985 for item 1). Then, difficulties can be interpreted in the standardized scale. Mplus actually provides transformed difficulty values in its output. In IRT, the difficulty of 0 indicates that the difficulty of the item is the same level as the mean of the latent trait. In other words, a respondent with the "average" level of trait has a 50% chance of endorsing the item. For item 1, because its item difficulty was 0.985, the item is relatively difficult to be endorsed; examinees about 1 *SD* higher than the mean trait level have 50% chance of endorsing the item. If the trait level of an examinee is lower, then the probability of endorsing the item will be lower than 50%. On the other hand, item 2 is an easy item. It takes trait level of 1.3 *SD*s lower than the mean trait level to have 50% chance of endorsing the item. For higher trait levels, the probability of endorsing the item will be much higher and approaches 1.0 as the trait level increases. In a process of scale development, items with considerably low discrimination (e.g., below 0.30 in the fully standardized scale) or extremely easy or difficult items (e.g., absolute value of difficulty greater than 2.0) should be flagged for potentially being removed from the scale.

IRT can be extended in a similar way as we demonstrated in previous sections, such as evaluation of factor loadings (item discriminations) in a multidimensional case, a MIMIC modeling for DIF detection, and a multiple-group CFA for factorial invariance study. Another useful note for Mplus is that it does not limit the number of response categories to two. It detects the number of response categories from the data, and the user does not have to specify such information. Note that the number of threshold parameters is the number of response categories minus 1. So, when items have more than two response categories, more than one threshold parameter will be estimated. Moreover, a scale can contain a mixture of items with different numbers of response categories, and Mplus can handle such a case without any additional specifications.

However, one needs to be cautioned that if items have different numbers of response categories, derivation of reported scores should not be based on summed total scores. Rather, scoring should rely on the factor scores of the IRT model, ξ_j, which is sometimes referred to as "theta-scores" in IRT literature. Scoring based on IRT models is beyond the scope of this book, and readers interested in IRT scoring and more details on IRT models are referred to excellent textbooks on IRT, such as Embretson and Reise (2000).

CONCLUSION

Our attempts have been to provide a good overview of factor analytic procedures in a context of test/instrument score validation. We covered both EFA and CFA. One critical question is which one should be utilized, EFA or CFA. In general, choice between the two should depend on whether we have a specific theory about the factor structure for the data. As mentioned earlier in this chapter, when we do have such a theory, CFA is a better choice. On the other hand, when we do not have such a theory, EFA is a better choice. Given that rapid assessment instrument (RAI) development should be based on a clearly defined domain and subdomains, our choice is CFA as a primary tool for RAI development. EFA can still be utilized as a supplement tool to identify potential problems, such as flagging items as we demonstrated in this chapter. However, we believe CFA should remain as a primary tool in scale validation process. Readers who wish to attain broader knowledge in factor analysis are referred to other overview articles on factor analysis (e.g., Kahn, 2006) and excellent textbooks of factor analysis (e.g., Brown, 2006; Gorsuch, 1983; B. Thompson, 2004).

7

Integration and Enhancement of Psychometric Evidence

INTEGRATING PSYCHOMETRIC EVIDENCE

As we have shown, development and validation of rapid assessment instruments is an ambitious task requiring clear thinking, carefully executed methodology, and sophisticated interpretation of complex and potentially contradictory results. Making sense of the wide range of information generated about scales and their performance requires a creative approach balancing respect for conventions and standards with an appreciation for their limitations.

In this final chapter, we summarize some of the critical concerns we've previously detailed and attempt to provide some realistic guidance on making final decisions regarding scale composition, structure, interpretation, and application. It is rare for a carefully conducted validation study to completely "fail." Still, developers should be prepared to honestly critique what has (and has not) been achieved, to present findings so that their methods can be replicated by interested others, and to provide appropriate guidance to those who will use the measure in practice or research contexts.

TYING IT ALL TOGETHER

From start to finish, an abundance of evidence is established on the focus, coherence, and functioning of a scale. Pieces of the puzzle range from the clarity of its conceptualization through the intuitive and subjective impressions it prompts to the consistency and accuracy of scores on its items and domains. As we wrote in Chapter 1, assembling all of this information is not an entirely linear process. Neither is it purely conceptual or quantitative. While we have tried to show an integrated sequence and progression, we've also noted that developers need to envision future, "late-stage" steps in the process (i.e., issues in an oblique vs. orthogonal factor rotation) from the very beginning. Deciding whether a construct lends itself to uni- or multidimensional measurement will shape the development of item pools, instructions to expert review panelists, and the selection of convergent and discriminant construct validity indicators and will have implications for scale utility and burden. Knowing who the ultimate respondents are likely to be will color the reading level of scale items and the dialect included, will determine who should be recruited for large-sample validation, and will guide future decisions regarding score interpretation and social validity. Holding all of this together seems (and is) a large task. As summarized in Figure 7.1, the major topics to be balanced are many. Although the sequence of topics in the figure reflects our ordering of them in the preceding chapters, here we will point out how that flow might be adjusted in the actual execution of a study.

CONSTRUCT CONCEPTUALIZATION

Finding the focus for construct conceptualization is usually much more time-consuming than developers imagine. Particularly when the construct in question is subjective, abstract, and can only truly be expressed secondarily, through the self-reporting of the respondent. As we have shown, wrestling with constructs like self-efficacy is considerably more challenging than counting consumption of cigarettes.

Responsibility for "getting it right" when deciding what to measure, how, and for whom ultimately falls to the scale developer. Pulling it

Chapter	Component
2	Consider what to measure, how, and for whom
	Select scale structure and format, considering readability, scale length, and burden
	Create scale items and response formats, considering scoring and interpretation
3	Design validation study
	Determine sample: who, how, how many
	Develop data collection instrument: components, layout, length, sequence
	Anticipate recruitment and training of associates, labor and costs, data entry and management
4	Examine evidence of reliability
	Determine appropriate forms: test/retest, interrater, internal consistency
	Compute and interpret coefficients (i.e. coefficient alpha, *SEM*)
	Consider implications for item retention or deletion
5	Examine evidence of validity
	Determine appropriate forms: face, content, convergent and discriminant construct, criterion
	Compute and interpret coefficients (i.e. means, correlations)
	Consider implications for item retention or deletion, and interpretations of scale scores
	Assess scale sensitivity and specificity
6	Examine factor structure
	Determine appropriate technique: CFA, EFA, or both
	Compute and interpret coefficients (i.e. correlations, factor loadings, Kaiser criterion, fit indices)
	Consider examination of item invariance
	Consider implications of response option level of measurement
	Consider implications for item retention or deletion, factor structure, scale score interpretation, and instrument application

Figure 7.1 Components of scale development.

off, however, is almost never a solo achievement. Flexibility and genuine humility are assets when receiving critique on a first draft of items. The time and trouble taken to identify and recruit focus group members or expert panelists can only pay off if their feedback is thoughtfully considered in shaping the item pool adopted for validation. At the same time, such "small sample" input might also be taken with a grain of salt. Presumably, the developer has spent considerable time reviewing the conceptual and empirical literature, knows a thing or two about the "real-world" context in which a construct will be applied, and is something of an expert is his or her own right. Consequently, the first "hard call" in scale development can come early when weighing whether or not to drop, add, or reword items based on such initial feedback. In this context, examination of face and content validity, which is detailed in Chapter 5, is actually conducted near the end of initial instrument design.

As indicated earlier, these decisions will be easier if the focus group members or panelists were carefully selected to begin with and given very clear instructions for their tasks. As in all other aspects of validation, separating signal from noise will be easier if there are fewer reasons to doubt the integrity of the information being assessed.

DESIGNING THE VALIDATION STUDY

Methodological decisions in psychometric studies are just as important as selecting and operationalizing the target construct. At this stage, much hard work has already been accomplished, and the emphasis shifts to thinking through each step in establishing evidence of reliability and validity. The capacity to see the big picture becomes crucial, as the developer envisions sampling; composition, layout, length, and sequence of the data collection instrument; and all the issues and aspects of actual data collection.

Many things can go wrong, and in some cases, the only way to correct for errors is to start over with a fresh sample, fresh site, or revised data collection instrument. Some errors (i.e., mishandling of respondents, failing to follow through on procedures for informed consent, or protection of respondents' identities) can even trigger requirements for event reporting to institutional review boards. All of these can be costly, so the motivations to anticipate and avoid them are huge.

As indicated in Chapter 3, so-called clinical samples are almost always preferable to nonclinical samples, although the latter can and do have their place. We have tried to show that firm standards for determining sample size remain elusive. An active debate continues in the literature, and developers should be mindful not only of minimal requirements of the statistical procedures they plan but also the preferences and biases of the venues where they intend to publish or apply their findings. Acknowledging that there may be more than one "acceptable" decision does not free developers from providing a good defense of whatever position they ultimately take. When it comes to sampling, developers must justify their decisions about desirable respondent characteristics and show that they have meaningfully considered or included potential respondents in scale development and design and have respected both informed consent and voluntary participation in sample selection.

The actual, complete data collection instrument becomes a project in itself, requiring thoughtful anticipation of variables needed to test validation hypotheses, identification and incorporation of suitable standardized instruments and single-item indicators, and consideration of how components are positioned in relation to each other. As we wrote in Chapter 3, there is a large literature on content and layout of surveys, including implications for probable response rates and biases.

Although these issues may seem less critical than those we have previously considered, short-changing the attention paid to them can bring a heavy price. If the data collection instrument is confusing, lacks sufficient "white space," or causes distress by the way topics are worded or placed, then all the previous effort can go down the drain. Piloting an initial version of the instrument on a small sample can be just as important as the use of focus groups and expert panelists when designing the new scale. Getting an accurate estimate of time needed for completion can help in gauging respondent burden, and learning where phrases or instructions are confusing can lead to debugging before the major commitment to full-scale validation is made.

If research associates are needed to help in data collection, then training them in all aspects of the process is crucial. Mistakes or outright violation of procedures approved by an institutional review board (IRB) for research with human participants can lead to unnecessary loss or even forfeiture of data. Obviously, the old saying that "an ounce of prevention is worth a pound of cure" applies when it comes to making sure everyone involved understands the study procedures and is prepared to follow through.

The same goes for training of those who will enter and manage data for analysis. There is little more regrettable than learning that accurately collected data was sloppily entered or cleaned, leading to misleading or critically flawed analyses. Often, mistakes like these can be corrected but not without considerable delays and costs. It's worth noting here that delegating can be dangerous, as developers who place too much faith in the competence of associates risk coming to false conclusions about the strengths or weaknesses of their measures. Once peer-reviewed and published, these errors may live on indefinitely in the literature, misleading many about the merits of a scale.

EVIDENCE OF RELIABILITY

One of the first fully quantitative steps in examining psychometric evidence is to estimate the reliability or consistency of scale responses. The evidence will indicate whether or not the developer has been on the right track in creating an item pool reflecting a common construct. Interpreting coefficient α and α-if-item-deleted statistics can guide retention of strong items and flag weak ones for potential deletion. The analyses are easy to produce, and the interpretations are generally straightforward. All of this is initially provisional, however, because such examinations are limited to considering how responses to items within a specific pool relate to a total score based on them and do not address whether and how their responses might relate to other components of a multidimensional scale. Still, if the larger plan for initial analyses is to proceed with a confirmatory factor analysis (CFA), finding strong α coefficients in an early run can be encouraging, as they suggest that some of the intended structure for the new scale may be present. Items flagged as "problematic" at this stage can be tracked in subsequent analyses to see whether evidence continues to "stack up" against them or whether an apparently weak contribution in this context is offset by strengths in others.

Therefore, early estimates of reliability are both informative and inconclusive. They illustrate the interdependent nature of psychometric evidence, as they address only a piece of a larger and much more complex picture. Computations of the standard error of measurement (*SEM*) are best reserved until after other considerations have been factored in, and the developer wishes to close the reliability discussion with calculation and assessment of this feature.

EXAMINING FACTOR STRUCTURE

Although we reserve detailed coverage of factor structure for Chapter 6, conventionally, it is often the next step in examining psychometric evidence. And the results obtained may prompt a reconsideration of scale (and subscale) composition, leading to reanalysis of internal consistency. In the best of all possible worlds, developers get strong, confirming evidence at each step of scale analysis. When this ideal is achieved, describing the methodology in replicable form is straightforward, and others can easily follow along as decisions regarding scale composition and characteristics emerge. When, as is more often the case, assessment of factor structure identifies "imperfections" in the form, for instance, of weak loadings, cross-loadings, or poor fit indices, then a more complex process is engaged. The corresponding decisions on item retention or deletion, respecification of hypothesized measurement models, or the search for meaning in a newly emerging set of factors (e.g., resulting from an exploratory factor analysis), can create a confusing web of overlapping analyses.

Although there are no fast and firm answers, we have attempted to summarize key considerations in selecting a factor analytic technique. The most basic of these is whether to begin with an exploratory or confirmatory approach, and both have their defenders. In general, it seems reasonable to apply confirmatory techniques when analyzing scales developed from specific conceptual or theoretical bases and to use exploratory techniques when such initial analyses fail or when there was no prior conceptual foundation. As we have illustrated, there are also good grounds for deviating from these views, and ultimately, we leave the decision to the developer. Whichever approach is taken, factor analysis applies increasingly sophisticated tools to answering the very basic question of how many constructs are captured by a scale. Whether these confirm the constructs originally intended or discover others emergent in respondents' scores is ultimately less significant than whether the developer had good reason to select whichever approach was applied and the skill to interpret the results accurately.

As detailed in Chapter 6, determination of scale structure can be further complicated by concerns for differences influenced by the level of measurement built into response options or variations associated with specific respondent characteristics like cultural identification or primary language. We have illustrated techniques for accounting for both of these concerns, and developers should not underestimate the sophistication required to interpret findings appropriately. Finding statistically significant variability in item responses across language groups, for instance, will not necessarily lead to conclusions that the observed effects are practically significant. In other words, as with interpretations of coefficients discussed elsewhere in this text, developers should avoid jumping to the conclusion that when a sophisticated analytic technique yields statistically significant results, changes in scale composition are inevitable. As with items "flagged" as problematic in content validity or reliability analyses, indications of imperfections emerging here should also be considered with the larger psychometric picture in mind. What is gained and what is lost by altering scale composition based on any single indicator?

The challenges for the developer are twofold: to apply good standards in the use of decision rules associated with each form of analysis and to carefully log these decisions referencing the data guiding them, the sequence in which they were implemented, and the resulting interpretations. See the *Standards* (c.f. American Educational Research Association et al., 1999) for detailed conventions on clear reporting of both methods and their resulting evidence.

EVIDENCE OF VALIDITY

Throughout this text, we have emphasized the broad interpretation of construct validation and the long history of its evolution in psychometric literature. Already in this chapter we have considered the place of several forms of validity evidence in the development of a rapid assessment instrument (RAI). Here, our emphasis is to briefly acknowledge that in the practical order of things, it is only *after* the item pool for a scale has been conceptually affirmed, *after* initial assessments of its reliability have been considered, and *after* its factor structure has been determined that it really makes sense to consider the accuracy of meaning associated with scale scores. In these terms, evidence of convergent, discriminant, and criterion validities are reserved until other fundamental characteristics have been established. Doing so beforehand would be premature, as examining the association of vaguely established scale scores with other validation indicators could become irrelevant if some of the items contributing to those scale scores were later abandoned or realigned.

In a sense, reaching the stage in analyses where testing convergent, discriminant, and criterion-based hypotheses becomes defensible is good cause for some early celebration. The content of a RAI has been intuitively affirmed by experts, and its scores have been shown to cluster consistently in anticipated or newly emergent patterns. Not bad (and sadly, after all this work, reducible to a single sentence!). Still, developers may draw a big breath of anticipation here, because the icing on the cake turns out to be pretty important. This is when quantitative evidence for whether and how well the scale measures what it was intended to measure is finally examined.

As we have shown, constructing these hypotheses is a major challenge in itself. A lot has been written on considerations in identifying what factors should and should not correlate with others, and the literature is often thin or inconclusive. When good theory does exist, available standardized scales may not. When scales are identified, they may be unsuitable for the population of interest, too long, or too expensive to be included in the data collection instrument. We remind readers of the financial advisers' maxim that "past performance is no guarantee of future success," meaning here that even when instruments were included based on their track record elsewhere, their performance in the present context cannot be taken for granted. A recheck of their reliability in the validation sample is a minimal cross-check before their use in testing subsequent hypotheses, and the results should be included in written reports.

Single-item indicators are one plausible alternative. Their low burden is an obvious strength, but their lack of established meaning in the literature is an offsetting weakness. Between the challenges of identifying theoretically and empirically sound relationships and finding suitable measures to reflect them, developers may have struggled to get the right materials in place during data collection.

Conducting the tests themselves is reasonably straightforward, and we have provided some general guidelines for interpreting and reporting evidence of convergent and discriminant construct validity. Beyond that, developers may also have bases for examining evidence of criterion validity. In our brief discussion of scale sensitivity and specificity, we have illustrated some techniques for determining how accurately scale scores can be applied to diagnostic decisions. Details on determination of cut scores, like the identification of population prevalence rates, are beyond the scope of this text but can become relevant when assessing receiver operating characteristics. Interested readers are encouraged to dig further, beginning with the references provided.

BALANCING EVIDENCE AND PRAGMATICS

When developers are satisfied that their measure meets basic psychometric standards, they may find themselves in a position some would consider a luxury: making an additional round of decisions on final scale composition based on pragmatics. All things being equal, shorter scales are preferable to longer ones, as are measures that are easier to score and interpret (Hudson, 1982a). Although length, readability, and burden are of no value when a scale lacks evidence of reliability and validity, for scales that have those qualities, trade-offs can be considered. What is the ultimate the impact of adjusting a 23-item scale (11 items in one factor and 12 in another) to a 20-item scale with 10 items in each factor? If the α coefficients in the first format were 0.93 and 0.92, respectively, and once recalculated for the shorter version were 0.90 and 0.91, what real loss was incurred? If fit indices in a CFA have not appreciably suffered, and if inspection of item content reveals that nothing essential has been lost, then all factors considered together may support the decision to accept a slightly weaker set of psychometrics in return for a scale that is a little shorter and a little easier to use. Although this would hopefully have been examined beforehand, the result may even reduce a little unnecessary redundancy in item content.

Considered from the other point of view, a scale with exceptional (or even just adequate) psychometrics is useless if it is too long or too complicated to be appealing to the desired audience. What satisfies an academic might be irritating or anxiety-provoking to an intended respondent. The point (and this links back to the expectation that developers anticipate all aspects of scale validation while still in the design stage) is that the real value in a scale is in its capacity to give respondents a way to show or tell us how they really are. Lacking psychometrics, the scale will not be credible to researchers or practitioners. Failing to consider the needs and circumstances of those who administer, interpret, or take the scale may derail data collection entirely and stop the validation process in its tracks. As in all aspects of psychometrics, a balanced approach to design and, ultimately, to decisions on final scale composition is key. And the happiest endings are often driven by careful consideration from the start.

ENHANCING PSYCHOMETRIC EVIDENCE

In a sense, much of the material covered in this text amounts to "the basics," which is appropriate, we hope, for a pocket guide. Much can be accomplished using these techniques and strategies. Increasingly, however, developers recognize the need to tailor measures to specific target groups. The resulting scales are built to reflect particular gender, ethnic, or age perspectives, for instance, or are validated to yield reasonably comparable results across diverse contexts and characteristics. Succeeding in these goals requires attention to a host of details, including an appreciation of what is needed to bridge differences attributable to varying world views, problem definitions, and intended applications of new scales. We touch briefly here on a few relevant points.

Increasing Emphasis on Diversity: Translation and Cross-Cultural Assessment

Motivations to enhance evidence of validity in these ways are in part an outgrowth of the increasing appreciation for diversity within Western cultures and of the recognition that many problems confronting the social, behavioral, and health sciences cut across ethnic, cultural, and national boundaries. Scales built to accurately reflect such problems may have added advantages as they promote cross-cultural understanding and provide tools for comparing the impacts of programs and policies initially designed in one setting and implemented in another.

The debate over universal vs. culturally relevant ethics and standards is complex, intense, and well beyond the scope of this text (c.f. Healy, 2007; International Federation of Social Workers, 2005). Suffice it to say that scale developers engaged in multicultural or international work will find their efforts both welcome and vigorously critiqued as affected populations try to make sure their views and characteristics are respected and not misrepresented.

For evidence of the growing interest in and sophistication surrounding these topics, we can look to the rich literature on translation and cross-cultural validation (c.f. van de Vijver & Tanzer, 2004; van de Vijver & Poortinga, 1997; van de Vijver & Hambleton, 1996). A special issue of *Medical Care* (Teresi, Stewart, Morales, & Stahl, 2006) focused on techniques for establishing evidence of cross-cultural equivalence in health-related measures, overviewing both qualitative and quantitative methods in a series of articles with broad application to related fields. The explosion of psychometric studies addressing cross-cultural concerns is impressive and encouraging, detailing—to name only a few—measures of depressive symptoms among Vietnamese Americans (Tran, Ngo, & Conway, 2003), youth quality of life for Latino children and adolescents (Chavez, Matías-Carrelo, Barrio, & Canino, 1006), and Arabic versions of quality-of-life measures for general populations or people with particular diseases (Halabi, 2006).

In their taxonomy of bias and equivalence, van de Vijver and Tanzer (2004) summarize what are at once highly intuitive and complex topics that, like other aspects of psychometric jargon, overlap in ways that require careful attention from cross-cultural scale developers. Bias can be thought of as "the generic term for nuisance factors in cross-cultural score comparisons" (2004, p. 120), rendering inferences invalid because score differences based on the poorly conceptualized scales do not correspond to actual respondent differences on the trait or ability of interest. Equivalence (illustrated in Chapter 6) can be thought of as the opposite of bias, and is demonstrated quantitatively when individual item responses are shown not to vary meaningfully where scale scores in referent groups are held constant. Both of these concepts must be considered when establishing evidence of cross-cultural validity.

Three forms of bias in scale development are proposed (van de Vijver & Poortinga, 1997). *Construct bias* occurs when the target construct is not experienced or understood in the same ways across groups of interest. Tran, Ngo, & Conway (2003), for instance, concluded that when describing depression, somatic complaints ("nerves, headaches, and 'problems of the heart,'" p. 56) were much more common among Vietnamese people than their Western counterparts. *Method bias* may be problematic across all items in a scale when cultural factors unrelated to the construct of interest impact scores differently across groups. Comfort with response options, or different views on the appropriateness of self-disclosure, for example, can affect scale scores for reasons that have little to do with the actual subject of measurement. Chavez et al. (2007) changed the position and anchoring of response options originally structured as semantic differentials to improve comfort and ease potential confusion among Latino respondents. *Item bias* (often referenced as differential item functioning, or DIF) occurs when "different groups with the same score on the construct, commonly operationalized as the score on the instrument, do not have the same expected score on (individual) item(s)" (van de Vijver & Poortinga, 1997, p. 30). We have previously discussed this as the topic of item *invariance*, demonstrated when individual item scores are shown not to vary, and establishing the conceptual and empirical link with scale equivalence. Teresi (2006) provides a detailed synopsis of the problem and potential remedies drawing on studies in health assessment.

Returning to van de Vijver and colleagues' taxonomy, there are also three types of equivalence. *Construct equivalence* (also called structural or functional equivalence) is achieved when the understanding of a construct and the term(s) typically used to describe it are fundamentally the same from culture to culture (van de Vijver & Tanzer, 2004). Its opposite, construct *inequivalence*, exists when cultural understandings and expressions vary. Reflecting on what it means to be a "good" son or daughter, for example, might lead to very different conclusions in Western as contrasted to Eastern cultures. *Measurement unit equivalence* exists when the units carry the same meanings and interpretations across cultures. In the same way that we cannot compare temperatures reflected as Fahrenheit or Celsius scores without appropriate conversions, we risk measurement inequivalence if we assume that differentiations based on "none," "a little," "a lot," or "all" mean the same thing from one group to another. Finally, *scalar equivalence* (or *full-scale* equivalence) is achieved when measures across groups or contexts have the same origin (e.g., representation of complete absence of the quality of interest) and unit of measurement (e.g., using a Celsius scale to measure temperature in both settings). Unless it can be shown that item responses do not systematically favor one group over another, understandings of real cross-cultural differences or similarities in scale scores cannot be achieved. When fully realized, scalar equivalence "assumes completely bias-free measurement" (2004, p. 122). This seeming abstraction is nevertheless the ideal in cross-cultural instrument development.

Sources of measurement bias and strategies for identifying it have been usefully summarized in a number of the references cited here. The reader is referred to them for greater detail. Many of the recommended remedies begin in careful translation, including clear thinking about whether the initial goal is to *apply* (literally translating an existing instrument from one language to another),*adapt* (modifying stimuli, response options, or both to achieve a new scale that is similar but not exactly matched to the original), or *assemble* (essentially abandoning the substance and form of the original scale and building a new measure more suited to capturing closely related constructs in a new culture) (van de Vijver & Hambleton, 1996).

We will illustrate translation processes a bit further later. Meanwhile, one very useful caution can be drawn from Halabi's (2006) development of Arabic quality-of-life measures. In an admirable and carefully conducted study, the author concluded that "thirteen Arabic disease-specific versions of the Quality of Life Index are ready for use with Arabic speaking clients anywhere in the world" (p. 609). This prompted a thoughtful critique, as Rassool (2006) sought to respectfully place some boundaries on Halabi's claim. Summarizing the great complexity of Arabic cultures and language, he cited work from the National Resource Center for Translation and Interpretation, writing that "Translation, of course, is an impossible task. No version of any sentence in one language can possibly capture the semantic richness, phonic structure, syntactic form and connotative allusiveness of a sentence in another language" (Petrey, 1984, in Rassool, 2006, p. 610). Having made his point, he concluded by admiring the methodological rigor attempted and lauding what was "only the beginning of this challenging endeavor" (2006, p. 611).

Psychometric studies conducted on diverse samples take on multiple levels of complexity as all of the steps previously described are reconsidered in light of challenges posed by engaging diverse groups. Construct conceptualization must be filtered through values and practices specific to the reference groups; biases toward and risks associated with disclosure or candor must be taken into account; and methodological issues such as ownership or sharing of data, use of incentives for respondents, and interpretation of meaning when data are analyzed all become crucial.

All-in-all, this is no simple task. And the degree to which developers succeed in recruiting appropriate participation of reference group members and following through on commitments to respect principles of cross-cultural collaborations can make or break the ultimate interpretation and utility of the new measure.

BILINGUAL VALIDATION

Throughout these chapters, many of our illustrations have been built around two scales, the Family Responsibility Scale (FRS) and the Parental Self-Care Scale (PSCS). Evidence of validity for both measures was originally examined on bilingual (Spanish and English) samples, as detailed in their primary references (Abell, Ryan, & Kamata, 2006; Abell, Ryan, Kamata et al., 2006). In Chapter 6, we illustrated techniques for examining item invariance where the goal was to determine whether English and Spanish versions of the scales based on the same items were functionally equivalent. Here, we concentrate briefly on steps taken during the design phase to create item pools capturing the same constructs for both groups.

Translation Processes

Most scale developers are not linguists, although they would do well to recruit their support when undertaking a bilingual validation. Unexamined conventions in word usage, generally taken for granted by the dominant culture in any setting, can lead not only to misinterpretations of meaning but to reinforced experiences that those who view themselves as "in charge" of a particular situation are actually clueless of what is really going on in a cross-cultural exchange (Dominelli, 2004). Whether or not this is intentional, the consequences can be severe. If recognized early, there may be time for correction. If not, scale development can proceed through many steps before the unfortunate realization that poorly chosen wording in the beginning has resulted in an item pool that fails to really capture the reference group's experience.

Zometa, et al. (2007) provided some excellent examples in an instrument developed for the U.S. Centers for Disease Control and Prevention to assess HIV/AIDS knowledge and attitudes. They determined that *zancudo* was a better term than *mosquito* in Spanish for questions about the HIV transmission myth involving an "insect that sucks blood from people" (p. 237). Similarly, they chose the Spanish word *chorro* over the phrase *los tomaderos de agua* for referring to drinking water out of a fountain, because the former term was more commonly used by adolescents, a key target group for the developers' risk assessment and prevention goals.

In her thesis emphasizing clear communications in health education materials, Diệu-Hiền (2002) provides an excellent summary of potential translation pitfalls and strategies for avoiding them. These reflect and are usefully augmented by the 22 guidelines formulated by the International Test Commission, providing recommendations on translation context, instrument development and adaptation, administration, and documentation/score interpretation (Vijver & Hambleton,1996; Hambleton, 1994).

Observing that words or concepts only achieve meaning when anchored in their cultural and social contexts, Diệu-Hiền advises that translators must not only be fluent in at least two languages but also familiar with the subject matter of the target material. This became clear when attempting to discuss oral sex as a component of HIV risk prevention, only to learn that in Vietnamese, the phrase had no meaning, as "sex" was interpreted exclusively to mean penetrative intercourse. A translator must understand not only the formal meanings of terms, but also the potential for their being misunderstood or misinterpreted in specific contexts.

People using translators (rather than performing the task themselves) are advised to evaluate the language skills of the translator, considering how each language was acquired and which is primary, and to assess his or her bicultural skills, determining the settings and types of interactions in which they were engaged. The goal is to be assured of technical ability but, beyond that, to gain comfort with the way a translator approaches the understanding of context-specific meaning. As illustrated by Zometa et al. (2007), more than one word may technically "do the job," but digging a little deeper reveals that one particular form is much more likely to capture the desired information.

For scale developers, taking care to get it right in the beginning can be challenging, particularly when they know the many methodological steps required down the road and feel impatient to get going. The bottom line regarding enhancement of evidence in these ways is that haste really can make waste. In responding to growing demands for scales suitable for multilingual and cross-cultural applications, developers must accept the reality that achieving the desired ends means avoiding short cuts and settling into a sustained process where attention to detail is critical.

REVISITING VALIDATION: RAISING EXPECTATIONS AND MAXIMIZING GAINS

Throughout this text, we have attempted to balance a holistic, integrated view of psychometrics with an appreciation for both the evolution of its history and the shortcomings faced by developers working within the current "state-of-the-art." Establishing evidence of scale score validity, sometimes considered a straightforward, even mechanical process, is in fact a nuanced, subtle weaving together of seemingly disparate information. And how do we account for all that "residual error," anyway?

Some of the tools and information we might desire are still evolving. Guidelines for applying statistical techniques and criteria for judging the adequacy of coefficients are continually advancing. The "gold standard" desirable for most criterion-based evidence of validity does not, in many cases, exist (Pepe, 2002), leaving developers with more approximations than absolutes against which to gauge their success. Although the central concepts of validation have remained relatively stable over the last 50 years, the methods available to assess them have expanded considerably, and many theoreticians and analysts have applied themselves to better understanding what we can and cannot claim about our ability to ground and objectify the subjective characteristics and capacities of others. This dynamism is what keeps the field so exciting.

It is a good thing, too, as many of those closest to the challenge have thought of validity as an unending process (c.f. Goldstein & Simpson, 2002; Nunnally & Bernstein, 1994). Starting with the acknowledgement that all psychometrics are sample-dependent, we are forced to recognize that even a very successful validation study applies only to those who were included or, where probability sampling was involved, to those from whom the sample was drawn in a given place and time. Broad replication of validation studies is rare, with the exception of the relatively small set of measures adopted as standards in their fields. And even those become eventually dated as the effort of further studies is abandoned or the basis on which a scale was built becomes irrelevant with changing times.

As indicated in our brief discussion on diversity, scales are almost never one-size-fits-all. The increased attention to matching all aspects of scale development to the diverse needs of intended users is necessary and welcome. But what should we be aiming for to justify all this effort?

BEYOND ENLIGHTENMENT TO INCREMENTAL VALIDITY

Unlike its spiritual interpretation, where the term means no less that the realization of truth, enlightenment in a measurement context refers to "an unbounded prediction" (Stickle & Weems, 2006, p. 214). Based on a scale score, we can know that an individual has particular tendencies or characteristics but not know exactly when or how they will be expressed. We gain a foothold on information but must acknowledge that its utility remains a bit unknown.

This goes to the heart of Witkin's question as introduced in Chapter 1 (2001, p. 104): "What can the test tell me beyond what I already know or could know about this individual?"

For Stickle and Weems, incremental validity means that for a scale to have value, it "has to give us information over and above what we have or could obtain in a cost and time-efficient manner by other means" (2006, p. 215). To learn, as did researchers validating a measure of pediatric anxiety, that "in fact, the single parent-reported item 'My child is shy' may be sufficient to signal the need for further assessment" (Bailey, Chavira, Stein, & Stein, 2006, p. 518) can be a bit of a let-down for developers and lead measurement critics to wonder what has really been achieved.

However, before we jump to conclusions, it may be best to remember that incremental validity, like the provisional and limited findings of all empirical research, rises or falls on the persistence of scale developers willing to put their assumptions to the test. Seen in a certain light, providing others with reliable and valid means to reveal something specific and clear about their experiences or abilities is a form of service. Finding the words that express just so an inner process, a point of vulnerability, or a latent strength can guide assessment and intervention and help keep all parties honest about what they are and are not about. In the process, RAIs may in fact play a meaningful part in enhancing understanding and directing change. Kept in perspective and interpreted with care, there is nothing so wrong with that.

Appendix

1. Mplus syntax for the first step in DIF detection with MIMIC model.

```
TITLE:      PSCS final 3 factor model with DIF
            analysis -Step 1

DATA:       FILE IS PSCS_combined.dat;

VARIABLE:   NAMES ARE x1-x30 group;
            USEVARIABLES ARE x1-x10 x12 x14-x17 x22
            x23 x26 x29 x30 group;

MODEL:      ksi1 BY x1-x10;
            ksi2 BY x12-x17;
            ksi3 BY x22-x30;

            ksi1 ksi2 ksi3 on group;
            x1-x30 on group@0;

OUTPUT:     STDYX;
            modindices;
```

2. Mplus syntax for the second step in DIF parameter estimation with MIMIC model.

```
TITLE:   PSCS final 3 factor model with DIF
         analysis -Step 2

DATA:    FILE IS PSCS_combined.dat;
```

```
VARIABLE:   NAMES ARE x1-x30 group;
            USEVARIABLES ARE x1-x10 x12 x14-x17 x22
            x23 x26 x29 x30 group;

MODEL:      ksi1 BY x1-x10;
            ksi2 BY x12-x17;
            ksi3 BY x22-x30;

            ksi1 ksi2 ksi3 on group;
            x1 on group@0;
            x2 on group;
            x3-x4 on group@0;
            x5 on group;
            x6-x30 on group@0;

OUTPUT:     STDYX;
            modindices;
```

3. Mplus syntax for the completely invariant multiple-group CFA model.

```
TITLE:      PSCS final 3 factor model - completely
            invariant MG

DATA:       FILE IS PSCS_combined.dat;

VARIABLE:   NAMES ARE x1-x30 group;
            USEVARIABLES ARE x1-x10 x12 x14-x17 x22
            x23 x26 x29 x30 group;
            GROUPING is group (1=English, 2=Spanish);

MODEL:      ksi1 BY x1* x2-x10;
            ksi2 BY x12* x14-x17;
            ksi3 BY x22* x23-x30;
            ksi1@1;
            ksi2@1;
            ksi3@1;

MODEL SPANISH:

OUTPUT:     STDYX;
            modindices;
```

4. Mplus syntax for the variant factor loading multiple-group CFA model

```
TITLE:   PSCS final 3 factor model - variant
         loadings

DATA:    FILE IS PSCS_combined.dat;
```

```
VARIABLE:    NAMES ARE x1-x30 group;
             USEVARIABLES ARE x1-x10 x12 x14-x17 x22
             x23 x26 x29 x30 group;
             GROUPING is group (1=English, 2=Spanish);

MODEL:       ksi1 BY x1* x2-x10;
             ksi2 BY x12* x14-x17;
             ksi3 BY x22* x23-x30;
             ksi1@1;
             ksi2@1;
             ksi3@1;

MODEL SPANISH:
             ksi1 BY x1* x2-x10;
             ksi2 BY x12* x14-x17;
             ksi3 BY x22* x23-x30;

OUTPUT:      STDYX;
             modindices;
```

5. Mplus syntax for the multiple group CFA model—variant factor loading only in the first latent factor.

```
TITLE:       PSCS final 3 factor model - variant
             loadings
             Only in the first factor

DATA:        FILE IS PSCS_combined.dat;

VARIABLE:    NAMES ARE x1-x30 group;
             USEVARIABLES ARE x1-x10 x12 x14-x17 x22
             x23 x26 x29 x30 group;
             GROUPING is group (1=English, 2=Spanish);

MODEL:       ksi1 BY x1* x2-x10;
             ksi2 BY x12* x14-x17;
             ksi3 BY x22* x23-x30;
             ksi1@1;
             ksi2@1;
             ksi3@1;

MODEL SPANISH:
             ksi1 BY x1* x2-x10;

OUTPUT:      STDYX;
             modindices;
```

References

Abell, N. (2001). Assessing willingness to care for persons with AIDS: Validation of a new measure. *Research on Social Work Practice, 11*(1), 118–130.

Abell, N., McDonnell, J., & Winters, J. (1992). Developing a measure of children's prosocial tendencies: An initial validation of a self-report instrument. *Journal of Social Service Research, 3/4*(16), 19–48.

Abell, N., Rutledge, S. E., & Whyte, J. (2007). Validation of the HIV/AIDS Provider Stigma Inventory. *Unpublished Manuscript.*

Abell, N., Ryan, S., & Kamata, A. (2006). Assessing capacity for self-care among HIV+ heads of household: Bilingual validation of the Parental Self-Care Scale. *Social Work Research, 30,* 233–243.

Abell, N., Ryan, S., Kamata, A., & Citrolo, J. (2006). Bilingual validation of the Family Responsibility Scale: Assessing stress among HIV+ heads of household. *Journal of Social Service Research, 32*(3), 195–212.

American Association of Social Workers. (1929). *Social casework, generic and specific: An outline. A report of the Milford Conference,* New York.

American Educational Research Association, American Psychological Association, & National Council on Measurement in Education. (1999). *Standards for Educational and Psychological Tests.* Washington, D.C.: American Educational Research Association.

Angoff, W. H. (1988). Validity: An evolving concept. In H. Wainer & H. Braun (Eds.), *Test Validity* (pp. 19–32). Hillsdale, NJ: Lawrence Erlbaum.

Anthony, E. J. & Cohler, B. J. (Eds.). (1987). *The Invulnerable Child.* New York: GuilfordPress.

Arbuckle, J. L. (2006). *Amos 7.0 User's Guide*. Chicago: SPSS.

Aroian, K. J. & Norris, A.-E. (2004). To transform or not transform skewed data for psychometric analysis. That is the question! *Nursing Research, 53*(1), 67–71.

Bailey, K. A., Chavira, D. A., Stein, M. T., & Stein, M. B. (2006). Brief measures to screen for social phobia in primary care pediatrics. *Journal of Pediatric Psychology, 31*(5), 512–521.

Beck, C. T. & Gable, R. K. (2001). Further validation of the Postpartum Depression Screening Scale. *Nursing Research, 50*(3), 155–164.

Bentler, P. M. & Wu, E. J. C. (1995). *EQS for Windows User's Guide*. Encino, CA:Multivariate Software, Inc.

Berger, C. S. & Ai, A. (2000). Managed care and its implications for social work curricula reform: Policy and research initiatives. *Social Work in Health Care, 31*(3), 59–82.

Bloom, M., Fischer, J., & Orme, J. G. (2006). *Evaluating Practice: Guidelines for the Accountable Professional* (5th ed.). Boston: Pearson.

Bonett, D. G. (2002). Sample size requirements for testing and estimating coefficient alpha. *Journal of Educational and Behavioral Statistics, 27*(4), 335–340.

Bridges, K. & Goldberg, D. (1989). Self-administered scales of neurotic symptoms. In C. Thompson (Ed.), *The Instruments of Psychiatric Research* (pp. 157–176). New York: John Wiley & Sons.

Brown, T. A. (2006). *Confirmatory Factor Analysis for Applied Research*. New York: Gilford Press.

Buckey, J. W. (2007). *Factors Affecting Life-Sustaining Treatment Decisions by Health Care Surrogates and Proxies*. Unpublished Doctoral Dissertation, Florida State University, Tallahassee.

Butler, S. F., Budman, S. H., Fernandez, K. C., Houle, B., Benoit, C., Katz, N., et al. (2007). Development and validation of the Current Opioid Misuse Measure. *Pain, 130*, 144–156.

Campbell, D. T. & Fiske, D. W. (1959). Convergent and Discriminant Validation by the Multitrait-Multimethod Matrix. *Psychological Bulletin, 56*(2), 81–105.

Cattell, R. B. (1966). The scree plot for the number of factors. *Multivariate Behavioral Research, 1*, 245–276.

Charter, R. A. (2001). Damn the precision, full speed ahead with the clinical interpretation. *Journal of Clinical and Experimental Neuropsychology, 23*(5), 692–694.

Clark, L. A. & Watson, D. (2003). *Constructing validity: Basic issues in objective scale development*. Washington, D.C.: American Psychological Association.

Chavez, L.M., Matías-Carrelo, L., Barrio, C., & Canino, G. (2007). The cultural adaptation of the Youth Quality of Life Instrument-Research Version for Latino children and adolescents. *Journal of Child and Family Studies*, 16, 75–89.

Cohen, F., Nehring, W., Malm, K., & Harris, D. (1995). Family Experiences When a Child is HIV-Positive: Reports of Natural and Foster Parents. *Pediatric Nursing*, 21(3), 248–254.

Cohen, J. A. (2003). Managed care and the evolving role of the clinical social worker in mental health. *Social Work*, 48(1), 34–43.

Comrey, A. L. (1988). Factor-analytic Methods of Scale Development in Personality and Clinical Psychology. *Journal of Consulting and Clinical Psychology*, 56(5), 754–761.

Concept Systems Incorporated (2006). *Facilitator training seminar manual*. Ithaca, New York: Concept Systems.

Conley, T. B. (2005). Evaluating rapid assessment instruments' psychometric error in a practice setting: Use of receiver operating characteristics analysis. *The Journal of Evidence-Based Social Work*, 2(1/2), 137–154.

Corcoran, K. & Fischer, J. (1987). *Measures for Clinical Practice: A Sourcebook*. New York: The Free Press.

Cornelius, D. S. (1994). Managed care and social work: constructing a context and a response. *Social Work in Health Care*, 20(1), 47–63.

Conigrave, K. M., Hall, W. D., & Saunders, J. B. (1995). The AUDIT questionnaire: Choosing a cut-off score. *Addiction*, 90, 1349–1356.

Cronbach, L. J. & Meehl, P. E. (1955). Construct Validity in Psychological Tests. *Psychological Bulletin*, 52(4), 281–302.

Davison, M. L. (1983). *Multidimensional Scaling*. New York: Wiley.

Derogatis, L. R. & Lynn II, L. L. (2006). Screening and monitoring psychiatric disorder in primary care populations. In M. E. Maruish (Ed.), *Handbook of Psychological Assessment in Primary Care Settings* (pp. 115–152). Mahwah, NJ: Lawrence Erlbaum Associates.

DeVellis, B. M. & DeVellis, R. F. (2001). Self-efficacy in Health. In A. Baum, T. Revenson & J. Singer (Eds.), *Handbook of Health Psychology* (pp. 235–247). Mahwah, NJ: Lawrence Erlbaum Associates.

DeVellis, R. F. (2003). *Scale Development: Theory and Applications* (2nd ed.). Newbury Park: Sage.

DeVellis, R.F. (2006). Classical test theory. *Medical Care*, 44 (11, Suppl 3), s50–s59.

DeVon, H. A., Block, M. E., Moyle-Wright, P., Ernst, D. M., Hayden, S. J., Lazzara, D. J., et al. (2007). A psychometric toolbox for testing validity and reliability. *Journal of Nursing Scholarship*, 39(2), 155–164.

Dieu-Hien, H. T. (2002). *Lost in translation: How translation procedures impact the transfer of meanings in printed health education materials.* Unpublished Masters Thesis, University of Washington, Seattle, WA.

Dillman, D. A. (2007). *Mail and Internet Surveys: The Tailored Design Method* (2nd ed.). Hoboken, New Jersey: John Wiley & Sons.

Dominelli, L. (2004). Crossing international divides: Language and communication within international settings. *Social Work Education, 23*(5), 515–525.

Early, T. J. (2001). Measures for Practice with Families from a Strengths Perspective. *Families in Society, 82*(3), 225–232.

Edmunds, H. (1999). *The Focus Group Research Handbook.* Lincolnwood, IL: NTC Business Books.

Embretson, S. & Reise, S. (2000). *Item Response Theory for Psychologists.* Mahwah, NJ: Lawrence Erlbaum Associates.

Feinauer, L. L. & Stuart, D. A. (1996). Blame and Resilience in Women Sexually Abused as Children. *American Journal of Family Therapy, 24*(1), 31–40.

Finch, H. (2005). The MIMIC model as a method for detecting DIF: Comparison with Mantel-Haenszel, SIBTEST, and the IRT likelihood ratio. *Applied Psychological Measurement, 29,* 278–295.

Fischer, J. (1976). *The Effectiveness of Social Casework.* Springfield, IL: Thomas.

Fischer, J. & Corcoran, K. (2007a). *Measures for Clinical Practice and Research* (Vol. 1). New York: Oxford.

Fischer, J. & Corcoran, K. (2007b). *Measures for Clinical Practice and Research: A Sourcebook* (4th ed.). New York: Oxford.

Gallop, R. J., Crits-Christoph, P., Muenz, L. R., & Tu, X. M. (2003). Determination and Interpretation of the Optimal Operating Point for ROC Curves Derived Through Generalized Linear Models. *Understanding Statistics, 2*(4), 219–242.

Gilgun, J. F. (2004). Qualitative methods and the development of clinical assessment tools. *Qualitative Health Research.Special Issue: Models for Illness, 14*(7), 1008,1019.

Glaros, A. G. & Kline, R. B. (1988). Understanding the accuracy of tests with cutting scores: The sensitivity, specificity, and predictive value model. *Journal of Clinical Psychology, 44*(6), 1013–1023.

Goldberger, L. & Breznitz, S. (Eds.). (1993). *Handbook of Stress: Theoretical and Clinical Aspects.* New York: The Free Press.

Goldstein, J. M. & Simpson, J. C. (2002). Validity: Definitions and applications in psychiatric research. In M. Tsuang & M. Tohen (Eds.), *Textbook in Psychiatric Epidemiology* (2nd ed., pp. 149–163). New York: John Wiley & Sons.

Gordon, W. E. (1965). Knowledge and value: Their distinction and relationship in clarifying social work practice. *Social Work, 10*(3), 32–39.

Gorsuch, R. L. (1983). *Factor Analysis* (2nd ed.). Hillsdale: Erlbaum.

Groves, R. M., Fowler, J., Floyd J., Couper, M. P., Lepkowski, J. M., Singer, E., et al. (2004). *Survey Methodology*. Hoboken, N.J.: John Wiley & Sons.

Guadagnoli, E. & Velicer, W. (1988). Relation of sample size to the stability of component patters. *Psychological Bulletin, 103*, 265–275.

Guion, R. M. (1980). On Trinitarian Doctrines Of Validity. *Professional Psychology, 11*(3), 385–398.

Guttman, L. (1954). Some necessary conditions for common-factor analysis. *Psychometrika, 19*, 149–161.

Halabi, J.O. (2006). Psychometric properties of the Arabic Version of the Quality of Life Index. *Journal of Advanced Nursing, 55*(5), 604–611.

Hambleton, R.K. (1994) Guidelines for adapting educational and psychological tests: A progress report. *European Journal of Psychological Assessment, 10*(3), 229–244.

Healy, L. M. (2007). Universalism and cultural relativism in social work ethics. *International Social Work, 50*(1), 11–26.

Hendrickson, A. E. & White, P. O. (1964). Promax: A quick method for rotation to oblique simple structure. *British Journal of Mathematical Psychology, 17*, 65–70.

Hirsch, E. D., Jr., Kett, J. F., & Trefil, J. (Eds.). (2002). *The New Dictionary of Cultural Literacy* (3rd ed.). Boston: Houghton Mifflin Company.

Holbert, R. L. & Stephenson, M. T. (2002). Structural equation modeling in the communication sciences, 1995-2000. *Human Communication Research, 28*(4), 531–551.

Hsiao, J. K., Bartko, J. J., & Potter, W. Z. (1989). Diagnosing diagnoses. *Archives of General Psychiatry, 46*, 664–667.

Horn, J. L. (1965). A rationale and test for the number of factors in factor analysis. *Psychometrika, 30*, 179–185.

Hu, L.-t. & Bentler, P. M. (1999). Cutoff criteria for fit indexes in covariance structure analysis: Conventional criteria versus new alternatives. *Structural Equation Modeling, 6*(1), 1–55.

Hudson, W. W. (1978). First axioms of treatment. *Social Work, 23*(1), 65.

Hudson, W. W. (1982a). Scientific imperatives in social work research and practice. *Social Service Review, 56*(2), 246–258.

Hudson, W. W. (1982b). *The clinical measurement package: A field manual*. Homewood, IL: Dorsey.

Hudson, W. W. & Nurius, P. S. (1988). Computer-based practice: Future dream or current technology? *Social Work, 33*(4), 357–362.

Humphreys, L. G. & Montanelli, R. G. (1975). An investigation of parallel analysis criterion for determining the number of common factors. *Multivariate Behavioral Research, 10*, 191–205.

International Federation of Social Workers. (2005). Global standards for the education and training of the social work profession [Electronic Version]. Retrieved May 4, 2008, from http://www.ifsw.org/cm_data/GlobalSocialWork-Standards2005.pdf

Jackson, D. L. (2001). Sample Size and Number of Parameter Estimates in Maximum Likelihood confirmatory factor analysis: A Monte Carlo investigation. *Structural Equation Modeling, 8*(2), 205–223.

Jackson, D. L. (2003). Revisiting sample size and number of parameter estimates: Some support for the N:q hypothesis. *Structural Equation Modeling, 10*(1), 128–141.

Johnsen, J. A., Biegel, D. E., & Shafran, R. (2000). Concept mapping in mental health: Uses and adaptations. *Evaluation and Program Planning, 23*, 65–75.

Jöreskog, K. G. & Sörbom, D. (1996). *LISREL 8: User's Reference Guide.* Chicago: Scientific Software International.

Kahn, J. H. (2006). Factor Analysis in Counseling Psychology Research, Training, and Practice: Principles, Advances, and Applications. *Counseling Psychologist, 34*(5), 684–718.

Kaiser, H. F. (1958). The varimax criterion for analytic rotation in factor analysis. *Psychometrika, 23*, 187–200.

Kane, M. & Trochim, W. M. (2007). *Concept mapping for planning and evaluation.* Thousand Oaks, CA: Sage.

Kamata, A. & Bauer, D. J. (2008). A note on the relation between factor analytic and item response theory models. *Stuctural Equation Modeling, 15*, 136–153.

Kamata, A. & Vaughn, B. K. (2004). An introduction to differential item functioning analysis. *Learning Disabilities: A Contemporary Journal, 2*, 49–69.

Kane, M. N., Hamlin, E. R., & Hawkins, W. (2000). Perceptions of Field Instructors: What Skills Are Critically Important in Managed Care and Privatized Environments? *Advances in Social Work, 1*(2), 187–202.

Kline, R. B. (2005). *Principles and Practices of Structural Equation Modeling* (2nd ed.). New York: Guilford.

Kraemer, H. C., Kazdin, A. E., Offord, D. R., Kessler, R. C., Jenson, P. S., & Kupfer, D. J. (1999). Measuring potency of risk factors for clincial or policy significance. *Psychological Methods, 4*(3), 257–271.

Krueger, R. A. & Casey, M. A. (2000). *Focus Groups: A Practical Guide for Applied Research* (3rd ed.). Thousand Oaks, CA: Sage.

Kruskal, J. B. & Wish, M. (1978). *Multidimensional Scaling.* Beverly Hills, CA: Sage.

Kutchins, H. & Kirk, S. A. (1997). *Making Us Crazy: DSM, the Psychiatric Bible and the Creation of Mental Disorders.* New York: The Free Press.

LeCroy, C. W. & Krysik, J. (2007). Understanding and interpreting effect size measures. *Social Work Research, 31*(4), 243–248.

Link, B. G. & Phelan, J. C. (2001). Conceptualizing Stigma. *Annual Review of Sociology, 27,* 363–385.

Link, B. G., Yang, L. H., Phelan, J. C., & Collins, P. Y. (2004). Measuring Mental Illness Stigma. *Schizophrenia Bulletin, 30*(3), 511–541.

Long, J. S. (1997). *Regression Models for Categorical and Limited Dependent Variables.* Thousand Oaks: Sage.

MacCallum, R. C., Browne, M. W., & Sugawara, H. M. (1996). Power analysis and determination of sample size for covariance structure modeling. *Psychological methods, 1*(2), 130–149.

MacCallum, R. C., Widaman, K. F., Zhang, S., & Hong, S. (1999). Sample size in factor analysis. *Psychological methods, 4*(1), 84–99.

Marsh, H. W., Ellis, L. A., Parada, R. H., Richards, G., & Heubeck, B. G. (2005). A short version of the Self Description Questionnaire II: Operationalizing criteria for short-form evaluation with new applications of confirmatory factor analysis. *Psychological Assessment, 17,* 81–102.

Maydeu-Olivares, A., Coffman, D. L., & Hartmann, W. M. (2007). Asymptotically distribution-free (ADF) interval estimation of coefficient alpha. *Psychological methods, 12*(2), 157–176.

McPhail, S. M. (2007). Development of validation evidence. In S. M. McPhail (Ed.), *Alternative Validation Strategies: Developing New and Leveraging Existing Validity Evidence* (pp. 1–25). New York: Jossey-Bass.

Messick, S. (1989). Validity. In R. L. Linn (Ed.), *Educational Measurement* (3rd ed., pp. 13–103). New York: MacMillan.

Messick, S. (2003). Validity of Psychological Assessment: Validation of Inferences from Persons' Responses and Performances as Scientific Inquiry into Score Meaning. In A. E. Kazdin (Ed.), *Methodological Issues and Strategies in Clinical Research* (pp. 241–260). Washington, D.C.: American Psychological Association.

Michalski, G. V. & Cousins, B. (2000). Differences in stakeholder perceptions about training evaluation: A concept mapping/pattern matching investigation. *Evaluation and Program Planning, 23,* 211–230.

Mosier, C. I. (1947). A critical examination of the concepts of face validity. *Educational and Psychological Measurement, 7,* 191–206.

Muthen, B. O. & Muthen, L. K. (2007). Mplus (Version 5). Los Angeles, CA: Muthen & Muthen.

Neuman, K. M. (2003). Developing a comprehensive outcomes management program: A ten step process. *Administration in Social Work, 27*(1), 5–23.

Nugent, W. R. (1992). Psychometric characteristics of self-anchored scales in clinical application. *Journal of Social Service Research, 15*(3–4), 137–152.

Nunnally, J. C. & Bernstein, I. H. (1994). *Psychometric Theory*. New York: McGraw-Hill.

Nyblade, L. C. (2006). Measuring HIV Stigma: Existing Knowledge and Gaps. *Psychology, Health, and Medicine, 11*(3), 335–345.

O'Connor, B. P. (2000). SPSS and SAS programs for determining the number of components using parallel analysis and Velicer's MAP test. *Behavior Research Methods, Instruments, and Computers, 32*, 396–402.

O'Connor, B. P. (2001). EXTENSION: SAS, SPSS, and MATLAB programs for extension analysis. *Applied Psychological Measurement, 25*(1), 88.

Orwell, G. (1946). *Animal Farm*. New York: Harcourt Brace.

Parker, R. & Aggleton, P. (2003). HIV and AIDS-related Stigma and Discrimination: A Conceptualization Framework and Implications for Action. *Social Science and Medicine, 57*, 13–24.

Pepe, M. S. (2002). Receiver operating characteristic methodology. In A. E. Raftery, M. A. Tanner & M. T. Wells (Eds.), *Statistics in the 21st Century* (pp. 60–66). Boca Raton: American Statistical Association.

Pfeiffer, S. I. & Petscher, Y. (2008). Identifying young gifted children using the Gifted Rating Scales-Preschool/Kindergarten Form. *Gifted Child Quarterly, 52*(1), 19–29.

Rassool, G. Hussein (2006). Commentary on Halabi J.O. (2006) Psychometric properties of the Arabic version of the Quality of Life Index. *Journal of Advanced Nursing, 55*(5), 610,611.

Richmond, M. (1917). *Social Diagnosis*. New York: Russell Sage Foundation.

Rubio, D. M., Berg-Weger, M., Tebb, S. S., Lee, E. S., & Rauch, S. (2003). Objectifying content validity: Conducting a content validity study in social work research. *Social Work Research, 27*(2), 94–104.

Russell, D. W. (2002). In Search of Underlying Dimensions: The Use (and Abuse) of Factor Analysis in Personality and Social Psychology Bulletin. *Personality and Social Psychology Bulletin, 28*(12), 1629–1646.

Rutledge, S. E., Abell, N., Padmore, J., & McCann, T. (2007). AIDS Stigma in Health Services in the Eastern Caribbean. *Manuscript submitted for publication*.

Saleeby, D. (2002). *The Strengths Perspective in Social Work Practice*. Boston: Allyn and Bacon.

Santor, D. A. (2005). Using and evaluating psychometric measures: Practical and theoretical considerations. In J. Miles & P. Gilbert (Eds.), *A Handbook of Research Methods for Clinical and Health Psychology* (pp. 95–109). Oxford: Oxford University Press.

Sapnas, K. G. & Zeller, R. A. (2002). Minimizing sample size when using exploratory factor analysis for measurement. *Journal of Nursing Measurement, 10*(2), 135–154.

Schaefer, M. A., Schmidt, B., & Wynd, C. A. (2003). Two quantitative approaches for estimating content validity. *Western Journal of Nursing Research, 25*(5), 508–518.

Shern, D. L., Trochim, W. M. K., & LaComb, C. A. (1995). The use of concept mapping for assessing fidelity of model transfer: An example from psychiatric rehabilitation. *Evaluation and Program Planning, 18*, 143–153.

Springer, D., Abell, N., & Hudson, W. W. (2002). Creating and validating rapid assessment instruments for practice and research: Part 1. *Research on Social Work Practice, 12*(3), 408–439.

Springer, D., Abell, N., & Nugent, W. (2002). Creating and validating rapid assessment instruments for practice and research: Part 2. *Research on Social Work Practice, 12*(6), 805–832.

Springer, D. W. (1998). Validation of the Adolescent Concerns Evaluation (ACE): Detecting indicators of runaway behavior in adolescents. *Social Work Research, 22*, 241–250.

Stevens, J. (1996). *Applied Multivariate Statistics for the Social Sciences* (3rd ed.). Mahwah, NJ: Lawrence Erlbaum.

Stickle, T. R. & Weems, C. F. (2006). Improving prediction from clinical assessment: The roles of measurement, psychometric theory, and decision theory. In R. R. Bootzin & P. E. McKnight (Eds.), *Strengthening Research Methodology: Psychological Measurement and Evaluation* (pp. 213–230). Washington, D.C.: American Psychological Association.

Strauss, A. & Corbin, J. (1998). *Basics of Qualitative Research* (2nd ed.). Thousand Oaks, CA: Sage.

Strom-Gottfried, K. (1997). The implications of managed care for social work education. *Journal of Social Work Education, 33*(1), 7–18.

Tate, R. (1998). *An Introduction to Modeling Outcomes in the Behavioral and Social Sciences* (2nd ed.). Edinis, MN: Burgess.

Teresi, J.A. (2006). Overview of quantitative measurement methods: Equivalence, invariance, and differential item functioning in health applications. *Medical Care*, 44(11, Suppl 3), s39–s49.

Teresi, J.A., Stewart, A.L., Morales, L.S., & Stahl. S.M. (2006). Measurement in a multi-ethnic society: Overview to the special issue. *Medical Care, 44*(11, Suppl 3), s3–s4.

Thompson, B. (2004). *Exploratory and Confirmatory Factor Analysis*. Washington, D.C.: American Psychological Association.

Thompson, M. D. M. (2007). Trauma Resilience Scale for Children: Validation of protective factors associated with positive adaptation following violence. Unpublished doctoral prospectus. Florida State University.

Tran, T.V., Ngo, D., & Conway, K. (2003). A cross-cultural measure of depressive symptoms among Vietnamese Americans. *Social Work Research, 27*(1), 56–64.

Trochim, W. M. (1989). An introduction to concept mapping for planning and evaluation. *Evaluation Program Planning, 12*, 1–16.

Van Brakel, W. H. (2006). Measuring Health-Related Stigma: A Literature Review. *Psychology, Health, and Medicine, 11*(3), 307–334.

van de Vijver, F. & Hambleton, R.K. (1996). Translating tests: Some practical guidelines. *European Psychologist, 1*(2), 89–99.

van de Vijver, F. & Poortinga, Y.H. (1997). Towards an integrated analysis of bias in cross-cultural assessment. *European Journal of Psychological Assessment, 13*(1), 29–37.

van de Vijver, F. & Tanzer, N.K. (2004). Bias and equivalence in cross-cultural assessment: An overview. *European Review of Applied Psychology, 54*, 119–135.

Weert-van Oene, G. H., Buwalda, V. J. A., Havenaar, J. M., Swildens, W., van Keijzerswaard, A., & Schrijvers, A. J. P. (2006). Demand-oriented care: The development and validation of a measuring instrument. *Social Psychiatry and Psychiatric Epidemiology (41)*, 215–220.

Witkin, S. L. (2001). The measure of things. *Social Work, 46*(2), 101–104.

Yang, L. H., Kleinman, A., Link, B. G., Phelan, J. C., Lee, S., & Good, B. (2007). Culture and Stigma: Adding Moral Experience to Stigma Theory. *Social Science and Medicine, 64*, 1524–1535.

Zimbalist, S. E. (1977). *Historic Themes and Landmarks in Social Welfare Research.* New York: Harper & Row.

Zometa, C. S., Dedrick, R., Knox, M. D., Westhoff, W., Siri, R. S., & Debaldo, A. (2007). Translation, cross-cultural adaptation and validation of an HIV/AIDS knowledge and attitudinal instrument. *AIDS Education and Prevention, 19*(3), 231–244.

Index